The Sage Dictionary of Health and Society

The Sage Dictionary of Health and Society

Kevin White

SAGE Publications

London ● Thousand Oaks ● New Delhi

First published 2006

Apart from any fair dealing for the purposes of research
or private study, or criticism or review, as permitted under
the Copyright, Designs and Patents Act, 1988, this
publication may be reproduced, stored or transmitted in
any form, or by any means, only with the prior permission
in writing of the publishers, or in the case of reprographic
reproduction, in accordance with the terms of licences
issued by the Copyright Licensing Agency. Inquiries
concerning reproduction outside those terms should be
sent to the publishers.

 SAGE Publications Ltd
1 Oliver's Yard
55 City Road
London EC1Y 1SP

SAGE Publications Inc.
2455 Teller Road
Thousand Oaks, California 91320

SAGE Publications India Pvt Ltd
B-42 Panchsheel Enclave
Post Box 4109
New Delhi 110 017

British Library Cataloguing in Publication data

A catalogue record for this book is available
from the British Library

ISBN 0 7619 4115 0
0 7619 4116 9

Library of Congress Control Number available

Typeset by C&M Digitals (P) Ltd., Chennai, India
Printed on paper from sustainable resources
Printed in Great Britain by The Cromwell Press Ltd, Trowbridge, Wiltshire

Contents

On writing a dictionary of health social sciences

If you open this book looking for Oxford English Dictionary type definitions you will be disappointed. Rather, in this dictionary I have attempted to show how critical medical anthropologists, sociologists, historians and philosophers of medicine use words to discuss healthcare and healing systems. Psychological and sociobiological concepts are also included, though usually contrasted with sociological accounts. This is because they make the same assumptions that medicine does about sickness, illness and disease: that they are a product of nature, existing independently of social life, and that they are essentially individual events, the product of the individual's biology or psychological characteristics. So the dictionary provides an account of how words are used in the social sciences when exploring the activities of professional medical workers, patients' experiences of disease, or alternative understandings of the causes of sickness, illness and disease. Thus many of these usages are at odds with both common-sense usage and medical usage. From a social sciences perspective, disease, for example, is not regarded as just the simple, or even complex, malfunctioning of the body. Rather, depending on the perspective of the social scientists under consideration, it is the product of what is defined as disease, its social distribution, and treatment processes, of the wider structures of power relationships in society. As an example, taking four major social science approaches to explaining disease will illustrate the point.

Marxists argue that the cause of disease can be attributed to the alienating features of life in a capitalist society. Those among the unskilled and manual labouring sections of the workforce die earlier, and of more preventable conditions, than those in managerial and professional sectors. Those at the top also receive better and earlier treatment for their condition, thus enhancing their longevity. Feminist sociologists point to subordination of women in a patriarchal society, arguing that the focus on women's bodies by the medical profession, and especially the medicalization of their reproductive capacity, is in fact an exercise in social control. Foucauldian sociologists argue that medicine is part of a centralized administrative state apparatus which sorts and classifies the population to police deviance. Moreover, modern societies have been so successful in constructing an understanding of what is normal, based on medical and psychiatric definitions, that we have internalized these norms, and actively police ourselves. Thus in this analysis the focus on fitness, body weight, jogging and diet – healthism – are aspects of social control by the psy-professions, though we experience them as freely chosen pastimes or reasonable concerns about our physical and psychological well being. Even those sociologists who view medicine in a favourable light, for example Talcott Parsons, argue that despite its overt role of caring and curing, the fundamental role of the medical profession is to guard entry into the sick role and to maintain individuals at a level to competently perform their social roles. So something that is taken for granted by the medical sciences and in common usage, disease, as an objectively existing disorder, is for the health social sciences very problematic. Disease and how an individual experiences it, is the product of the organization of the economy, the gendered division of labour, the division between the private world of the home and the public world of work, the ranking of ethnic groups into status hierarchies and the impact of class membership on life chances. It is not an accident of biology or nature.

This leads social scientists from a wide range of perspectives to argue that the problems of our society which are usually dealt with by medical practitioners should be seen as social issues. They argue that in contemporary society many conditions which have their origin in society – learning disabilities for example – are medicalized and turned into 'natural' conditions which obscure the social processes producing them. So while there is a wide range of social science perspectives on health and illness – the Parsonian, interactionist, social constructionist, Foucauldian and feminist – they all distance themselves from the medical model of disease. This is because of three central aspects of medical thought. First, it is biologically reductionist, reducing human action to its lowest common denominator, its claimed understanding of the body, and separating the experience of sickness, illness and disease from their social location. Second, the medical model, developing out of the Cartesian separation of mind and body, is mechanistic and behaviouristic, conceptualizing disease as an event that happens to parts of the body and not an experience that involves the whole person. Third, the medical model is scientistic, applying the methods of the natural sciences – designed to examine an inert nature – to human beings who actively and meaningfully construct their environment. The use of statistical definitions of disease, in particular, leads to definitions of disease as deviations from a norm that takes no account of the individual's experience of the condition. Thus in the medical approach sickness, illness and disease are things that happen to the body, independently of its social location and the subjectivity of the individual, to be treated using drugs and high cost technology.

The development of the social science approach, in general, develops out of a long tradition of social medicine, derived from Frederick Engels and Rudolf Virchow, which takes as its premise that health and illness are the product of social, political and economic relationships. Rather than point to the individual's body, or to germs as the sole cause of disease they identified the social environment as the source of sickness and ill health. Along with others in the sanitary movement such as Booth, Snow, and the Webbs, the solution proposed for ameliorating disease was to clean up the slums, keep water fresh and uncontaminated by sewage, and enforcing the hygienic production of foodstuffs.

These early social, political and economic analyses of the causes of disease are backed up by historical analyses of the negligible role of organized medicine in contributing to the health of the population in the nineteenth and twentieth centuries. Rather than the triumphal overcoming of diseases as a consequence of great men, having great breakthroughs, in great institutions, as Whig histories of medicine would have it, it was precisely urban reform and control over working conditions that transformed the health of the population. As the historical epidemiologist Thomas McKeown has demonstrated, environmental and social reforms counted for more in the development of contemporary health standards than any breakthroughs around the germ theory of disease, the formation of the medical profession, or developments in medical technology. The work of Archie Cochrane in Britain in post-World War II continued to testify to the limited or unknown utility of much medical practices and the need for the development of evidence-based medicine if medicine's claim to be a science was to have any basis. Coupled with Ivan Illich's analysis of modern medicine as iatrogenic there developed a powerful critique of claims of the medical profession to be the practitioners of the humane application of science in society. The medical profession and its activities came to be seen as part of the problem rather than a solution to the problems of sickness and disease in society. This orientation was given substantial impetus with the development of the antipsychiatry movement, which argued that the 'diseases' of psychiatry were in fact labels attached to deviant individuals for the purposes of social control; and that the treatment processes were there to ensure the smooth functioning of bureaucracies such as hospitals and asylums, rather than the cure of individuals. The publication of Eliot Freidson's *Profession of Medicine: A Study of the Sociology of Applied Knowledge*, and *Professional Dominance*, both in 1970 marks the consolidation of the sociology of medicine (the contrast is with sociology in medicine) into an examination of medicine, medical knowledge and medical practices. Freidson's argument is that the medical profession dominated the health sector, not because it was the humanitarian scientific elite it claimed to be, but because it was politically well organized. Consequently it has excluded competing medical knowledges and practitioners, obtained a monopoly of practice guaranteed by the state, has autonomy over its own work practices, and defines for the wider society the issues that it has control over. The achievements of the profession have little to do with its professionalism and more to do with its economic and political power.

The key to this position, and to the development of the health social sciences by the early 1980s, is that it does not allow that medicine has a pure, scientific knowledge base. It calls into question medicine's claims to reflect an objective underlying reality, and argues that the conceptual categories of medicine, the diagnostic categories of disease and treatment patterns are themselves a product of social life. While this argument is often identified in the work of Foucault, and in social constructionist accounts of medical knowledge and technology, it has had a subterranean history in the sociology of health throughout the twentieth century, in the work Bernhard Stern in the United States, Ludwig Fleck in Germany, and Georges Canguihelm and Gaston Bachelard in France. In this perspective the point is not to counterpoise medicine as a natural science with contaminating social factors but to see them as mutually constitutive of each other.

While the development of the sociology of medical knowledge, the historical sociology of health, and the development of a sceptical attitude to the claims of medicine were central to the development of a social science approach to medicine, there were also factors at work intrinsic to the social sciences. The dream of a scientific account of society – in the sense of being on par with the methods and findings of the natural sciences – had been central to Durkheim and Marx, albeit from different political perspectives. Coupled with the rise of statistics and the need for the welfare state to have access to information about large numbers of people, quantitative, large scale surveys became the dominant form of social science research in the post-World War II period. However from the 1970s onwards sociologists became more and more critical of the positivist tradition of quantitative research and more interested in the philosophy of the social sciences. Weber's work in particular, with its neo-Kantian epistemology (put crudely, that the mind shapes reality rather than reality shaping the mind) experienced a resurgence in Britain leading to an emphasis on interpretive, qualitative sociology, conducted with the aim of explaining not only the regularities of social life, but also understanding the subject's world view. This development resonated with the pragmatism of the American sociological tradition – from Peirce, Dewey and Mead – crystallizing in the Chicago school, and fed into the development of ethnomethodology and phenomenological sociology, through the work of Schutz in the United States. These developments echoed the demise of Parsons' structural functionalism and a rejection of grand theorizing in favour of grounded theory: exploring what actually was happening in various social sites and institutions.

Health sociologists thus turned to studying the experience of illness and disease, the informal structures of hospitals and asylums, as in the work of Erving Goffman, of the experience of disease as stigma, or the social organization of dying. Social science enquiries into the working of society came to be based more on ethnographies, case studies and to use qualitative techniques of investigation such as participant observation, in-depth interviews, and focus groups. These types of studies often supply very rich empirical case studies which may not be generalizable, and may be vulnerable to the charge that they overlook the workings of powerful groups and institutions in society.

Along with these intellectual developments, and central to compiling this dictionary has been the social and political changes in Western capitalist societies since the late 1970s. Political sociologists of health have demonstrated that with the winding back of the welfare state, more and more of the services that it used to provide – in shorthand, the social wage – have to be provided by individuals in the home, especially women, and by communities as they are exhorted to develop their social capital to make themselves healthy. The corporatization of health services, the privatization of state facilities, and the outsourcing of activities once supplied by the state have had a major impact on the structure of the medical profession, leading to deskilling and proletarianization, as well as restricting access to services to those in a position to take out private health insurance. The introduction of market principles – funder–provider splits, case mix and diagnostic related groups – into state institutions such as hospitals has led to degradation of nursing work and conditions, as patients, doctors and nurses meet production targets. Many sociologists argue that the 'new public health', with its emphasis on lifestyle factors and risks, feeds into this neoliberalism, individualizing and depoliticizing the political, environmental and economic causes of disease.

There has been ongoing debate about the impact of these and other social changes – an increasingly educated public, scepticism about the appropriateness of much medical interventions based on drugs and technology, the rise of complementary and alternative medicines – on the medical profession. With changes in the economic environment, the rise of entrepreneurial medicine, and the ongoing commodification of healthcare, doctors perform more and more as employees than as freestanding professionals. This proletarianization, or alternatively, deprofessionalization, has suggested that the end of medical dominance is nigh. However the situation is not clear cut: doctors still retain considerable independence in their clinical work; and empowered patients do not seem to be fundamentally challenging medicine, but want more of it delivered on their terms. The rise in complementary medicine in part reflects this ambiguous relationship to the medical system. Users of complementary medicine are usually not rejecting orthodox medicine, but seeking supplementary treatments and therapies. The health consumer movement and the concept of the empowered patient have meant that there has been considerable research into the doctor–patient relationship, with Parsons' original model of the passive patient and the active doctor seriously questioned. Many current research projects into the doctor–patient relationship emphasize negotiation and interaction of the doctor and patient over treatment and therapies. This is especially the case in the context of the rise of chronic illness where patients may be on equal footing or have greater knowledge of their condition than their doctor.

This dictionary is a product of these intellectual and social changes. It grows principally out of my parent discipline, sociology, and my experience as a sociologist of health over the better part of twenty years. In writing it I drew on my own work in political sociology, the sociology of the health professions, the sociology of medical knowledge, the historical sociology of healthcare and the medical profession and the medicalization of social problems. I also reviewed leading textbooks in the fields of anthropology of health, the social psychology of health, health administration, public health, the social history of health and medicine and epidemiology. From these, doing a rough and ready frequency count I identified words that cropped up across these different disciplines (for example, medicalization) as well as words specific to the discipline (say epidemiological polarization in epidemiology). This resulted in the over 900 head words in this dictionary. Wherever possible I tried to track a word to its original usage, often without success, sometimes with (for example, Jarvis' Law). Except where I have directly quoted an author, the text is my own, and I have not consulted other dictionaries of health sociology except fleetingly (for example, Cockerham, W. and Ritchey, F. (1997) *Dictionary of Medical Sociology*, Westport: Greenwood Press). This seemed to me to be the easiest way to avoid plagiarism. At one point I was bemoaning my fate in attempting this project and someone in a bar suggested using the web. While not a Luddite this had never occurred to me. However it was not particularly useful, since it constantly provided me with screeds of course outlines in which my word appeared. The only truly memorable event in using it was tracking down the entries for Kinsey, and Masters and Johnson, who do not rate a mention in any contemporary study of sexuality that I could find – it is remarkable how short lived fame is! So most of the research was done in the old fashioned way, trudging back and forth to the library and ransacking my office shelves for examples of the use of words.

A good deal of the dictionary was written as 'word trees' that is, of interlinked words – for example, all the entries relating to profession were written in sequence, and most of the entries in the philosophy of social science, as were entries on the social construction of technology, the historical sociology of health and the sociology of scientific knowledge. Hence, following the links is a good way to pick up the full usage and complexity of a term. Because so many sociologists have contributed to the sub-discipline, I restricted entries for individuals to those who are dead. So to my professional colleagues, if you are disappointed not to have an entry under your own name, be grateful: at least you are alive.

The writing of this dictionary has very much been the product of my own intellectual biography. My undergraduate career spanned the mid-1970s at the height of the debates around scientific and humanist Marxism, and the role of class analysis in the social sciences. I was fortunate at Flinders University in my lecturers Professors Ivan Szelenyi, Bob Holton, and Allan Patience. As I started my PhD Professor Bryan Turner was appointed and became my supervisor as I pursued research into the historical formation of the medical profession, using a sociology of knowledge framework to examine the ways in which the germ theory of disease was mobilized to consolidate the nascent professions' claim to be the arbiter of health and disease. My first appointment, to teach the history and philosophy of medicine at Wollongong University, in the then Department of the History and Philosophy of Science (now science and technology studies) immersed me in the sociology of scientific knowledge and the sociology of technology. I benefited enormously from working with John Schuster, Ev Richards, Brian Martin and Terry Stokes. I then moved to New Zealand to the Department of Sociology and Social Work at Victoria University of Wellington. New Zealand fully embraced the neoliberalist revival of the late 1970s and early 1980s and provided a microcosm of changes to the welfare state and the introduction of market principles to the healthcare sector. My political sociology of healthcare systems and an interest in comparative healthcare systems were fostered by interactions with Professor Peter Davis (now Christchurch), while my colleagues at VUW, Professor Mike Hill, Drs Claire Toynbee, David Pearson and Bob Tristram, along with Barry Doyle, provided a rich sociological environment in which to work. At the Australian National University I have enjoyed the colleagueship and friendship of Dr Owen Dent, Stephen Mugford, Jack Barbalet and Professor Frank Lewins (to whom I owe the opening line of this introduction). I would also like to sincerely thank Dr Thomas Mautner, Department of Philosophy, ANU who provided often very funny feedback on an early draft of parts of the dictionary. Thomas' sense of humour, as the only other person I have met who has taken on a dictionary (*A Dictionary of Philosophy*. Cambridge, MA: Blackwell, 1996) was far more important in keeping me going than he would realize. Dr Alison Rawling (whose PhD I supervised and who is now also a medical practitioner) tried to steer me in the direction of the interesting usages of some medical terminology.

Academic writing by definition is a solitary exercise, but one's intellectual formation is the product of the intellectual communities that nourish and shape us and I sincerely thank the above institutions and colleagues, as well as my students, for their input and support. One way or another this dictionary would not have been written without the love and support of Dr Elizabeth Coleman. Elizabeth heard my first halting efforts at many of the definitions, talked through the logic of the dictionary with me, played tennis, shared beers, and by her own example as a scholar, kept me committed to doing my best in this book. She also had the good humour during my pensive silences, when she asked what I was thinking about, not to be offended by answers such as the entry on the body, or what to do about all the 's's that needed filling in! This dictionary is for her. And always there are my children: Claire, Michael and David. Hi guys.

From the perspective of specialists in the wide range of health social sciences covered in this dictionary, the errors will be glaring. (I cannot repeat the description of my first attempts at critical medical anthropology provided by Professor Hans Baer!) I apologise in advance. However, I hope its failings are balanced by the effort to chart the dynamics of the health social sciences and that in the future updated versions will rectify the most immediate faults.

A

ABNORMAL The diagnoses in clinical medicine of a patient or group in the population as deviating from the medical definition of **normal**. In **Foucault's** sociology the proposition is that concepts of normality are constructed by state and professional healing and helping occupations to facilitate the regulation of the population. Thus the contrast with abnormality is not 'normal' but the processes of normalization, in which individuals internalize professionally defined and enforced norms of behavior and regulate themselves (**Bachelard**; **bodyism**; **Canguihelm**; **fitness**; **normal**; **psy-professions**; **somatization**; **technologies of the self**).

ABNORMAL ILLNESS BEHAVIOUR A diagnosis in psychiatry based around a dispute between the doctor and the patient about whether the patient is sick or not. Either the doctor thinks that the patient has no underlying pathology despite the patient's claim to the contrary, or the patient denies the doctor's diagnosis that they are clinically sick. While the diagnosis is usually one determined by a psychiatrist, it is not an unusual characteristic of the doctor–patient relationship, particularly when it involves contested diseases, such as chronic fatigue syndrome, or diseases which may take a long time to be diagnosed, such as multiple sclerosis (Pilowsky, I. (1978) 'A general classification of abnormal illness behaviour', *British Journal of Medical Psychology*, 51: 131–7) (**chronic fatigue syndrome**; **consultation**; **diagnostic limbo**; **diagnostic shock**; **doctor–patient relationship**; **normal**; **Parsons**; **sick role**).

ABORIGINAL HEALTH SERVICES Established in the 1970s by the Australian Federal government and individual Australian states, specific education and health promotion programmes aimed at Australia's indigenous population. These programmes were set in place but have been unsuccessful in dealing with Aborigines' morbidity and mortality rates: fetal death rate of 14.4 per 1000 live births, compared with 6.8 for non-indigenous births; deaths from infectious disease are 14.7 times higher for Aboriginal males and 17.6 times higher for females than the non-indigenous population; life expectancy is 14–18 years lower for Aboriginal males and 16–20 years lower for females than for the non-indigenous population (**African Americans**; **American Indians**; **Canadian Inuits**; **Hispanic Americans**; **New Zealand Maori**).

ABORIGINALS   The indigenous populations of colonized countries. Aboriginality is a marker for poorer health status and shorter life span in all cases and their condition has been captured in the idea that they constitute a third world in the first. Common to all Aboriginal cultures are a distrust of Western medical practices (combined with a rejection of their medical practices by Westerners); poor levels of funding for healthcare; a problem of attracting medical practitioners to their communities; and poor transportation and remote living conditions (Young, E. A. (1995) *Third World in the First: The Development of Indigenous Peoples.* London: Routledge) (**Aboriginal Health Services; African-Americans; American Indians; Canadian Inuit; indigenous peoples; New Zealand Maori**).

ABORTION   The spontaneous expulsion or deliberate removal of the fetus before gestation is complete. Made illegal in the USA and the UK in the 1860s with the support of many early feminists, and forbidden by the Catholic Church in 1869. Anti-abortionists claim that all human life is sacred from inception. Pro-abortionists are either those who want reform so that abortion is acceptable when the life or mental health of the mother is at risk or those who argue that a woman should have full control over her body and should be able to have an abortion on demand. Struggles over the control of women's reproductive capacity have been central to the development of **feminism** and its medicalization widely criticized. When abortion is made illegal, as in Romania in 1966, the impact on maternal mortality is huge, as women source illegal, backyard terminations. In the Romanian case maternal mortality rose by 40 per cent over five years, and by 1989 was ten times higher than in any other Western country. Following the legalization of abortion in 1989 the maternal mortality rate was almost halved within a year (World Development Report. (1993) *Investing in Health: World Development Indicators.* New York: Oxford University Press) (**childbirth**; **life**; **new reproductive technologies**).

ACCIDENT PRONENESS   A psychological theory that explains industrial accidents as a consequence of individual predisposition to cut corners and take risks at work. It overlooks the fact that workers have very little control over the rate and speed of their work, nor over the control of safety features, such as machinery guards or other safe work conditions. It also overlooks the fact that since many of these events are preventable they are not accidents at all (**blame the victim**; **Engels**).

ACCOUNTS OF ILLNESS   In contrast to medicine in which the clinical interview elicits from a patient biological signs and symptoms of disease, qualitative researchers in health studies focus on the individual's experience of illness and sickness and how they actively make sense of it in the stories they tell both to other ill and well people. The ways in which individuals provide accounts of their illness are structurally determined (**agency**). Those with the strongest sense of control over what it is that is happening to them, and who cope best with the diagnoses of disease, also tend to be placed higher in the social structure, that is, have better access to information, time and money to cope with their condition, and therefore have a stronger sense of **locus of control (biographical disruption; chronic illness; clinical narratives; narrative accounts of illness; theodicy).**

ACID RAIN   The product of industrial pollution, a combination of sulfur dioxides and nitrous oxides, it degrades the environment and contributes to respiratory problems. In a **risk society** the source of the pollution may be hundreds or even thousands of miles away **(life scapes; materialist analyses; popular epidemiology).**

ACUPUNCTURE   The Chinese practice of inserting needles at what are held to be 'energy' points in the human body. It has been argued that the metaphor of the body as possessing specific points of vitality and power was derived from the structure of the Chinese economy, which was based on granaries and irrigation. At the cultural level Chinese medicine conceptualized disease as the outcome of social instability, caused by individual behaviour. The therapy was to drive out demons or magical influences with spears, which evolved into the use of needles at specific points of the human body (Unschuld, P. (1985) *Medicine in China: A History of Ideas*. Berkeley, CA: University of California Press) **(Chinese medicine).**

ACTION BASED METHODS/RESEARCH   Research, in the **qualitative** tradition, that has as its goal the transformation of the situation it is investigating, with an aim to improving the quality or delivery of services, or the experience of life events. It sees the researcher and the researched as working on a joint enterprise, with the researcher abdicating their role as expert. Action researchers tend also to focus below management level in addressing issues, seeking to find out about and transform the issues of participants in organizations. The contrast is with positivist research, in which the researcher stands apart from the subject under investigation (McNiff, J. (1995) *Action Research for Professional Development: Concise Advice for New Action Researchers*. Dorset: Hyde Publications) **(bias; positivism).**

ACTOR-NETWORK THEORY   An approach in the sociology of science, which argues that scientific knowledge, rather than being discovered, is produced out of the interactions of researchers, instruments, and their laboratories. The theory has been particularly important in the anthropology of science, in which Western science is approached on the same basis as an anthropologist would investigate other indigenous knowledge systems (Latour, B. (1987) *Science in Action*. Cambridge: MA: Harvard University Press) **(Fleck; medical technology; social construction; constructionism; social construction of technology approach).**

ADDICT   Central to construction of the 'drug problem' is the concept of the addict as personality characteristic. Late nineteenth-century medical practitioners looked on opiates and narcotics favourably and as an important part of their treatment regime. In the 1930s, the US Department of Health took the position that the drug addict had a psychopathic personality, was potentially a criminal and had sociopathic tendencies. The Harrison Act of 1914 made opiates and narcotics available only on prescription and criminalized addiction, and in 1934 the American Psychiatric Association's diagnostic handbook listed it as a psychiatric disease. The impact was to drive drugs underground to become the centre of huge illegal activities. While individuals can become addicted to legally prescribed drugs they are not classified as 'addicts' (Berridge, V. and Edwards, G. (1987) *Opium and the People: Opiate Use in Nineteenth Century England*. New York: St Martin's Press) (**addiction**; **alcoholism**; **medicalization**).

ADDICTION   Psychologists, medical practitioners and psychiatrists explain addiction as: a chemical process, in that some people's brains are such that they are chemically programmed to become addicted to some substances; a psychodynamic process, that is, based on unresolved underlying tensions in the person's life; or, in the social learning approach, the product of the individual's upbringing where they have learnt inappropriate forms of behaviour. From a health studies perspective, these approaches are all variants on approaches that **blame the victim**. Sociologists have demonstrated that rates of addiction are highly correlated with

the experience of inequality. The poor, the disadvantaged, the unemployed and the homeless, as well as those in low status jobs – the socially excluded, with low social support and high stress – are most at risk of addictive behaviours. Furthermore addiction should not be considered as a **lifestyle choice** but the product of social relationships (**health determinants**; **social exclusion**; **social inequality**).

ADVANCED CARE DIRECTIVES   Instructions to medical personnel prepared in advance by the patient in the event of developing a terminal illness or experiencing a life threatening injury. The patient may designate another person to make decisions about their treatment if they are unable to make or communicate their decisions. Under the 1990 Patient Self-Determination Act (USA) all patients entering a health institution funded by Medicare or Medicaid, must be supplied with information about advanced care directives (**death**; **do not resuscitate**; **euthanasia**; **hospice movement**; **life**; **physician assisted suicide**).

ADVERSE DRUG REACTIONS   The recognized health damaging consequence of taking a medically prescribed drug. By contrast medical professionals define adverse drug reactions as side effects and as acceptable, though uncomfortable, for the patient. The size of the problem is significant, with the former chief executive of SmithKline Beecham, a major international pharmaceutical company, George Poste, estimating 100,000 deaths annually from adverse drug reactions in the United States (Poste, G. (1998) 'Molecular medicine and information-based targeted healthcare', *Nature Biotechnology*, 16: 19–21) (**iatrogenic iatrogenesis**).

AFFECT MANAGEMENT The idea that we systematically manage our emotions in social interactions. The idea in general has always been part of **symbolic interactionist** accounts of social life, and particularly in the work of **Erving Goffman** (1969) *The Presentation of Self in Everyday Life* (Harmondsworth: Penguin). Similarly, Strauss pointed to 'sentimental work' and to the way in which nurses had to manage their emotions in the face of unexpected deaths in hospitals (**dying trajectories**). In more recent literature a distinction is made between emotional labour, in which, as part of our employment, we must manage our presentation of self, and emotion work, which is part of our interaction in the domestic sphere. The concept has had wide application in the sociology of nursing (Hochschild, A. (1983) *The Managed Heart: Commercialization of Human Feeling*. Berkeley: University of California Press) (**doctor/nurse game**; **emotions**; **nursing**).

AFRICAN AMERICANS Organized medicine is both shaped by and shapes racism, prejudice and discrimination. In America medically legitimated knowledge has been used to subjugate African Americans and to justify their unequal social status. The impact on their health status has been devastating: they are at 1.5 per cent higher risk of dying from the major causes of death than Caucasians. They are at higher risk of all preventable illnesses: hypertension, substance abuse, kidney disease and heart disease. Approximately 1 in 10 have diabetes, while tuberculosis rose by 26 per cent between 1985 and 1992. African American women die at the rate of 4:1 compared with Caucasian women, while African American men die almost ten years earlier than their white counterparts. The AIDS virus is also distributed by **ethnicity** with 53 per cent of all AIDS carriers being African American women and adolescents. 'The problems that beset African American communities seem to be nearing genocidal proportions' (Tomes, H. (1998: 25) 'Health status and needs of diverse communities,' in V. Cancela, J. Chin and Y. Jenkins (eds), *Community Health Psychology*. New York: Routledge) (**Hispanic Americans**).

AGE In Western societies the biological length of a person's existence measured in years. From a sociological perspective biological age is not necessarily equated with social functioning and the impact of 'age' is mediated by political and economic factors, such as compulsory schooling, voting and retirement ages. From a political economy and feminist perspective definitions of age and experiences of the ageing process are shaped by labour market requirements and the requirements of socially defined masculine and feminine social roles (Estes, C. (1979) *The Ageing Enterprise*. San Francisco: Jossey Bass) (**ageing**; **intergenerational conflict**; **triple jeopardy**).

AGEING   In a taken for granted sense the biological and psychological experience of the lifecycle from birth to death. Psychological theories focus on the role of the individual, in for example, **disengagement theory** which emphasizes the 'natural' and inevitable separation of the individual from social roles. On the other hand, activity theories emphasize the continuities of the ageing person with their life-time roles, counteracting ageist stereotypes of the elderly as of little or no social value. However, psychological theories, based on biological assumptions, study the ageing process in the absence of any account of the impact of the differential and unequal impact of class, gender and ethnicity on ageing populations, particularly women (Estes, C. and Linkins, K. (2000) 'Critical perspectives on health and aging', in G. Albrecht, R. Fitzpatrick and S. Scrimshaw (eds), *The Handbook of Social Studies in Health and Medicine*. London: Sage).

AGEISM   The ascription of negative social characteristics to the chronologically old that have embedded in them unwarranted assumptions of decline, dependency and despondency (**Alzheimer's disease**; **ageing**; **disengagement theory**; **gerontology**; **intergenerational conflict**).

AGENCY   A term used by sociologists to capture the idea that individuals have scope for action notwithstanding the way that they are constrained by social structures. Talcott Parsons for example argued that sickness could be considered a form of motivated deviance, that is, the individual's response to social strain. In particular he saw the nuclear family as a major social structure, which, because of its intense demands around childrearing and the maintenance of adult personalities, we as destructive. Thus individuals did not respond passively to their social roles but negotiated and challenged them (**Parsons**; **sick role**; **voluntaristic theory of action**).

AGE-SPECIFIC RATE   The number of cases per 100,000 persons per year for a specific, narrow age range. Five-year groups are commonly used.

AGE-STANDARDIZED RATE   A procedure whereby weighted averages of age-specific rates are used to modify rates to a standard population in order to minimize the effects of differences in the age composition of specific populations. For example, since cancer is more common in older age groups, a population that is older will have a higher crude incidence rate. Age standardized rates allow comparisons of groups of people from different backgrounds and age structures.

AGORAPHOBIA   From the Greek meaning literally fear of the market place, a diagnosis in psychiatry of an inability, usually in women, to leave the house. In sociological accounts its origins lie in the development of occupations that drew women out of the home at the end of the nineteenth century and the beginning of the twentieth century (for example, clerking, school work and nursing). This development in the labour market simultaneously challenged the authority of the Victorian husband, who perceived himself demeaned by having a working wife who had independence from him, and set up tensions for the women who were torn between going out to work and keeping a good home. One solution – both for the women who experienced this tension and for their husband who wanted to retain control over them – was to medicalize the wife, such that she could not leave the home: she was diagnosed as having agoraphobia (de Swann, A. (1981) 'The politics of agoraphobia: on changes in emotional management', *Theory and Society*, 10: 359–85) (**drapetomania**; **hysteria**; **masturbatory insanity**).

AIDS   (Acquired Immune Deficiency Syndrome) referred to as HIV/AIDS (**ARC**). Commonly accepted to be a disease caused by the human immunodeficiency virus (HIV) and first diagnosed in 1979–80 in the USA. Although from the start the disease was found in heterosexual and monogamous gay men it was linked to promiscuous gay lifestyles and originally called Gay Related Immune Deficiency (GRID). It is a prime example of the blending of moral prejudice and claimed scientific facts in the labelling and stigmatizing of a 'deviant' group. It is of considerable interest to sociologists of medical knowledge who have shown the contingent nature of claims about AIDS; historians of medical science, who have

demonstrated the close interface between explanations of AIDS and cultural values related to sexuality; and gay activists who have contested the professional knowledge-claims of medical science. The medical community has itself been deeply divided about the cause of AIDS with some denying the role of HIV altogether; and many third world countries have refused to accept the diagnostic label on the grounds that it masks the politics of imperialism, starvation and poverty (Epstein, S. (1996) *Impure Science: AIDS, Activism, and the Politics of Knowledge*. California: University of California) (**morality and medicine**).

ALCOHOLISM   The disease model of alcoholism has provided sociologists with an example of the development of medical thought in the twentieth century. Alcohol in the nineteenth century was conceptualized in terms of its effects on the body. The body was an object on which disease could be mapped. In the twentieth century the technical medical discourse merged with psychological discourse to make compassion and the social aspects of medical care part of the skill of medical practice. In the **biopsychosocial** model socio-moral judgements joined with the biophysical and fused to make a new medical discourse in which the patient's subjectivity was as much a focus as their biology. In this model alcoholism is a failure to cope with social roles, manifest in addictive behaviour with biological outcomes. (Arney, W. and Bergen, B. (1984) *Medicine and the Management of the Living*. Chicago:

University of Chicago Press) (**gambling**; **medicalization**; **repetitive strain injury**).

ALIENATION   Marx's account of the experience of work under capitalism. Workers are alienated in four inter-related ways: 1 from what they produce; 2 from control over the production process; 3 at the fundamental level the worker is alienated by having to sell what makes him or her human, his or her labour power; and 4 from other workers. Lack of autonomy at work, lack of control over the production process and separation from fellow workers are all now supported in empirical research as causes of disease (Karasek, R. and Theorell, T. (1990) *Healthy Work: Stress, Productivity and the Reconstruction of Working Life*. New York: Basic Books) (**Engels**; **job strain**; **Marx**; **occupation and health**).

ALLIED HEALTH WORKERS   A term used to describe all those who work under the control and at the direction of legally qualified medical practitioners (**medical dominance**).

ALLOPATHY/ALLOPATHIC   The noun and adjective for Western medical practitioners, who emphasize their secular, scientific training in natural sciences and locate disease in the individual's body. The individualistic and biologistic (**Cartesian**) definitions of health and disease have been challenged from their inception by those who emphasize the social determinants of health and disease, and who argue that the claimed 'scientific' status of medical knowledge obscures a range of **social** control functions in which definitions of disease are often thinly veiled descriptions of the failure to perform social roles. Ironically, given its current dominance, the term was coined by one of the fiercest opponents of orthodox medicine in the USA, Samuel Hahnemann (1745–1843), to distinguish it from his holistic homeopathic method (**homeopathy**; **morality and medicine**; **social construction/ constructionism**).

ALMA ATA DECLARATION   The World Health Organization's statement of 1978 which aimed for the 'attainment by all peoples of the world by the year 2000 of a level of health that will permit them to lead a socially and economically productive life' through the provision of primary healthcare 'made universally accessible to individuals and families in the community and by means acceptable to them, through their full participation and at a cost that the community and the country can afford' (World Health Organization (1978) *Alma-Ata. Primary Health Care (Health for All Series No. 1)*. Geneva: World Health Organization). Given the distance between the rhetoric and the resources of many countries it is not surprising that the goal remains unfulfilled (**Ottawa Charter**; **World Health Organization**).

ALTERNATIVE MEDICINE   The use of drugs or therapies that are not supported by allopathic medicine. The best known are **homeopathy**, **chiropractic osteopathy**, **acupuncture** and herbalism, though in popular usage the practice of alternative medicine extends to self-administered vitamin supplements. The definition of a healthcare practice as 'alternative' is a political and economic accomplishment of orthodox medicine. It results in specific national struggles by these alternative practitioners to resist this designation and to obtain a state licence to practise. In Australia, for example, chiropractic is legally recognized as a form of medicine, while in the UK homeopathy is recognized. Paradoxically 'alternative' medicine shares many of the characteristics of orthodox medicine, seeing disease as natural, focusing on the individual rather than social factors as the source of disease, and increasingly being dependent on a wide range of preparations marketed by multinational drug companies (Fulder, S. (1996) *The Handbook of Alternative and Complementary Medicine*. Oxford: Oxford University Press) (**allopathy/allopathic; complementary/alternative medicine**).

ALTRUISM   Putting others' needs ahead of one's own. In **sociobiology** this is explained in terms of enhancing the likelihood of one's genetic contribution to the human species, that is, such acts that make a person more attractive to a member of the opposite sex. In Durkheim's sociology it is a product of too much social integration, and can lead an individual to commit altruistic suicide, sacrificing themself on behalf of the group (**anomie; Durkheim; suicide**).

ALZHEIMER'S DISEASE   The gradual loss of memory, and the ability to perform cognitive functions such as abstract thought.

In its final stages the person loses all mental faculties. In the USA it is estimated to affect 20 per cent of the population over 85 years old. 'Grey' activists see it as a diagnostic category of gerontology which fuels ageist assumptions about the inevitability of dependency and decline in old age (Friedan, B. (1993) *The Fountain of Age*. New York: Simon and Schuster) (**ageing; ageism; gerontology**).

AMERICAN INDIANS (AMERINDIANS)   The discovery of the Americas by Columbus in 1492 unleashed the diseases of Europe on a population with little or no resistance. In combination with the onslaught of European culture and technology the 'columbian exchange' of disease (smallpox for syphilis) wreaked havoc on the populations of North and South America (Arnold, D. (1988) *Imperial Medicine and Indigenous Society*. Manchester: Manchester University Press). Amerindians share with other **indigenous peoples** poor health in comparison with the surrounding population: life expectancy of 66.3 years compared with the US average of 75 years; 25 per cent living in poverty; heart disease and cancer are the leading causes of death; and HIV/AIDS and hepatitis C are rapidly increasing (Grim, C. (2003) 'Health of American Indians and Alaska Natives', *BMJ USA*, 3: 242–3).

AMERICAN MEDICAL ASSOCIATION   Founded by **allopathic** medical practitioners in 1848 to represent the interests of 'regular' medical practitioners who identified themselves with scientific medicine (**Flexner Report**). Its control over the certification of who is allowed to practise medicine allows it to define as **alternative** those forms of health practice which do not meet its criteria of scientificity. Politically, the association has always resisted any form of state provided medicine, seeing it as socialistic, and undermining the **fee-for-service** basis of the supply of medical services (**perverse incentives**; **supplier induced demand**).

AMERICAN PSYCHIATRIC ASSOCIATION Founded in 1844 at a meeting of thirteen superintendents of hospitals for the insane. Benjamin Rush (1745–1813) wrote the first American textbook on psychiatry, *Medical Inquiries and Observations upon the Diseases of the Mind* (Philadelphia, 1812). He continued the tradition of attempting to shock or frighten the mentally ill, if not into cure, at least into submissiveness, inventing the tranquillizing chair, which was in keeping with other treatments such as the gyrating chair or the sudden plunging of the patient into cold water. Its handbook *The Diagnostic and Statistical Manual* (now in its fourth revised edition) lists all those conditions held to be psychiatric diseases. It is a source of considerable controversy since many of its diseases – and those excluded from it – are often seen to be reflections of contemporary culture. Homosexuality for example was voted out of the *Manual* in the mid-1970s (**antipsychiatry**; **Bedlam**; **Diagnostic and Statistical Manual**; **mental illness**; **Pinel**; **post traumatic stress disorder**; **Tuke**).

ANALYTIC INDUCTION A form of theory generation involving close examination of a phenomenon which allows for generalization to other like phenomena. Used in **grounded theory** approaches to research the aim is to generate hypotheses out of the data rather than forcing the data into a pre-existing theoretical framework. Most health social studies adopt this approach. The approach is rejected by all those who favour quantitative methods and theory testing research (**Chicago School of Sociology**; **positivism**; **qualitative research**).

ANATOMO-POLITICS In Foucault's work an aspect of **disciplinary power**, the internalization of scientific concepts of health and normality which are administered by professional groups on the basis of their claim to scientific knowledge. The development of biopower started in the eighteenth century with the state's recognition that healthy individuals and healthy populations were necessary for the well being of the state. Thus a focus on the body developed, to be managed and controlled. The development of the **psy-professions** (medicine, penology, sexology, psychology, sociology and psychiatry) from the end of the nineteenth century is the culmination of this process, with individuals constituted as self-managing, according to the dictates of medicine (**abnormal**; **biopolitics**; **biopower**; *Birth of the Clinic, The*; **Foucault**; **healthism**; **morality and medicine**; **surveillance**; **technologies of the self**).

ANATOMY The structure of the body and the medical discipline which studies the structure of the body, taught through dissection. The development of anatomy is important on two counts in the history of British medicine. The first is that the anatomists were not members of the College of Physicians or of the Company of Barber Surgeons. Rather they worked in private schools and hospitals. Thus the development of British medicine was the development out of empirical work, rather than derived from the 'scientific' revolution of the late seventeenth century, or the 'philosophic' revolution of the sixteenth century (**Whig histories of medicine**). The second is that it was the site of enormous public resistance to the development of medicine, and of the right of medicine to take the body in death (Linebaugh, P. (1988) 'The Tyburn riot against the surgeons', in Hay, D. (ed.), *Albion's Fatal Tree*. London: Penguin) (**cadaver**).

ANDERSON, ELIZABETH GARRETT (1836–1917) First English woman doctor and first woman member of the British Medical Association, obtaining the degree of Doctor of Medicine from Paris and appointed lecturer in medicine at the London School of Medicine for Women. She founded the St Mary's Dispensary for Women (1866), and the New Hospital for Women and Children. A leading suffragist, inspired by **Elizabeth Blackwell** she was a member of the committee which produced the first petition for woman's suffrage, presented to J. S. Mill in 1866 (**Mary Wollstonecraft**).

ANOMIE From the French sociologist **Émile Durkheim** who argued that with the development of industrial society and the breakdown of traditional society individuals could lose their sense of what was right and what was wrong, that is, find themselves in a state of 'normlessness'. This was a consequence of the increasingly specialized division of labour, the growth of an urban population and the loss of community, and the general decline of religion. At its worst it results in anomic suicide, that is, suicide induced in the individual by a society that has lost its way (**social pathology**; **suicide**).

ANOREXIA NERVOSA Medically defined as a disorder of body image in which a 'normal' weight or emaciated person 'feels' or is sure that they are fat, leading to self-starvation. The condition was given its medical label in 1874 by Sir William Gull and is now seen as a psychiatric disorder, with the therapy being hospitalization and forced feeding. There are clear sociological correlations for the condition: the person is young (usually under 30), female and from a high socio-economic group. Feminist sociologists argue that anorexia is the result of the contradictions of modern patriarchal societies where young women are supposed to be at once sylph-like as well as voluptuous, a paradox that neither they nor their bodies can sustain. In the context of this structural contradiction a viable response is to control the one thing they that perceive to be under their control, their appetite, and since with weight loss they cease to menstruate, their sense of self as sex-object (Orbach, S. (1981) *Fat is a Feminist Issue*. NY: Berkeley) (**binge-purging**; **bulimia**; **obesity**).

ANTHROPOLOGY OF HEALTH Anthropologists usually study traditional, non-industrial societies examining their cultural patterns and belief systems, and show how these are reflected in their medical systems. Anthropologists who turn their attention to the West argue that our medical beliefs are similarly cosmological structures which reflect our societies' understanding of the world (**biological anthropology**). They do not see Western medicine as 'better' but just different. One of the key differences from traditional forms of healing is the attempt in Western medicine to separate the meanings of illness for the sufferer from an allegedly pure biological base, thus creating a dualism between illness and disease (Kleinman, A. (1980) *Patients and Healers in the Context of Culture*. Berkeley: University of California Press) (**medical anthropology**; **medical anthropology, critical**).

ANTIBIOTICS Chemical substances produced by micro-organisms and capable of preventing the development of other micro-organisms. It is widely believed in popular and scientific Western medicine to have brought the infectious diseases of the late nineteenth and early twentieth centuries under control. However, **Thomas McKeown**, a historical epidemiologist, has demonstrated that their impact on these diseases was negligible and that health was improved by control over food, water and living conditions (McKeown, T. (1979) *The Role of Medicine*. Princeton: Princeton University Press) (**bacteriology**; **magic bullet**; **social medicine**).

ANTIPSYCHIATRY Erving Goffman's book *Asylums* (1961, NY: Doubleday and Co.) opened up the critique of medicine as a value-loaded system of social control operating under the guise of scientificity. He was followed by what is now called the antipsychiatry movement (Cooper, D. (1967) *Psychiatry and Anti-psychiatry*. London: Tavistock) particularly identified with the works of Thomas Szasz (1971, *The Manufacture of Madness: A Comparative Study of the Inquisition and the Mental Health Movement*. London: Routledge and Kegan Paul) and R. D. Laing (1961, *The Divided Self: An Existential Study in Sanity and Madness*. London: Tavistock). They argued that the categories that medicine uses to label a person, that is the disease labels, do not necessarily have an underlying biological reality but reflect the social values and prejudices of medical professionals (**labelling theory**). They held that this was particularly the case when the diseases were psychiatric and no physical basis for them could be established. Furthermore psychiatry was seen as a form of political oppression. As Laing put it: 'I do not myself believe that there is any such "condition" as "schizophrenia". Yet the label is a social fact. Indeed this label as a social fact is a political event' (Laing, R. D. (1964) 'What is schizophrenia?', *New Left Review*, 28: 63–9, p. 64). The antipsychiatry movement provided the environment for the first English understandings of Foucault's work, especially **Madness and Civilisation** (mental illness; therapeutic community).

ANXIETY   A term in Freudian psychoanalysis, which included castration, separation, depressive, paranoid, phobic and objective anxiety. **Freud** suggested that anxiety was a product of a repressed libido (that is, sex drive); that it was a repetition of the birth experience; or that it was the ego responding to emotional conflict. Anxiety, unlike fear, is not focused but a pervasive sense of apprehension or unease, and hence open to a wide range of interpretations. In psychology, in learning theory, it is a conditioned drive to alert the person to avoid a stimulus. In existential philosophy it is the consequence of confronting the meaninglessness of existence. In current social science the question is whether or not it is a biological universal or a culturally shaped emotion, with the evidence pointing to it being a specific European-American phenomenon (Tuma, H. and Mazur, J. (1985) *Anxiety and Anxiety Disorders*. New York: L. Erlbaum).

APANTHROPY   Aversion to society or human companionship. Put here for sociologists who may suffer from it, but not know what it is.

APOTHECARIES   Prior to the late nineteenth century, medicine was organized into the College of Physicians, who monopolized practice in the cities, particularly London, the Company of Barber Surgeons and apothecaries. Apothecaries were the general practitioners of the day though scorned by the physicians and surgeons since they not only diagnosed, but also prescribed and dispensed drugs for a fee (**Apothecaries Act**).

APOTHECARIES ACT   The attempt by the General Pharmaceutical Association, in 1815, to gain state mandated standards of entry to the occupation and to prohibit unqualified practitioners. This is the beginning of the introduction into English law of the concept of a qualified or registered medical practitioner and was consolidated with the Medical Act of 1858, allowing the General Medical Council the right to control who could practise medicine (Waddington, I. (1973) 'The struggle to reform the Royal College of Physicians 1767–1771: a sociological analysis', *Medical History*, 17: 107–26) (**credentialism; Flexner Report; medical dominance; occupational closure; professionalization**).

ARC (AIDS-RELATED COMPLEX)   AIDS in itself does not kill people; however by weakening the body's immune system it allows the development of a wide range of infections, the combination of which are fatal and are called AIDS-related complex.

ASBESTOSIS   A terminal disease of the lungs caused by exposure to asbestos. Of interest in the area of occupational health and safety because of the power of employers to avoid responsibility for the condition. They have successfully argued that there was a predisposing factor in individual workers rather than anything in their employment conditions that gave rise to the disease (Smith, B. (1981) 'Black lung: the social production of disease', *International Journal of Health Services*, 11 (3): 343–59) (**blame the victim**; **occupational disease**).

ASCLEPIUS   In ancient Greek mythology, the first medical practitioner, pursuing an empirical orientation to the diagnosis and treatment of an individual's disease. The other mythological origin of medicine is associated with the goddess Hygia, with her followers taking an approach that emphasized the impact of the environment on the collective health of the population. She is the origin of 'hygiene' and of public health. These contradictory origins, the one individualistic, the other collectivist, have shaped the history of Western medicine (Dubos, R. (1959) *Mirage of Health: Utopias, Progress and Biological Change*. London: George Allen and Unwin) (**hygiene**; **sanitation**).

ASIAN HEALING SYSTEMS   The basic essences of the body are Qi (wind), blood and yin and yang qualities. Hot and cold, and male and female elements must be kept in balance to be healthy. Causes of disease are wind, moisture and toxins. Too little yin produces dryness and heat, for example a cough and a temperature, while too little yang results in a loss of vitality and strength. Keeping the balance between

yin and yang is the basis of health (**Chinese medicine**).

ASPERGER'S SYNDROME   A psychiatric diagnosis of children, usually between 5 and 9 years of age and more commonly in boys, of a qualitative impairment in social interactions, such as eye-to-eye gaze, facial expression and body postures. Named for Hans Asperger who first diagnosed it in 1944, though not a diagnostic category in the United States until the 1980s, when his work became available in translation. Once thought to be very rare it is now widely diagnosed, though the symptoms may be very mild and difficult to diagnose. Initially explanations focused on the role of the mother and a failure to bond between the parent and child, though currently a genetic explanation is being developed. Because there are no clinically identifiable causes, and because the diagnosis is so insecure, sociologists argue that it can be analysed as the **medicalization** of socially inappropriate behaviour (**attention deficit disorders**; **autism spectrum disorders**; **behavioural disorders**; **labelling theory**; **learning disabilities**).

ASSISTED REPRODUCTIVE TECHNOLOGIES (ARTS)   A range of medical interventions – from hormone treatment through to artificial insemination – to induce pregnancy. In 1995, 6.2 million American women reported reduced fertility with 44 per cent presenting to a medical practitioner. With the rise of the idea that everything is amenable to a 'technical fix' infertility has been transformed from a natural condition into a medical problem. Its **medicalization** enshrines cultural concepts of a woman's role as mother (Donchin, A. (1996) 'Feminist critiques of new fertility technologies: Implications for social policy', *Journal of Medicine and Philosophy*, 21: 475–98) (**childbirth**; **new reproductive technologies**; **reproduction**).

ASYLUMS Institutions for those diagnosed as mentally ill (**Bedlam**). In the 1970s following the **antipsychiatry** movement and cost saving initiatives in government spending there was a move to return these individuals to the community. This 'decarceration', unaccompanied by a transfer of resources, left individuals to fend for themselves, and 'community care' rapidly became 'community neglect' (Scull, A. (1984) *Decarceration: Community Treatment and the Deviant*. Cambridge: Polity) (**care in the community**; **deinstitutionalization**; **total institution**).

ATTACHMENT THEORY Developed by John Bowlby in the 1960s and 1970s identifies as crucial for emotional development the role of bonding between mother and infant, and as developed in health sociology provides a pathway for explaining health in later life. Bowlby's work was a combination of psychoanalysis and ethology, the study of animal behaviour. Following reactions from the women's movement Bowlby came to accept that men could mother too (Bowlby, J. (1979) *The Making and Breaking of Affectional Bonds*. London: Tavistock) (**Barker hypothesis**;

life course analysis; separation anxiety; social support).

ATTENTION DEFICIT DISORDERS First classified as a psychiatric disorder in the third edition of the *Diagnostic and Statistical Manual of the American Psychiatric Association* in 1981 as attention deficit/hyperactivity disorder, that is, as one condition with two different manifestations. DSM-III, revised in 1987, distinguished them as two different conditions, while DSM-IV (1994) has reclassified them as the same disorder. The condition is one of 'developmentally inappropriate inattention and impulsivity', that is, the classification of inappropriate behaviour as a disease. It thus represents the **medicalization** of a condition and its changing diagnostic criteria have been analysed to demonstrate the political and social construction of the disorder. Although there are no biological tests for the condition it is treated with a prescribed drug, Ritalin (Conrad, P. (1976) *Identifying Hyperactive Children: The Medicalisation of Deviant Behaviour*. Massachusetts: D.C. Heath and Company) (**autism spectrum disorders**; **behavioural disorders**; **labelling theory**; **learning disabilities**; **post traumatic stress disorder**).

AUSTRALIAN MEDICAL ASSOCIATION Founded in 1962, out of the Australian branch of the British Medical Association, to represent the interests of the medical profession. A vociferous opponent of government involvement in the medical professions' activities, it hotly opposed the establishment of a universal free healthcare system after World War II, and supports a **fee-for-service** and private health insurance system. Australia's healthcare system was aptly described by Sir Theodore Fox in the *Lancet* in 1963 as 'private practice publicly supported', a situation in which the medical profession has benefited enormously. As with the medical profession in other Western countries there are challenges to its dominance from consumer groups, the feminist movement and with the rise of corporatization, the increasing proletarian-ization of the medical workforce (**depro-fessionalization; Medibank; medical dominance; perverse incentives; supplier induced demand**).

AUTHORITY   Max Weber distinguished authority, the compliance with orders because they are perceived as legitimate, from power, forcing someone against their will to comply. Weber distinguished irra-tional forms of authority – tradition, doing things because they have always been done this way, and charisma following an inspiring leader – from **rational legal authority**, a codified set of rules, as for exam-ple in a **bureaucracy (hospitals; substantive rationality)**.

AUTISM SPECTRUM DISORDERS   Also known as pervasive developmental dis-order, the diagnosis ranges from profound withdrawal through to virtually normally functioning individuals with Asperger's syndrome. Sociologists have argued that the diagnosis, since it is based on behav-ioural observation, may be explained in terms of the medicalization of inappropri-ate social behaviour (**Asperger's syndrome; attention deficit disorders; learning disabil-ities; medicalization**).

AUTOPSY   The dissection of the body to establish the cause of death. Important in the history of Western medicine as the focus of conflict between the Church and the developing medical profession, involv-ing control over definitions of **death** and the **body (anatomy)**.

AYURVEDIC MEDICINE   Derived from the Sanskrit 'veda' for knowledge and 'ayus' for longevity. Unlike Western medicine Ayurvedic teaching is a holistic perspec-tive on the healthy life. The three basic bodily humours (dosas) – wind, bile and phlegm – are counterparts of wind, sun and moon. The body is made up of chyle, blood, flesh, fat, bone, marrow and semen. The medical system is located within a Hindu religious philosophy of birth, renunciation, and the maintenance of the balance of the soul (Porter, R. (1997) *The Greatest Benefit to Mankind*. London: Harper Collins) (**Asian healing systems; Chinese medicine**).

B

BACHELARD, GASTON (1884–1962)
French historian and philosopher of
science who along with **Canguilhelm**
argued that scientific developments were
'epistemological ruptures' and not progressive developments. Thus the history of
science was the history of discontinuities.
His work had a major impact on **Foucault**
who used the concept of epistemological rupture to challenge linear, progressive
histories of the development of Western
knowledge, and particularly medical
knowledge (Bachelard, G. (1968) *The
Philosophy of No*. Trans. G.C. Waterson.
New York: Orion Press) (**Fleck**; **Kuhn**;
social history of medicine; **Whig histories
of medicine**).

BACTERIOLOGY The study of bacteria,
especially as they relate to the spread
of disease. Their discovery by Pasteur
(1822–1895) the French chemist produced the spur for the development of the
germ theory of disease, that is, that disease
is caused by an invading micro-organism
which infects the body. The development
of the germ theory meant that the social
and political aspects of the causes of disease were obscured (**antibiotics**; **McKeown**;
social medicine; **Virchow**; **Whig histories
of medicine**).

BAREFOOT DOCTOR An initiative of the
Chinese Cultural Revolution in the 1960s
in which local people received basic medical training and thereby provided the
rural population with access to basic
medical services.

BARKER HYPOTHESIS From the work of
epidemiologist David Barker on the fetal
origins of disease, suggesting that life-time
patterns of health are laid down in the
womb (Barker, D. (1994) *Mothers, Babies
and Disease in Later Life*. London: BMJ
Publishing Group). This has led to a reductionist account of the 'biological pro-
gramming' of health at birth, with the
implication that it is an individual, biological phenomenon unrelated to social
factors. In contrast, health sociologists argue
that far from being simply biological, poor
fetal development is linked to class position, which in turn in later life exposes
individuals to hazardous lifestyle factors. It
is the interaction of the biological with the
social that has to be accounted for, and
not the assertion of a biological inevitability to disease (Blane, D. 'The life course,
the social gradient and health', in M. Marmot
and R. Wilkinson (eds), *Social Determinants
of Health*. Oxford: Oxford University
Press) (**life course analysis**).

BEDLAM   The first psychiatric institution for the insane in Britain, the Hospital of St Mary of Bethlehem. Founded in 1247, but established as an asylum in 1547 by Henry VIII, the insane were treated with deprivation and shock. In the nineteenth century it was the focus of reform as humane care for the insane replaced public exposure and confinement in chains. The claim of a progressive development in the treatment of the insane was the target of Foucault's (1961) *Madness and Civilisation* (London: Tavistock) (**American Psychiatric Association; asylums; Dix; Foucault; Pinel; Tuke**).

BEDSIDE MEDICINE   In the history of medicine the term used to designate the situation of medical practice in the eighteenth century. It was one in which the elite, powerful patients dominated the lower-status, poorer doctor. The model of illness in this period reflected the concerns of the patient who was treated in a holistic way. With the development of **hospital** medicine patients lost power to the rising medical profession. Along with this went a redefinition of disease as a purely physical event, independent of the patient's social location. In turn this has been supplanted by laboratory medicine in which both the doctor and the patient have become subservient to laboratory tests rather than clinical judgement (Jewson, N. (1976) 'The disappearance of the sick man from medical cosmology 1770–1870', *Sociology*, 10 (2): 225–44) (**medical technology; profession; Whig histories of medicine**).

BEHAVIOURISM   A highly influential stream of thought in psychology in the mid-twentieth century. Behaviourists argue that psychology can become a science if it focuses on the external behaviour of people and rejects any analysis of mental events, emotions or feelings. Largely based on animal studies of rats and pigeons, it is rejected in sociological accounts of human action (**behaviour modification; empiricism; voluntaristic theory of action; Watson**).

BEHAVIOUR MODIFICATION   Based on the **behaviourism** of J. B. Watson a clinical technique alleged to be able to modify an individual's reactions to stimuli, particularly that they could be desensitized to things that they fear. At its height under the impact of B. F. Skinner and Clark Hull it was claimed that all forms of human behaviour could be manipulated via stimulus–response reactions. In works of fiction such as Aldous Huxley's *Brave New World*, and George Orwell's *1984*, it was presented as a tool of a totalitarian state to ensure conformity and compliance.

BEHAVIOURAL DISORDERS   A wide range of conditions in which the individual fails to conform to 'normal' expectations, developmentally, educationally, or interpersonally. Empirically, sociologists examine these conditions as aspects of the **medicalization** of life and of the **social control** functions of medical professionals (**abnormal; attention deficit disorders; Asperger's syndrome; autism spectrum disorders; labelling theory; learning disabilities**).

BELMONT REPORT   The report of the National Commission for the Protection of Human Subjects of Biomedical and Behavioural Research, published in 1979. It lays down the basic ethical principles for medical research in the US: that there be respect for the autonomy of the person, beneficence, that is, to do no harm, and that the findings of research be used justly (**bioethics; ethics, medical; Helsinki Declaration; Hippocrates; Nuremberg Code; Tuskegee syphilis experiment**).

BENCHMARKING   The commitment to introduce the best standards of international practice into an organization, such as a hospital. It is usually done in the guise of the new public management, in which market approaches are applied in public institutions, on the grounds that this will make them more efficient and businesslike (Cairney, P. (2002) 'New public management and the Thatcher healthcare legacy', *British Journal of Politics and International Relations*, 4: 375–98) (**clinical pathways; corporatization; neoliberalism; new public management; privatization**).

BENTHAM, JEREMY (1748–1832)   The founder of utilitarianism, and author of *Introduction to the Principles of Morals and Legislation* (1789), a philosophy that states that each individual's pursuit of happiness will produce the happiness of the greatest number. Bentham devised the model of the **panopticon**, a form of prison, in which the prisoners do not know when they are being observed and therefore at all times have to assume that they are under observation. This

leads to the internalization of social control. Foucault argues that this is now a central feature of modern societies such that we now police ourselves, monitoring our thoughts, behaviour and body in the context of a medicalized net of social relationships (Goodin, R. (1995) *Utilitarianism as a Public Philosophy*. Cambridge: Cambridge University Press) (**carceral society; Foucault; medicalization; psy-professions; technologies of the self**).

BEREAVEMENT   Following the work of Kubler-Ross in the 1960s, grief over death became acceptable in the West. Kubler-Ross identified the stages of grief as denial that the person is dead, anger with the person for dying, explained by Kubler Ross as the outcome of things that have been left unsaid, bargaining, depression and finally acceptance of the situation (Kubler Ross, E. (1969) *On Death and Dying*. London: Tavistock) (**death; hospice movement**).

BEST-CARE PRACTICES   The claim by medical practitioners to have the clinical freedom to act in the best interests of their patients, independently of considerations of cost. In Max Weber's terms they are guided by 'wertrational' principles, action guided by an orientation towards valued ends, and come into conflict with bureaucratic concerns guided by 'zweckrational' principles, that is, rule following in a bureaucratic hierarchy (**authority; bureaucracy; critical theory**).

BIAS   In positivist social science the claim that the researchers' subjectivity has to be controlled so as to allow for 'objective' scientific findings to emerge. The pursuit of objectivity has been criticized by those in the qualitative tradition of research who emphasize the contextual nature of knowledge. Feminist sociologists, for example, argue that the research process is built on trust and empathy, and that the production of knowledge is a joint venture of the researched and the researcher (Oakley, A (1981) 'Interviewing women: a contradiction in terms', in H. Roberts (ed.), *Doing Feminist Research*. London: Routledge and Kegan Paul). Jürgen Habermas has argued that the aim of social science research is empathy and understanding, rather than explanation and prediction, and that objectivity is a impossibility in the social sciences (Habermas, J. (1972) *Knowledge and Human Interests*. London: Heinemann). It is often assumed that if the results are statistical this in some way frees them from bias. However over thirty-five sources of bias have been demonstrated in statistical research as a consequence of selection, classification or confounding of data (Sackett, D. (1979) 'Bias in analytic research', *Journal of Chronic Disease*, 32: 51–63) (**action based methods/research**; **positivism**; **verstehen**; **Weber**).

BINARY OPPOSITIONS　　The division of the natural and social worlds into opposites, for example male/female, reason/emotion, able-bodied/disabled body, healthy/sick, or young/old with the privileging of one – the former – over the latter. Dualisms such as these are central to Western ways of thinking, taken as they are to reflect real differences in nature. Such simple divisions obscure the complexity of social relationships and exclude those in the latter categories from a full participation in social life (**ageism**; **Cartesian**; **disability**; **gender**).

BINET, ALFRED (1857–1911)　French psychologist at the Sorbonne who formulated the IQ test. Widely adopted by educational reformers it was standardized by Lewis Terman at Stanford University, hence the Stanford-Binet IQ test (**IQ controversy**).

BINGE-PURGING　　The act of gorging on food and then inducing vomiting, self-administering laxatives or undertaking excessive exercise to prevent weight gain. Foucauldian **feminists** argue that binge-purging may be either the act of a rebellious subject, flaunting societal dictates of appropriate usage of food, or of a docile subject attempting to conform to what they think is the appropriate body image (Eckermann, E. (1997) 'Foucault, embodiment and gendered subjectivities', in A. Petersen and R. Bunton (eds), *Foucault, Health and Medicine*. London: Routledge) (**anorexia nervosa**; **bulimia**).

BIOETHICS　　The study of moral issues raised by medical research, technological developments and the rights of individuals and groups, particularly around reproduction, life and death. Many of these issues are specific to social groups. **New reproductive technologies** and their impact are specific to women, while the conduct of unethical research based on racist assumptions is of concern to black Americans (**Belmont Report; eugenics; new genetics; Nuremberg Code; Tuskegee syphilis experiment**).

BIOGRAPHICAL DISRUPTION   With the increase in chronic illness, and the extension of life after the diagnosis of a terminal illness, individuals now experience ongoing status as a sick person. This may positively or negatively affect their sense of self, and a new identity has to be created and managed to allow the continual presentation of the self. In doing so, individuals tell stories that repair the damage done to them, both physical and psychological, and attempt to reconstitute their biography as meaningful (Williams, G. (1984) 'The genesis of chronic illness: narrative reconstruction', *Sociology of Health and Illness*, 6: 175–200) (**chronic illness; disease identity dependency; narrative accounts of illness; quest narratives; stigma**).

BIOLOGICAL ANTHROPOLOGY   A branch of anthropology, also called physical anthropology, that studies human beings in the context of their links with the animal world, adopting an evolutionary perspective and closely allied to **sociobiology**. It is biologically **reductionist**, and in studying disease, ignores the social, political and economic factors which socially produce and distribute it (**anthropology of health; medical anthropology**).

BIOLOGICAL DETERMINISM   The claim that some characteristics of human beings are given in nature, and therefore are unchangeable. It provides conservatives with an argument that inequality is natural and inevitable. In its political form it leads to **eugenics**, the claim that the 'unfit' should not be allowed to produce offspring. The opposite is **cultural determinism**, which argues that human beings at birth are unfinished, and that their culture will determine their final characteristics, both psychological and biological. The debate has significant policy implications, since the biological determinist position suggests that little can be done if those experiencing ill-health are biologically programmed that way. Cultural determinists hold to the position that if our characteristics are socially shaped then they can be socially modified. The most significant arena for the debate in the late twentieth century has been over the heritability of intelligence (**IQ controversy; sociobiology**).

BIOLOGICAL HAZARDS   The explanation given for disease in biomedicine is that it is the product of external biological factors such as germs or viruses, that is, 'biological hazards'. The contrast is with the role ascribed to psychosocial and social epidemiological factors identified by the social sciences in explaining the production and distribution of disease (**health determinants; social support; stress**).

BIOLOGISTIC   A pejorative term used to describe the attempt by the medical sciences to reduce human experience to the biological workings of the body. Social scientists argue that the experience of the **body**, sickness and disease is mediated by social structures such as gender, class and ethnicity, and do not reflect in any immediate way the working of nature (**constructionism**; **disembodiment**; **reductionism**).

BIOMEDICAL CULTURES A concept in anthropology which highlights the fact that there are competing understandings of disease and illness co-existing along side the **medical model**. These include lay and folk understandings of illness in the West, as well as those alternative medical practices in developing countries, captured in the phrase 'medical pluralism', where an attempt is made to integrate indigenous healing systems with Western biomedicine (Leslie, C. (1980) 'Medical pluralism in world perspective', *Social Science and Medicine*, 14B: 629–42) (**lay referral system**; **shamanism**).

BIOMEDICAL MODEL Developing from the eighteenth century, the biomedical model explains disease as the working of lesions in the body, chartable by the doctor through the physical examination. It became institutionally located in the developing hospitals in France from the eighteenth century. The emphasis of biomedicine is the treatment of disease using the methods of the natural sciences (*Birth of the Clinic, The*; **Cartesian**; **Foucault**).

BIOMEDICINE Orthodox Western medical knowledge sometimes referred to as **allopathic**. Its key assumptions – that disease is a biological fact, that patients can best be examined using the methods of the natural sciences, and that effective treatment involves drugs, technology, surgery and **psychosurgery** – are widely criticized in health studies (**abnormal**; **clinical iceberg**; **disease**; **disembodiment**; **normal**).

BIOPOLITICS The linking of the human body to organized medical knowledge so as to achieve social control (**anatomo-politics**; **biopower**; *Birth of the Clinic, The*; **Foucault**; **morality and medicine**; **psy-professions**; **surveillance**).

BIOPOWER In **Foucault's** sociology the key to understanding social control in modern societies. Foucault argued that the new social and medical sciences of the nineteenth century – penology, criminology, sexology, psychiatry, psychology, sociology and medicine – operate as disciplines of **power/knowledge**. They are disciplines in the academic sense of claiming to have knowledge of how populations and individuals act and behave, and they are disciplines in the sense that they are empowered by the state to enforce compliance with normal behaviour (**abnormal**; **anatomo-politics**; **biopolitics**; *Birth of the Clinic, The*; **psy-professions**).

BIOPSYCHOSOCIAL The integration of sociological and psychological insights into

biomedicine. The development of the model was professional medicine's attempt to come to grips with the patient's experience and understanding of their illness, as well as seeing their illness as an aspect of their social location. Nevertheless the model fails to challenge the basis of medical practice in biology and is ultimately reductionist (Engel, G. (1977) 'The need for a new medical model: a challenge for biomedicine', *Science*, 196: 129–34) (**medicalization**; **mind–body relationship**).

BIOTECHNOLOGY   The interface between engineering and biology ranging from the stethoscope, the ultrasound, and the fetal monitor to the titanium hip, the pacemaker and the cochlea ear. These developments have led some to speculate on the disappearance of the body in modern techno-medicine. We now have bodies made with plastic, bionic/interchangeable bodies, and the virtual bodies of the new surgical techniques in which surgeons operate at a distance on TV screens of the patient's body. The body of the patient has been dissolved with the creation of hyper-real bodies of technological-human blend, such that the two cannot be distinguished (Williams, S. (1997) 'Modern medicine and the "uncertain" body: from corporeality to hyperreality', *Social Science and Medicine*, 45: 1041–9) (**body**; **cyborgs**; **disembodiment**; **medical technology**; **social construction of technology approach**; **visual imaging**).

BIRTH CONTROL   Measures taken to prevent conception. In early feminism (before the 1920s) this included abstinence and the refusal of conjugal rights to the husband. With the development of the pill in the 1960s freedom from the threat of pregnancy became a reality for women and fuelled the woman's liberation movement. Women's control over their reproductive capacity is central to all forms of **feminism (abortion**; **childbirth**; **radical feminism)**.

BIRTH OF THE CLINIC, THE   Foucault's account of the development of modern medicine in which he argues that medical knowledge, rather than being a steady progression of science, is historically and culturally specific. In it he documents the rise to power of the medical profession with the development of the medical gaze, that is, the **power/knowledge** to define life and death. Foucault locates in the development of medicine the first successful discourse to treat human beings as objects, producing a science of the individual. Central to *The Birth of the Clinic* is the concept of the gaze, by which Foucault means both the act of perception, but also a way of perceiving, of bringing something into existence. The medical gaze brings into existence the body of the individual and the fact of disease, an objective and independent entity, as something that happens to the individual. This allows Foucault to develop his argument that modern societies have power relations that involve the individual policing their own bodies and health status (**technologies of the self**), and provides the basis for **anatomo-politics** and **biopower** (Foucault, M.

(1973) *The Birth of the Clinic: An Archeology of Medical Perception*. London: Tavistock) (**Foucault; social construction/ constructionism**).

BLACK REPORT   One of the most important reports to come out of the UK in the twentieth century on the social patterning of illness and disease. It demonstrated the links between poverty, inequality and differential rates of disease in the population. Using the British Registrar-General's classification of occupation on death certificates it showed that those in classes IV and V (partly skilled and unskilled) were sicker and died earlier than those in classes I and II (professional and managerial). The report systematically reviewed the evidence for this correlation and rejected explanations that suggested that it was a statistical artefact, that it was a consequence of natural selection, or that it was a product of lifestyle choice. Rather it argued that the distribution of disease down the social system was the product of structural aspects of inequality such as patterns of property ownership and poverty. Because of its overwhelming demonstration of inequality in health and the links it made between wider social inequalities and health the Conservative Prime Minister Margaret Thatcher attempted to prevent its publication and it was only through the privilege of the House of Lords that Lord Black brought it to light (Department of Health and Social Security (1980) *Inequalities in Health: Report of a Working Group Chaired by Sir Douglas Black*. London: Department of Health Statistics and Surveys) (**health determinants; social inequality; Whitehall Studies**).

BLACKWELL, ELIZABETH (1821–1910) The first woman to gain an American medical degree and to have her name listed on the Medical Register, London. The author of, and the first to use the term 'medical sociology', *Essays in Medical Sociology*, published in 1902 (republished in 1977, AMS Press: New York), her major contribution was a scepticism about 'medical materialism' developing out of the mechanistic view of the body that bacteriological medicine was fostering. She founded the National Health Society of London and was one of the founders of the London School of Medicine for Women (Morantz-Sanchez, R. (1992) 'Feminist theory and historical practice: rereading Elizabeth Blackwell', *History and Theory*, 31: 51–69) (**Anderson; vitalism**).

BLAME THE VICTIM   Attributing to a person the cause of their own misfortune. A common strategy in conservative social policy which by focusing on the individual obscures the social, political and economic environment that shapes their actions. In the **new public health** individuals are blamed for their conditions for choosing an unhealthy **lifestyle**. The result is to excuse governments from taking action and thus to evade the costs of disease prevention (Ryan, W. (1971) *Blaming the Victim*. New York: Vintage) (**accident proneness; asbestosis; Engels; industrial disease; morality and medicine; social drift hypothesis; stigmatized risk group**).

BLUE CROSS/BLUE SHIELD US health insurance agencies that operate by collecting monies from individuals independent of their current healthcare requirements for utilization when needed (**health insurance; health maintenance organizations; uninsured**).

BODY In medicine, the body is the unproblematic basis of our natural, biological existence, and the site of disease (**Cartesian**). In the social sciences the argument is that our experience of, and knowledge of, our bodies is a product of our specific historical, cultural, political and gendered existence. In this sense the body is not a biologically objective entity but the canvas on which social relationships are painted. In classical sociology **Marx**, **Engels** and **Weber** demonstrated the shaping of the body as it was harnessed to the discipline of factory labour, and in this sense the malleability of its 'natural' form, which they took for granted. One of the earliest anthropological accounts of the body was produced by Marcel Mauss who noted that every aspect of bodily deportment – from breathing, through to marching and swimming – was specific to the society which produced it and reflected hierarchies of inequality, especially based around education levels (Mauss, M. (1973 [orig. 1935]) 'Techniques of the body', *Economy and Society*, 2: 71–88). Mary Douglas went on to argue that 'the social body constrains the way the physical body is perceived. The physical experience of the body, always modified by the social categories through which it is known,

sustains a particular view of society. There is a continual interchange between the two kinds of bodily experience so that each reinforces the categories of the other' (Douglas, M. (1973: 93) *Natural Symbols*. Harmondswoth: Penguin). Contemporary research goes further in rejecting the 'naturalness' of the body, providing alternative definitions and accounts of the body that highlight both the social shaping of our understandings of our body and our body as a lived reality. As Simone de Beauvoir, the French feminist philosopher put it: 'it is not the body-object described by biologists that actually exists, but the body as lived in by the subject' (de Beauvoir, S. (1953: 69) *The Second Sex*. London: Harmondsworth) (**embodiment**). Feminist analyses of medical representations of the body highlight the way in which **medicalization** produces women's bodies as sick and in need of constant care and surveillance (**Foucauldian-feminism**). At the cultural level women's bodies have been shown to be construed as inferior to men's, as less amenable to control and as dangerous (Grosz, E. (1994) *Volatile Bodies: Towards a Corporeal Feminism*. Sydney: Allen and Unwin). Historians, particularly those influenced by Foucault, have also demonstrated how specific religious, political and economic contexts produce our knowledge of the body (Feher, M. et al. (1989) (eds), *Fragments for a History of the Human Body*. (3 volumes). New York: Zone). In the context of medical thought Foucault argues that the crucial concepts of the body and disease must be seen as historical products.

In our culture we believe 'that the body obeys the exclusive laws of physiology and that it escapes the influences of history but this too is false. The body is moulded by a great many regimes' (Foucault, M. (1977) 'Nietzsche, genealogy and history', in D. Bouchard (ed.), *Language, Countermemory, Practice*. Oxford: Basil Blackwell) (**biotechnology**; **cyber-anatomies**; **cyborgs**; **embodiment**).

BODYISM   The imperative to control one's body in neoliberalism, where to fall sick, particularly of what are claimed to be lifestyle based diseases, is a failure to monitor oneself in the conduct of one's life as an active citizen. Being ill is a moral failure (Rosenberg, C. (1997) 'Banishing risk: continuity and change in the moral management of disease', in A. Brandt and P. Rozin (eds), *Morality and Health*. London: Routledge) (**fitness**; **habitus**; **Mauss**; **morality and medicine**; **self-care**; **somatic norms**; **technologies of the self**).

BODY MAINTENANCE   (**bodyism**; **citizenship**; **fitness**; **self-care**; **technologies of the self**).

BODY POLITICS   The idea of the body as resource for political mobilization around issues of inequality of access to social status and resources and, especially for disabled bodies and aged bodies (Elshtain, J. and Cloyd, J. (1995) *Politics and the Human Body*. Nashville, TN: Vanderbilt University Press). Nancy Henley's 1977 book, *Body Politics* (New Jersey: Prentice

Hall) described how in Western patriarchal society power relationships between men and women determine who can touch who, where and for what reason. Thus men in guiding women to restaurant tables exercise their dominance in physical touch (**somatic society**)

BOOTH, CHARLES JAMES (1840–1916) Author of the study *Life and Labour of the People in London* (1889–1891) in seventeen volumes, in which he demonstrated statistically the links between poverty and disease. The discovery of the social patterning of disease – its distribution correlating to poverty and housing conditions, as well as employment conditions – laid the basis for the public health movement. It was overtaken by the **germ theory** of disease, which by locating disease in the body of the patient, and developing drugs and technologies for cure, deflected attention from the social environment (**Chadwick**; **Engels**; **hygiene**; **Snow**; **social medicine**).

BRACKETING   (phenomenological reduction) At its simplest, the attempt by phenomenological researchers to suspend pre-existing knowledge, that is, the taken for granted reality, so as to achieve understanding from the perspective of the subject. In qualitative research it has been adapted to mean 'putting yourself in the place of the other', in an attempt to capture their view of the world, and while having origins in the work of **Max Weber**, was brought into American sociology by **Alfred Schutz** (**Husserl**; **qualitative research**; **verstehen**).

BREAST CANCER   Of particular interest to sociologists of scientific knowledge and feminist sociologists because of the wide range of medical opinions about the utility of mammogram screening for its early detection. Because of this uncertainty it is argued that breast cancer screening is a form of **surveillance medicine** and of the **medicalization** of women's bodies. In this perspective screening is 'a site for state, professional and male surveillance and control, through preventive services that many feel obligated to participate in' (McKie, L. (1995) 'The art of surveillance or reasonable prevention – the case of cervical screening,' *Sociology of Health and Illness*, 17: 441–57) (**mammography screening programme**; **surveillance medicine**).

BRITISH MEDICAL ASSOCIATION (BMA) Founded in 1832 as the Provincial Medical and Surgical Association, becoming the BMA in 1855, the first of the modern professional organizations and one whose power and influence in politics and policy other occupations have aspired to. The aims of the organization were to break the stranglehold of the Royal Colleges over the practice of medicine and to eliminate competition from unqualified practitioners (**medical dominance**). The success of the developing medical profession was marked by the monopoly over practice granted to it when the General Medical Council was established as a statutory body in 1858. Throughout its history the BMA has had a antagonistic relationship to state-based healthcare initiatives, arguing for the preservation of a private fee-for-service model. In Britain the **National Health Service** represented an uneasy truce between doctors and the state in the provision of healthcare (Lawrence, C. (1994) *Medicine in the Making of Modern Britain. 1700–1920*. London: Routledge).

BRITISH NATIONAL HEALTH SERVICE Legislation to extend state ownership and provision of health services in 1948 following long-standing recognition of problems of quality and access to health services exacerbated by World War II. It was hotly opposed by the **British Medical Association**, which saw it as turning doctors into state employees and threatening their professional status. In all events it did neither, but it did increase their income (Klein, R. (1989) *The Politics of the National Health Service*. London: Longman).

BRITISH NATIONAL INSURANCE SCHEME A health insurance scheme launched by British Prime Minister Lloyd George in 1911, and laying the foundation for the scheme operating today in the UK. The scheme did not bring about free healthcare for everyone. Only the worker who paid into the scheme was entitled to free medical care from a panel of doctors. His wife and children had to pay for treatment. Free medical care for everyone came about in 1948 with the introduction of the **National Health Service**.

BROWN LUNG DISEASE   (asbestosis).

BRUNONIANISM   A system of medicine named after the Scottish medical practitioner John Brown (1735–88) who argued that health was the outcome of an equilibrium between stimulus and excitability. Too much of one, or too little of the other, resulted in disease.

BUILDING   RELATED   ILLNESS   (BRI) Unlike **sick building syndrome**, BRI is the term used when symptoms of diagnosable illness are identified and can be directly attributed to airborne contaminants. Indoor air pollution comes from the manufactured products emitting volatile organic compounds (VOC). Other sources are contaminated air supplies from stagnant water lying in air-conditioning ducts, the cause of **Legionnaires' disease** (*Indoor Environmental Quality*. National Institute for Occupational Safety and Health, June 1997. http://www.cdc.gov/niosh/ieqfs. html) (**alienation**; **occupation and health**; **repetitive strain injury**).

BULIMIA   The diagnosis of an eating disorder, characterized by the excessive intake of food over a two-hour period, usually followed by self-induced vomiting or the consumption of laxatives, prolonged fasting or excessive exercise, to prevent subsequent weight gain. It may accompany anorexia nervosa. Statistical estimates of its prevalence range from 5–35 per cent of women aged 13–20 years in the USA having the condition. Feminist analysis points to the media's construction of the slender body as the ideal, the construction of a morbid fear

of weight gain, and the contradictory focus on women's role in the preparation of food for the family while she should watch her eating habits, as sources of tension which the individual cannot resolve. The result is that women are driven to consume food, but then need to rid themselves of it (Bordo, S. (1985) 'Anorexia nervosa: psychopathology as the crystallisation of culture', *The Philosophical Forum*, 17: 73–103) (**anorexia nervosa**; **binge-purging**).

BURDEN OF DISEASE   Epidemiologists examine the impact of disease and death in the population using measures of the 'burden of disease', that is, disability through ill-health and preventable death. These measures are: years of life lost due to premature mortality (YLL) and the impact of disability (YLD) – that is the number of healthy years that have been forfeited. YLL plus YLD gives the total number of years lost to disability and premature deaths (DALY). One DALY equals one year of life lost (**global burden of disease**; **quality adjusted life years**).

BUREAUCRACY   Institutional structures based on **rational legal authority** and argued by **Max Weber** to be the dominant form of social organization in modern society. A bureaucracy, as an **ideal type**, is characterized by: a division of labour based on specialization; a well-defined hierarchy of authority; a system of rules detailing the rights and duties of the office holder; explicit procedures for dealing with the work to be done; an impersonality of interpersonal relations; and selection and promotion based on technical competence. Hospitals as bureaucratic structures were the focus of much sociological analysis during the 1960s, examining the ways in which conflicts arose between physicians and the bureaucracy; and the ways, which in spite of appearances, individuals negotiated bureaucratic structures that got around the rules (Freidson, E. (1963) *The Hospital in Modern Society*. New York: Free Press) (**hospitals**; **total institution**).

C

CADAVER   A dead body. In the history of medicine important as the site of the dispute for cultural authority between the Church and medicine. The first documented public dissection of a body was in 1315 at Bologna, carried out by Mondolino de Luzzi, author of *Anatomia Mundini*, the first handbook of dissection, published in 1478 (**anatomy; bereavement; death**).

CANADIAN INUIT   An aboriginal people in Northern Canada who live above the tree line in Nunavit, the Northwest Territories, Northern Quebec and Labrador. As with other aboriginal peoples they have higher infant mortality and serious infectious disease rates. Tuberculosis is ten times higher than for Canadians (**Aboriginal Health Service; Aboriginals; African American**).

CANADIAN NATIONAL HEALTH INSURANCE A universal, taxation funded health insurance scheme implemented through the 1967 Medical Care Act. It provided the model for universal free health care like the Australian Medicare system.

CANADIAN PUBLIC HEALTH ASSOCIATION (CPHA)   Formed in 1912, a national, independent and not for profit voluntary organization. It advocates universal and equitable access to the basic conditions of life that are necessary to achieve health for all Canadians.

CANCER   Generic term for over 100 diseases characterized by malignant growth or development of tumours caused by uncontrolled and abnormal cell division. It may be spread to other parts of the body through the lymphatic system or the blood stream. It is the focus of enormous medical research, based on the assumption that its causes lie at the intracellular level of the body. In a health social sciences perspective cancer is of interest because of its social production, distribution, care and cure rates. For example, poor homeless men in Britain have twice the rates of tumours of the mouth and pharynx than would be expected in the male population. Survival rates from cancer are linked to socio-economic status, with those in the higher groups surviving them better and the poor die more of treatable cancers than the rich (Rosso, S., Faggiano, R., and Costa, G. (1997) 'Social class and cancer survival in Turin, Italy', *Journal of Epidemiology and Community Health*, 51: 30–4) (**breast cancer**).

CANGUIHELM, GEORGES (1904–95) Trained in medicine, Canguihelm taught history and philosophy of the life sciences at the Sorbonne, Paris, where he succeeded **Bachelard** and sponsored Foucault's doctoral thesis (which was published as *Madness and Civilisation*). He argued that what constituted a state of health or disease was the product of definitional processes of medicine rather than a biological fact. For Canguihelm medicine constructed its objects: 'There is a science of biological situations and conditions that are called normal' (Canguihelm, G. (1978; orig. 1943) *On the Normal and the Pathological.* Trans. C. R. Fawcett. Dordrecht, Holland: D. Reidel) (**Bachelard**; **Fleck**; **Foucault**; **Kuhn**; **morality and medicine**; **normal**).

CAPITALISM An economic system based on the ownership of private property and the pursuit of profit. In classical Marxism capitalist societies are composed of two classes. The dominant class, the bourgeoisie, owns the means of production, while the workers, the proletariat, owning only their labour power, sell themselves on the market to the bourgeoisie. Capitalists, to the extent that they can, will systematically sacrifice workers' health in the pursuit of profit, while in a Marxist analysis the medical profession acts as an agent of **social control** on behalf of the capitalist class to discipline the working class, particularly through its control of the sick certificate (Navarro, V. (1976) *Medicine Under Capitalism.* New York: Prodist) (**alienation**; **Black Report**; **class analysis**; **Engels**).

CAPITATION The payment system, used in the United Kingdom, of a fixed price per person treated by a general practitioner. In contrast to fee-for-service payment systems it reduces the incentive to oversupply medical services, and provides more space for GPs to practise health promotion and prevention as well as curative care. At the same time, it may also reduce the quality of the consultation through lessening its length, as GPs attempt to maximize their income by increasing their turnover. It also undermines patient care in terms of high-need patients with chronic illnesses (**fee-for-service**).

CARCERAL SOCIETY Foucault's concept of modern society. It is a prison in the sense that the **psy-professions** induce us to be our own agents of **social control**, so that we willingly comply with their definition of normality (**abnormal**; **Bentham**; **new public health**; **panopticon**).

CARDIOVASCULAR DISEASE Diseases of the heart widely held to be a consequence of well established **risk factors** and **lifestyle factors**. However, a large scale study of ischaemic heart disease in Poland found that those in the top socio-economic groups were dying less of heart attacks, but that an analysis of risk factors in their lifestyle accounted for less than half of this improvement. (Vertianen, E., Pekkanen, J. and Koskinen, J. (1998) 'Do changes in cardiovascular risk factors explain the increasing socioeconomic differences in mortality from ischaemic heart disease in Finland?', *Journal of Epidemiology and Community*

Health, 52: 416–19) (**multiple risk factor intervention trial**).

CARE IN THE COMMUNITY   With the rise of **neoliberalism** the assertion that the community should provide services to the sick, disabled and aged. The contraction of the welfare state has meant that care has been pushed back on to women in the home. Women are usually the primary caregivers, that is, they take responsibility for basic needs and act on behalf of the dependent. Secondary caregivers, usually other family members, provide intermittent support, and if men, indirect support usually of a financial sort. Sociological studies of caregivers have established the highly stressful nature of the caregiving role, especially for dependents with dementia, giving rise to an overload of tasks and responsibilities and causing conflict within the family. The caregiver has been referred to as the 'hidden patient' (Haug, M. (1996) 'Elements in physician/patient interactions in late life', *Research on Aging*, 18: 32–51) (**asylums; community; deinstitutionalization; health services; informal care; secondary care; social capital**).

CARTESIAN   The term to describe the way in which the thought of the French philosopher **René Descartes** (1594–1650) is used in the social sciences. It should be noted that this appropriation departs quite significantly from Descartes' own position. Cartesianism can be briefly summarized in terms of three main characteristics. First, it has a dualistic image of the person,

drawing a rigid distinction between consciousness and materiality, especially sharply distinguishing the mind and the body. This distinction has led to the formation of specialist academic disciplines with the consequence that the body is the subject of the natural sciences and the mind the subject of the human sciences. Given this premise it is difficult to recapture the totality of human experience. Second, it is reductionist in that priority in explaining human action is given to the material, physical basis of existence. This behaviourist emphasis means that it denies the salience of mental events. Thus, problems of meaning, and of subjective existence have been relegated to the unknowable, or at best, are only knowable in a limited and unscientific way. The focus of the social and natural sciences is on the empirically observable, and that about which causal laws, in a natural science sense, can be generated (**behaviourism**). Sociology as a discipline is at least partially a fight to put meaning and interpretation back into the equation. Third, it is positivistic. In positivism, since the claim is that science and the social sciences should only be dealing with physical realities, the argument is that the methods of the natural sciences – of observation, quantification, experiment and the search for regularities and laws – are the only legitimate ones for the study of human beings. While Cartesianism was an important rebuttal of metaphysical and theological explanations of social life, rejecting explanations that could not be grounded in its definition of empirical reality, it has led to an approach which overlooks the impact of social structures on individuals and of the role of consciousness in individual action.

CASE CONTROL STUDIES   A method in **epidemiology** for establishing the probable causal role of a specific factor in the cause of a disease. Cases, i.e. individuals with the disease (e.g. lung cancer) are compared with controls who do not have it, and a difference in behaviour between the two is then isolated (e.g. smoking) thereby establishing a causal link between smoking and lung cancer. The link is apparent because while based on quantitative data, it depends on a qualitative assessment of the situation because of problems with the concept of causality (Doll, R. and Hill, A. (1950) 'Smoking and carcinoma of the lung: preliminary report', *British Medical Journal*, 2: 739–48) (**causal inference; Popper; positivism**).

CASEMIX   An attempt to measure the production process in the healthcare system by categorizing each product, case or patient episode of care. Casemix classification schemes can be employed in a range of healthcare settings: resident classification scales are used as the basis for funding nursing homes; ambulatory patient groups for community care; and diagnosis related groups to fund public hospitals. Originally a concept in engineering, devised at Yale University in 1978, the Reagan administration in the USA adapted them for use as a cost saving measure in the American health insurance system, **Medicare**. It allows the caring aspects of health practices to be

commodified and measured in terms of time and outputs. Simultaneously it allows for greater control of medical professionals, with the organization of hospitals into clinical practice groups rather than medical occupations (Draper, M. (1992) *Casemix, Quality and Consumers*. Melbourne: Health Issues Centre) (**clinical pathways; diagnosis related groups; new public management**).

CASE RECORDS   The medical transcription of the patient's account of an illness. In the process the subjective position of the individual is converted into a medical condition under the control of the doctor (Waitzkin, H. (1991) *The Politics of Medical Encounters*. New Haven: Yale University Press) (**narrative accounts of illness**).

CASE STUDIES   Best understood in the qualitative health studies tradition as taking a single occurrence of a generally occurring event as an exemplar so as to gain a rich and deep insight into the event. One example is Prior's interviews with a single psychiatric patient over forty years, which can then be used to understand the experience of all psychiatric patients (Prior, P. (1995) 'Surviving psychiatric institutionalization: a case study', *Sociology of Health and Illness*, 17: 651–67) (**oral histories**).

CAUSAL INFERENCE   The claim to have established a link between a prior form of behaviour (e.g. smoking) and a later outcome (e.g. lung cancer). At one level causal inferences appear to be self evident, the object of quantitative research, and demonstrated by statistical relationships. However, there are complex epistemological issues involved, so much so that some philosophers have suggested abandoning the concept. There are two views of what constitutes a causal link. On the constant conjunction view we would say that for a causal relationship to exist Y always follows X. However, we would not want to say that night causes day, even though they are in constant conjunction. In the necessary connection view not only is X held to follow Y, but that X *must* be followed by Y. However, we can only infer that Y follows X. The element of necessity that is part of our ideas of cause and effect is not an empirical concept. In epistemology and in philosophy of science there is as yet no generally accepted theory of its nature. (Lincoln, Y. and Guba, E. (1985) *Naturalistic Inquiry.* Beverley Hills, CA: Sage) (**case control studies; Popper**).

CENTRE FOR DISEASE CONTROL AND PREVENTION (CDC)   The United States Federal agency in Atlanta, Georgia, that monitors disease in the interests of public health.

CHADWICK, EDWIN (1800–90)   Secretary to the Poor Law Commission, an inquiry in nineteenth-century Britain, into the links between industrialization, urbanization and poor health, and between the social conditions of an area and the population's health. While Chadwick's work lead to extensive social reform, he did not identify poverty as the source of disease but was motivated to

reduce the tax burden on the state of the sick. The report of the commission, *Report on the Sanitary Conditions of the Labouring Population* was published in 1842 and resulted in the Public Health Act of 1848 (Chadwick, E. (1965, orig. 1842) *Report on the Sanitary Conditions of the Labouring Populations in Great Britain.* Edinburgh: Edinburgh University Press) (Tesh, S. (1996) 'Miasma and "social factors" in disease causality: lessons from the nineteenth century', *Journal of Health, Politics, Policy and Law,* 20: 1001–31) (**Booth; Engels; Farr; miasma; sanitation; Simon; Snow; social history of medicine; social medicine**).

CHESS   (comprehensive health enhancement support system) A computerized system of integrated services designed to help individuals cope with a healthcare crisis or medical concern. Its website (http://chess.chsra.wisc.edu/chess) claims that: it provides timely, easily accessible resource information, social support decision making and problem solving tools; it combines various services and resources into one system, meeting the needs of various coping and information seeking styles; tailors and personalizes information and support to help users manage better their health and change behaviours that are harmful to their well being; protects privacy encouraging openness and honesty in dealing with health concerns; and presents reliable, well-organized, detailed 'health information' in a language comprehensible to individuals at most educational levels. It is claimed to illustrate the benefits of active **consumer**

participation resulting in improvements in quality of life and a decline in the experience of negative emotions (Gustafson, D., Hawkins, R., Rodberg, E., et al. 'Impact of a patient-centred computer based health information/support system', *American Journal of Preventive Medicine*, 16 (1): 1–9).

CHICAGO SCHOOL OF SOCIOLOGY An important intellectual centre for American sociology between 1920 and 1950. Its adaptation of G. H. Mead's concept of the self produced in interaction with others, and its adherence to pragmatism, that 'true' knowledge could not be known, but that what worked was the truth, was consolidated into symbolic interactionism by Herbert Blumer. This operated with a dynamic view of the self, a view that reality was fluid and constructed, and focused on the ways in which individuals attributed meaning, both to other individuals, and also to objects in their physical environment. In short, it was a form of **social constructionism**. Under the leadership of Robert E. Park (1864–1944) and E. Burgess (1886–1966) it laid the basis for ethnographical (**ethnography**) research in sociology. In this approach the emphasis was on the researcher participating in the social world of the researched. In health studies the best-known studies are of the socialization of medical students (Becker, H., Geer, B., Hughes, E., and Strauss, A. (1961) *Boys in White: Student Culture in a Medical School*. Chicago: Chicago University Press) and of **total institutions** such as mental asylums

(Goffman, E. (1961) *Asylums: Essays on the Social Situations of Mental Patients and Other Inmates*. New York: Anchor) as well as the social organization of dying. The contrast is with the sociology of Talcott Parsons, who in his **structural functionalism** sought to lay out a general theory of society, then to confirm it through observation. Symbolic interactionists, to the extent that they allowed that there could be a general theory of society, argued that it had to be built on the observation of social life as it happened (**analytic induction; dying trajectories; participant observation; qualitative research**).

CHILDBIRTH The World Health Organization has expressed concern about the continued technical intervention in pregnancy on no established medical grounds. For example, a study of ninety-eight hospitals and 3,160 low risk births found extensive evidence of unwarranted interventions in the delivery: routine ultrasound scanning, routine fetal electronic monitoring during birth, induction, the prone position during labour (when the evidence is that the upright position is better), operative vaginal birth, artificial rupture of the membranes, Caesarean section and episiotomy (Williams, F. et al. 'Intrapartum care for low risk primagravidas: a survey of interventions', *Journal of Epidemiology and Community Health*, 52: 494–500). Under the control of professional obstetricians childbirth has been turned into a medical event requiring substantial interventions, driven by technological advances and the birthing time defined by practitioners at their convenience (**medicalization; new reproductive technologies; reproduction**).

CHILE, HEALTH CARE   Chile's healthcare system developed out of a strong labour movement culminating in Chilean National Health Service (1952) which provided comprehensive health care for all citizens. Following the US inspired coup against the socialist/communist President Salvadore Allende and the installation of the dictator Augusto Pinochet the national system was dismantled. Using the right-wing economist Milton Freidman, Pinochet turned to a market based health system. The public health system was dismantled, the University of Chile's medical school had its budget reduced by 46 per cent and its staff by 40 per cent. Privatization and deregulation were systematically pursued. While the well to do experience healthcare standards like that of the US the poor and rural popu-lations endure high rates of infectious disease, malnutrition and infant mortality (Reichard, S. (1996) 'Ideology drives health care reforms in Chile', *Journal of Public Health Policy*, 17: 80–98) (**Cuba; epide-miological polarization; privatization**).

CHINESE MEDICINE   While often con-trasted with that of the West, Chinese medicine is not indigenous, but assimilated practices from **Ayurvedic medicine**, from Korea, Tibet, Persia and Arabia. The classi-cal tradition of Chinese medicine was laid down in the Han dynasty (206 BC–AD 220), where the need for a unified political system, a healthy body, and a healthy state intersected. Publications in this period – the

Inner Canon, the *Divine Husbandman's Materia Medica*, the *Canon of Problems* and the *Treatise on Cold-Damage Disorders* – are the basis of medical practice. At their core is the assumption that health is a product of harmony – within the body, and between the body and the environment. In the modern period the West from 1860 influenced Chinese medicine onwards, especially through the Chinese Medical Missionary Association (1886) and the Rockefeller-funded Chinese Medical Commission which attempted (as did the **Flexner Report** in the USA) to regularize medical education. By 1926 Western-style hospitals were in existence in 100 cities, and provided the basis for the post-1949 communist regime to develop a national healthcare system. While contemporary physicians must still study the *Canon*, they must also be trained in Western medicine (Porter, R. (1997) *The Greatest Benefit to Mankind*. London: Harper Collins) (**acupuncture**).

CHIROPRACTIC   An **alternative** form of healthcare practice involving spinal manipulation founded by American Daniel David Palmer (1845–1913). Chiropractic has provided sociologists of the medical profession one of the key examples of the resistance to **medical dominance** since it has with national vari-ations been licensed by the state in the USA (following extensive legal cases), Australia and Britain (Fulder, S. (1986) *The Handbook of Alternative and Complementary Medicine*. Oxford: Oxford University Press) (**osteopathy**).

CHRONIC ILLNESS   An ongoing condition of ill-health for which there is no medical cure, but which requires medical monitoring for example, diabetes, migraine, and epilepsy. Chronic illness has been conceptualized as 'biographical disruption' in the senses of 1 the disruption of everyday assumptions and actions about life; 2 disruptions in explanatory systems that require a rethinking of biography and self-concept; and 3 responses to the disruption (Bury, M. (1982) 'Chronic illness as biographical disruption', *Sociology of Health and Illness*, 4: 167–82) (**biographical disruption; disease identity dependency; liminality; narrative accounts of illness**).

CHRONIC FATIGUE SYNDROME (CFS)   The experience of persistent exhaustion. It is a disputed disease classification in that the patient's reported symptoms have no medically acceptable signs and symptoms, nor is there any medically accepted explanation of the cause of the condition. CFS can be seen to represent a fundamental clash between the experience of illness and the biomedical model with its definition of sickness as essentially biological. In this clash, where the individual's account cannot be accommodated by existing theories of disease, it is dismissed and they are denied access to the **sick role**. Clear differences in the treatment of men and women presenting with symptoms of chronic fatigue syndrome have been demonstrated, with well over two-thirds of women being diagnosed with a psychiatric disorder while less than a third of men are so diagnosed (Broom, D. and Woodward, R. (1996) 'Medicalisation reconsidered: toward a collaborative model of health care', *Sociology of Health and Illness*, 18: 357–78) (**abnormal illness behaviour; deviance; diagnostic limbo; miners' nystagmus; post traumatic stress disorder; repetitive strain injury**).

CHRONIC PAIN   Ongoing physical discomfort. While pain is a biological event its experience is social. The experience of pain has been shown to be determined by a variety of social and cultural factors. In a study where the pain levels would be, biologically speaking, similar for all respondents (herniated discs), it was found that different ethnic groups were more sensitive (Jews and Italians) or less sensitive to pain (white, Anglo-Saxon, Protestant, Americans). The study argued that cultural groups vary in the tolerance with which they will allow discomfort to be reported (Zborowski, M. (1952) 'Cultural components in responses to pain', *Journal of Social Issues*, 8: 16–30). Sufferers of chronic pain – rheumatoid arthritis for example – will attempt to pass as normal and to cover up their experience of pain. (Weiner, C. (1975) 'The burden of rheumatoid arthritis: tolerating the uncertainty', *Social Science and Medicine*, 9: 97–104). Yet other studies have demonstrated the impact of organizational structure on the experience and management of pain, as patients and staff in a hospital setting negotiate the condition (Fagerhaugh, S. and Strauss, A. (1977) *The Politics of Pain Management: Staff-Patient Interaction*. Menlo Park: Addison Wesley) (**negotiated order; pain**).

CIRCUMCISION (FEMALE)   The removal of some or all of the clitoris, labia minora and the labia majora. Performed on an estimated 80–114 million women in twenty-seven Eastern and Western African countries, and in parts of Malaysia and India. The procedure is to guarantee virginity, and is justified on religious grounds by some Jewish, Catholic and Muslim groups. It has adverse health consequences, and may result in chronic urinary tract infection, reduced fertility, urethral or bladder stones, excessive scar tissue formation and obstructed labour (Toubia, N. (1993) *Female Genital Mutilation: A Call for Global Action*. New York: Women Ink) (**female genital mutilation**).

CIRCUMCISION (MALE)   Removal of the prepuce, that is the foreskin of the penis, usually in infancy. It has been justified on religious grounds, that it will prevent the spread of venereal disease, and that it will inhibit masturbation. In Australia 15 per cent of males are circumcised, 20 per cent in Canada, and 60 per cent in the United States, where it has been described as 'cultural surgery'. Health complications include lacerations, skin loss, skin bridges, urinary retention, glans necrosis, penile loss, sepsis and gangrene (Wallerstein, E. (1985) 'Circumcision: uniquely American medical enigma', *Urology Clinics of North America*, 12: 123–32).

CITIZENSHIP   From the end of World War II through to the late 1970s individuals in Western societies could expect the **welfare state** to recompense their participation in the labour market with the provision of social goods, such as education, health and social welfare. However under the impact of **neoliberalism** these historic achievements of the working class and the women's movement have been reversed and the concept of citizenship has been reconstructed as 'active citizenship' in which the individual is increasingly responsible for themselves, operating in privatized education, health and welfare markets. This construction of active citizenship will have the specific outcome of increasing inequalities in health, especially for women who are disadvantaged in the labour market through their working life and are more dependent on the state sector, especially in old age (Esping-Andersen, G. (1996) (ed.), *Welfare States in Transition: National Adaptations in Global Economies*. Thousand Oaks, CA: Sage) (**ageing; healthism; market; self-care**).

CIVIL SOCIETY   That part of social life that escapes the control of the state and the constraints of the economic system. In health sociology it can be conceptualized as the arena of the **lifeworld** and the site for lay health practices. In contemporary neoliberal policies it is conceptualized as the community, which is responsible for the support and delivery of health services to its members (**community; lay culture; social capital**).

CJD   see **Creutzfeld Jakob Disease**

CLASS   In common usage the recognition that society is structured in a hierarchy of occupations with a descending scale, of income, prestige and education (**social gradient of disease**). The most widespread classification is the British Registrar General's: Class I Professional (lawyers, doctors, scientists); Class II Managerial (farmers, teachers, nurses, managers); Class III Skilled manual and non-manual (plumbers, drivers, tradespeople); Class IV Partly skilled (farm labourers, forestry workers, factory process workers); Class V unskilled (cleaners, road workers, labourers). The usefulness of this classification for health social scientists is that it is listed with the cause of death on death certificates allowing for a demonstration of the impact of **socio-economic inequality** on the health of the different groups (**Black Report; health determinants; social inequality; socio-economic status**).

CLASS ANALYSIS   In Marxist analysis class analysis produces a unitary theoretical explanation of the source of **inequality** around the ownership and non-ownership of private property. In this sense class is not a variable but constitutive of social relationships. In a capitalist society the pursuit of profit by the capitalist class means that it will seek to cheapen the cost of labour wherever it can. It will attempt to increase working hours, reduce wages, and lobby government for lower taxes. Each of these has an impact on health. At the level of workers, the removal of occupational health and safety regulations means increased injuries and deaths at work; the deregulation of environmental controls over pollution means environmental degradation; the deregulation of the preparation

of foodstuffs to reduce costs of their manufacture means increased food poisoning and death, especially for those most defenceless and most at risk: children and infants. Where capital successfully reduces the tax base it weakens state expenditure on public goods such as the health and welfare system (**ideology; social gradient of disease**).

CLINICAL DRUG TRIALS   The assessment of the safety and usefulness of drugs on human populations under strictly defined conditions. In the United States, the Food and Drug Administration use it as the basis for licensing and approval of a new drug. Feminists point out that many of the most important clinical trials are conducted without women subjects. The Physician Health Study of 1988 which is supposed to demonstrate the effect of aspirin on reducing the risk of cardiovascular disease is based on a study of 22,071 men; the Multiple Risk Factor Intervention Trial, which studied coronary heart disease risk factors was based on 15,000 men (**lifestyle choices**); and the Baltimore Longitudinal Study on Aging, carried out between 1958 and 1978 contained no women, and issued a report in 1984 on normal human aging that made no reference to women (Auerbach, J. and Figert, A. (1995) 'Women's health research: public policy and sociology', *Journal of Health and Social Behaviour*, 28: 115–31) (**clinical trial; placebo effect**).

CLINICAL EPIDEMIOLOGY   The application of the findings of epidemiology, that is population based trials of services and treatments, in the treatment of individuals. This may take the form of studies of the effectiveness and efficiency of health services, the application of the findings of randomized control trials to treatment issues, or the claim to base practice on evidence-based medicine. Whether or not data generated from population level studies can be applied at the individual level is highly problematic, since what is true of a group, is not true of individuals (**epidemiology**; **popular epidemiology**).

CLINICAL GAZE   A Foucauldian term for the power of the medical profession to define reality and **abnormality** over a wide range of social situations not limited to biology (Foucault, M. (1973) *The Birth of the Clinic*. London: Tavistock) (**medicalization**; **psy-professions**).

CLINICAL ICEBERG   The existence of high levels of morbidity (that is, symptoms of illness) in the community. The concept is based on the finding from community surveys that the general population reports high levels of illness without approaching medical professionals for treatment. In a classic study of 1,000 randomly chosen persons it was found that in the previous week almost all of them (954) reported at least one symptom of illness. One hundred and eighty-eight took no action; 562 treated themselves by taking rest or modified their diet, while 168 attended their GP, twenty-eight an outpatients clinic and five were admitted to hospital. The finding highlights the fact that people construct

and negotiate the meanings of their physical experiences in ways that do not just reflect a biomedical approach (Last, J. (1963) 'The iceberg: completing the clinical picture in general practice', *The Lancet* ii, 28–31; Wadsworth, M., Butterfield, W. and R. Blancy (1971) *Health and Sickness: The Choice of Treatment*. London: Tavistock) (**biomedicine; lay culture; lay referral system**).

CLINICAL MEDICINE   The development in the nineteenth century of medical practice, though with origins in fourteenth-century Padua, located in the hospital, synthesizing the observation of disease and built on a knowledge of anatomy based on dissection. This development transformed medicine from a gentlemanly practice, based on cultured learning into a science, based on surgical practice. In the UK its centre was Edinburgh University, which escaped the control of the Royal Colleges in London. The development of clinical medicine was the focus of Foucault's **The Birth of the Clinic** (**bedside medicine; social history of medicine; social medicine; Whig histories of medicine**).

CLINICAL NARRATIVES   An aspect of the **doctor–patient relationship**, the story that doctors tell their patient over time about their therapy and their condition. In this the 'voice of medicine' dominates, subsuming the patient's perspective (Mishler, E. (1986) *The Discourse of Medicine: Dialectics of Medical Interviews*. Norwood, NJ: Ablex). Clinical narratives are learnt as part of medical socialization, and enable the practitioner to control the course of the disease and the individual's reaction to it (Good, M. and Good, B. (1989) '"Disabling practitioners": hazards of learning to be a doctor on American medical education', *Journal of Orthopsychiatry*, 59: 303–9) (**accounts of illness**; **narrative accounts of illness**).

CLINICAL PATHWAYS Part of the **new public management**, the attempt to specify the treatment process for patients, to reduce treatment variability and to bring down costs by ensuring the discharge of patients from hospital within a set time period. At the same time, since clinical pathways are under the control of nurses, they can be seen as an attempt by nursing to assert itself against **medical dominance**, though in practice they have met medical resistance. They have also been called critical pathways, anticipatory recovery pathways, expected recovery paths, milestone action plans and multi-disciplinary care maps. The underlying assumption is that illness is an event, that it is predictable, that medicine is a science that can control it, and that managers can tie it to deadlines. (Zander, K. and McGill, R. (1994) 'Critical and Anticipatory Recovery Paths: Only the Beginning', *Nursing Management*, 25: 34–38) (**benchmarking**; **casemix**; **corporatization**; **diagnosis related groups**; **neoliberalism**; **privatization**).

CLINICAL TRIAL A prospective study comparing the effect and value of medical intervention(s) – technical, surgical or drug-based – against a control group in human populations. Thus in the trial of a new drug the patient population is divided into those who receive it and those who receive already established treatments and the two groups are then compared to see who fares best (**clinical drug trials**; **Cochrane centre**; **evidence-based medicine**; **placebo effect**; **randomized control trials**).

CLITORIDECTOMY The removal of the clitoris (**circumcision (female)**; **female genital mutilation**).

CLONING In genetics the process of duplicating biological material, coming to public attention with the cloning of the sheep Dolly in 1997 (*Nature*, 385: 810–13). There are three types of cloning. Recombinant DNA technology (also called DNA cloning or gene cloning) is the transfer of a DNA fragment from an organism to a self-replicating genetic element such as a bacterial plasmid. Reproductive cloning generates an animal that has the same nuclear DNA as another currently or previously existing animal. Therapeutic cloning is the production of human embryos for use in research. Notwithstanding media reports reproductive cloning has a high failure rate, with only one or two viable offspring for every hundred attempts, and of these, about 30 per cent are affected with 'large offspring syndrome', dying early of unexplained causes (**new genetics**).

COCHRANE, ARCHIE (1909–88) British epidemiologist and author of *Effectiveness* and *Efficiency: Random Reflections on Health Services* (1972, Nuffield Provincial Hospitals Trust). Cochrane's argument was that much of what passes for medical treatment has not been evaluated, and that since resources are limited, treatment should be limited to that which was demonstrably of use. He argued that **randomized controlled trials** were the gold standard to prove medical efficacy. His work led to the foundation of the **Cochrane Centre** (**casemix; clinical trial; health technology assessment; National Institute of Clinical Evidence**).

COCHRANE CENTRE   Named after the epidemiologist, **Archie Cochrane**, and founded in Oxford in 1993, the Centre brings together systematic and up-to-date reviews of randomized control trials of healthcare. These findings provide the basis for **evidence-based medicine**. While the centre fosters collaborative medical review groups around specific issues (e.g. coronary heart disease interventions) many of the social aspects of health related problems (e.g. suicide or the use of alternative health practices) are not amenable to randomized control trials, or do not attract funding for the conduct of trials. Those in other areas of healthcare do not accept the claim then that the Cochrane Centre produces the core of medical knowledge (Godlee, F. (1994) 'The Cochrane collaboration', *British Medical Journal*, 309: 969–70) (**casemix; health services evaluation; health technology assessment; National Institute of Clinical Evidence**).

CODING   In the positivist approach the application of a conceptual framework to the analysis of a document or situation (**content analysis**). In grounded theory coding moves from open, to axial and selective. Open coding is intensive analysis – often word by word – of a document to allow the concepts embedded in it to emerge, thus focusing the researcher in future data collection. Axial coding is the determination of a core category developed from open coding. Selective coding is the comparison of core categories with each other (Strauss, A. (1987) *Qualitative Analysis for Social Scientists.* New York: Aldine).

COGNITIVE DISSONANCE   A concept in psychology that when our attitudes and behaviour are not consistent we experience discomfort and act to change one or the other to bring them into line (Festinger, L. (1957) *A Theory of Cognitive Dissonance.* Stanford, CA: Stanford University Press).

COHORT STUDIES   The study of an entire section of a population. For example, the Nurses Health Study, using self-administered, mailed questionnaires surveyed 120,000 married nurses in the north eastern states of the United States. The original cohort study was the **Framingham Study** of the incidence of heart disease in a population (Dawber, T. (1980) *The Framingham Study.* Cambridge: Harvard University Press).

COMA   A deep state of unconsciousness. While still alive, the individual is unable to move or respond to the environment. Coma may be followed by a persistent vegetative state in which the individual loses their ability to think or be aware of their surroundings. Sleep patterns, breathing and circulation are not affected (**advanced care directives**; **death**; **do not resuscitate**).

COMMUNITY Following the World Health Organization's **Ottawa Charter** community development was heralded as a way of improving people's health. Strong communities would support individuals to make healthy **lifestyle** decisions. As the charter put it: 'health promotion works through concrete and effective community action in setting priorities, making decisions, planning strategies, and implementing them to achieve better health. At the heart of this process is the empowerment of communities, their ownership and control of their own endeavours and destinies'. However the approach has not been successful, largely given that public health policy is administered out of health departments still committed to the **medical model**. Its appeal to **neoliberal** governments was that it appeared to be a way of putting back on the community functions previously carried out by the welfare state (**civil society**; **social capital**).

COMMUNITY BASED LONG TERM CARE (CBLTC) Under **neoliberal** policies hospitals have been driven to discharge patients earlier and to reduce the length of stay creating the need for post-acute and ambulatory care services. The process of

caring for, and looking after these individuals, is labelled CBLTC, the burden of which falls mainly on women (**care in the community**).

COMMUNITY HEALTH CENTER In the United States, a federally funded initiative in the 1980s to provide primary healthcare facilities for low income areas. The programme was largely unsuccessful due to inadequate funding.

COMMUNITY HEALTH COUNCILS (CHC) An early development of the move to have consumer representation in healthcare services. They were established in the UK in 1974 to represent consumer views and interests in the National Health Service (**consumerism**).

COMMUNITY MEDICINE The attempt from the late 1970s to provide integrated primary care facilities in the community. The term 'public health medicine' was adopted by the Faculty of Community Medicine of the UK Royal College of Physicians.

COMMODIFICATION A Marxist concept for the process whereby parts of everyday life are converted into objects for sale on the market. In the health area the process includes the increasing need to buy medical services to gain better health status with fewer and fewer areas of non-market based resources available to individuals. In the past this worked in favour of the medical profession, developing a market for their services; now, however, with the development of corporate medicine and the **proletarianization** of the medical profession they too have become commodities on the labour market (**consumerism; corporate medicine; corporatization; medical-industrial complex; substantive rationality**).

COMPARATIVE HEALTH SYSTEMS　Initially spurred by the need to evaluate the New Deal policies of the 1930s in the USA and developed by Roemer in the 1950s into comparative systems analysis of the interactions between laissez-faire economies, welfare states and socialist economies and their interaction with the countries' status as affluent, developing or underdeveloped (Roemer, M. (1991) *National Health Systems of the World. Vol 1*. New York, Oxford University Press). In the 1960s and 1970s under the impact of Marxism the field focused on issues of equity and the distribution of resources and with explorations of alternatives to the health systems of capitalist social systems (Sidel, V. and Sidel, R. (1974) *Serve the People: Observations on Medicine in the People's Republic of China*. Boston: Beacon). With the rise of economic rationalism and neoliberalism in the 1980s, the move was to cost containment and the introduction of market principles, while current comparative work focuses on the effectiveness of interventions (Klein, R. (1991) 'Risks and benefits of comparative studies: notes from another shore', *Milbank Quarterly*, 69: 275–91) (**Chile; Cuba; healthcare systems**).

COMPENSATION NEUROSIS　A theory in psychiatry that individuals develop symptoms of illness to obtain payouts from their employers for causing their condition. It is seen as an attempt to obtain secondary gain, that is pecuniary or social benefits, from the **sick role** (**post traumatic stress disorder; repetitive strain injury**).

COMPLEMENTARY/ALTERNATIVE MEDICINE (CAM)　Healthcare practices which either attempt to supplement biomedical practices or reject them turning to other forms of healing. The growth of CAM is often analysed as an aspect of the decline of **medical dominance** (Tovey, P., Easthope, G. and J. Adams (2004) (eds), *The Mainstreaming of Complementary and Alternative Medicine*. London: Routledge) (**alternative medicine; deprofessionalization; proletarianization**).

COMPLEMENTARY MEDICINE　The use of drugs and treatments not accepted by orthodox medicine as scientific, with the aim, not of replacing orthodox forms of treatment, but of supplementing them. The main users are the middle classes, the well educated and more commonly women, usually in response to chronic conditions (Cant, S. and Sharma, U. (1999) *A New Medical Pluralism: Complementary Medicine, Doctors and the State*. London: Taylor and Francis) (**alternative medicine; deprofessionalization**).

COMPLIANCE　In the sociology of **Talcott Parsons** the acceptance of the doctor's orders as a condition of entry to the **sick role**. The changing context of the doctor–patient **relationship** with the rise of **consumerism** among a better educated public has led to a challenge to **medical dominance**. Current studies of the doctor–patient relationship suggest that patients and doctors may be more in partnership than either a relationship that is paternalistic or antagonistic (**consultation**).

CONSTRUCTIONISM Analysis of medical knowledge as socially produced, and reflecting social interests, rather than a correspondence with an independent biological reality. For example Marxist approaches demonstrate how capitalist social relations shape medical knowledge; feminist analysis show how women's bodies are constituted by patriarchal medical knowledge; and approaches influenced by Foucault argue that medical knowledge is produced in the administrative apparatus of the state and in the psy-professions (**feminism; Foucault; Marxist approaches; psy-professions; social construction/constructionism; strong programme in the sociology of scientific knowledge**).

CONSULTATION The meeting between a doctor and a patient. The dynamics of this relationship have changed over time, reflecting wider social changes. While **Parsons**, could conceptualize the doctor–patient relationship in the 1950s as the patient's following of doctors' orders in the presence of acute illness and as a condition of entry to the **sick role**, it is now understood to be a more fluid and negotiated relationship. Patients with chronic illnesses, for example, may be far more informed about their condition than their GP and negotiate to manage their condition in ways that suit them, thus reflecting a decline in medical dominance (Charles, C., Gafni, A. and Whelan, T. (1999) 'Decision-making in the physician-patient encounter: revisiting the shared treatment decision-making model', *Social Science and Medicine*, 49: 651–61) (**compliance; doctor–patient relationship; medical dominance**).

CONSUMER At its most general, those individuals who receive care and treatments directly from healthcare providers. The rise of the term 'consumer' reflects a move away from considering the sick person as the passive recipient of medical services to an active participation in the medical encounter. It is also linked to growth of the idea of a market for medical services and the decline of **medical dominance (citizenship; doctor– patient relationship; market**).

CONSUMER PARTICIPATION The participation in medical decision making by the patient in the selection of treatment alternatives. In 1978 the World Health Organization (WHO) in their **Alma-Ata Declaration** set out a vision for primary healthcare that stated that 'people have the right and duty to participate individually and collectively in the planning and implementation of their health care'. In 1986 the WHO developed the **Ottawa Charter** on Health Promotion in which consumer empowerment was identified as a central element in improved health and well being. In 1997 the Jakarta Declaration on Health Promotion in the twenty-first century recognized that health promotion is a process of enabling individuals to increase control over and to improve their health. However, given the knowledge imbalance between patient and doctor, many commentators are sceptical of patients' ability to enter meaningfully into dialogue, while the evidence for active participation by patients is sketchy (**CHESS**; **consumerism**) and little research has been carried out to demonstrate that consumer participation leads to better healthcare (White, D. (2000) 'Consumer and community participation: a reassessment of process, impact and value', in G. Albrecht, R. Fitzpatrick and C. Scrimshaw (eds), *Handbook of Social Studies in Health and Medicine*. London: Sage) (**health systems agencies**).

CONSUMERISM   On the one hand the growth of an educated public who demand an involvement in their medical treatment, involvement in health policy, planning, service delivery and evaluation. Patient activist groups see it as a source of **empowerment** redressing the power imbalance between doctor and patient. On the other, the attempt to bring down healthcare costs by governments by turning patients into active seekers of information on the market, the assumption being that they will search out the best services at the lowest cost (**citizenship**; **doctor–patient relationship**; **World Federation of Psychiatric Users**).

CONTAGIONISM   The theory that disease is communicated by contact between individuals infected with a condition. In the nineteenth century it was rivalled by miasmatic theories, which argued that disease was caused by the environment. What was at issue was the impact on business: contagion resulted in quarantine and the closing of ports and restrictions on movement; miasmatic theories involved cleaning up urban slums and controlling industry. Thus adherents of competing theories of disease were motivated by political and economic concerns rather than 'scientific' ones (Ackerknecht, E. (1948) 'Anticontagionism between 1821 and 1867', *Bulletin of the History of Medicine*, 22: 562–93) (**miasma**; **social medicine**).

CONTENT ANALYSIS   The analysis of texts (written and visual) in either a quantitative or qualitative tradition. In the quantitative, enumerative tradition, an objective analysis of texts is attempted, by measuring, for example, the frequency of words, the amount of space given to specific topics, and the way themes are presented. In this positivist vein validity, generalizability and replicability of the analysis are major concerns. In the qualitative tradition the researcher attempts not to impose a pre-existing set of categories on the data, but through intensive analysis to expose hidden levels of discourse embedded within it, of for example, sexism in medical journals (Koutroulis, G. (1990) 'The orifice revisited: portrayal of women in gynaecological texts', *Community Health Studies*, 24: 73–84) (**coding**; **deconstruction**; **discourse analysis**).

CONTEXT (frames).

CONTRACEPTION Chemical or physical measures taken to prevent conception. While practised in all societies the development of the pill in the 1960s was central to the women's movement in the West and enabled women to choose when and if to have children (**abortion**; **birth control**; **pregnancy**).

CONTRACTING OUT An initiative under the auspices of **neoliberalism** whereby the state puts out to the market activities it previously undertook. An example in health is the private management of publicly funded hospitals. It may also take the form of for profit contractual arrangements for the management of health and hotel services within hospitals. The process is also referred to as outsourcing (**corporatization**; **privatization**).

CONVALESCENCE In the past the period of recovery following entry into the **sick role**. With recent **welfare state** reforms the concept has been replaced by rehabilitation, to be undertaken by the patient at home, which legitimizes early discharge from hospital to save costs (Beckingham, C. (1995) 'Relinquishing the sick role: convalescence and rehabilitation', *Australian Journal of Advanced Nursing*, 12: 15–19) (**care in the community**; **hospital at home**).

CONVENIENCE SAMPLES The choice of subjects in a research project, because of the ease of access to them. The classic example is the compulsory participation of undergraduate psychology students in their lecturer's research projects. The contrast is with probability samples in which subjects are chosen to represent the whole population (**nonprobability sampling techniques**).

CONVENTIONALISM A perspective in **epistemology** that argues that phenomena can be explained equally well by a wide range of theories and that the adherence of a scientist to any particular explanation is the result of an agreement by the scientist's community to describe the world in this way. Thus scientific knowledge is always relative, always open to change, and does not reveal reality. The position underpins social constructionist accounts of medical knowledge and the **sociology of scientific knowledge**. In sociology the equivalent concepts are **thought style** or **paradigm** (**Fleck; Kuhn; Popper; social construction/ constructionism**).

CONVERGENT VALIDITY The argument that the use of multiple methods (e.g. quantitative and qualitative) and analysis at multiple levels (e.g. the biological, the psychological and the sociological) will produce the best fit with what can be known. In a study of induced abortion in Ecuador, for example, sixty-five families were observed, 3,000 women interviewed, local family planning clinics were observed and policy makers at the local and national level were interviewed to develop an overall picture of the social processes surrounding abortion. In this way an understanding of what abortion meant at the individual, through to the system level could be produced, providing rich in-depth data (Scrimshaw, S. (1985) 'Bringing the period down: government and squatter settlement confront induced abortion in Ecuador', in P. Pelto and W. de Walt (eds), *Macro and Micro Levels of Analysis in Anthropology.* Boulder CO: Westview Press) (**triangulation**).

CONVERSATIONAL ANALYSIS   Language is central to our daily lives and with it, from an ethnomethodological perspective, we construct meanings and realities. Ethnomethodologists study the structural organization of conversations, that is, their sequential organization, and ground their analysis in specific empirical situations. Thus ethnomethodologists seek to show how social reality is constructed at the micro level of interaction. (Silverman, D. (1993) *Interpreting Qualitative Data: Methods for Analysing Talk, Text and Interaction.* London: Sage). Feminist sociologists of conversation demonstrate how seemingly neutral words (e.g. mankind) have embedded in them the power relations of society (e.g. the use of 'mankind' makes women invisible). In this perspective, language reinforces the gendered inequalities of power that exist, though since we take it for granted, not in ways that are immediately obvious. These power relations between men and women are exacerbated when the social distance (e.g. between a woman patient and a male

doctor) is great (Davis, K. (1988) 'Paternalism under the microscope', in A. Todd and S. Fisher (eds), *Gender and Discourse: The Power of Talk.* Norwood, NJ: Ablett) (**ethnomethodology**; **microsociological**; **social distance**).

COPAYMENT   As part of **neoliberalism** and in an attempt to dissuade patients from using services, the amount the patient must pay for a medical service even though they have a national insurance system.

COPING   (**social support**; **stress**).

CORPORATE MEDICINE   The ownership of hospitals and medical services by for profit businesses. The development of corporate medicine since the 1980s represents a significant change to the organization and delivery of healthcare. No longer is health seen as a universal right guaranteed by the state but as a commodity for purchase on the market. Notwithstanding neoliberal rhetoric, corporate medicine is less efficient in the delivery of healthcare and costs more than healthcare delivered either by the state or the not-for-profit sector. In pursuit of profit corporate medicine shortens patient stays, and reduces the size of hospital staff. It results in the **proletarianization** of medical staff who as employees lose control of their clinical autonomy. It also skews the delivery of health services, electing to provide profitable day surgery, but not expensive accident and emergency services, which it leaves the state sector to pick up (White, K. and Collyer, F. (1998) 'Hospital care markets in Australia: ownership of the private hospital sector', *International Journal of Health Services*, 28 (3): 487–510) (**citizenship; medical-industrial complex; welfare state**).

CORPORATIZATION   With the support of conservative governments the entry of private investors into the public sector. The policy rests on a number of assumptions. First, that the market provides an economic discipline lacking in the public sector. Second, that a competitive market economy generates an output that is in equilibrium and therefore efficiently allocates resources. Third, that market principles, rather than government interventions, enable enterprises and organizations to operate more efficiently. Fourth, that larger, private sector corporations, for example, erstwhile public hospitals, with central planning, management and marketing and economies of scale, can produce goods and services with a lower price per unit, and can raise standards of services. All empirical studies to date show that these assumptions are unsupported. Corporatized and privatized health systems cost more, result in deteriorating working conditions, reduced access to care, a reduction in services, and the offsetting of debt to the next generation (White, K. and Collyer, F. (1997) 'To market, to market: corporatization, privatization and hospital costs', *Australian Health Review*, 20 (2): 13–26) (**contracting out; medical-industrial complex; neoliberalism; privatization**).

COSMETIC SURGERY   Surgical operations to change the shape and appearance of the body to meet the dictates of fashion or to repair appearance after accident. Over 4.6 million operations are carried out annually in the United States. Most operations are carried out on women as they attempt to meet patriarchal demands about the ideal feminine body type (Sullivan, D. (2001) *Cosmetic Surgery: The Cutting Edge of Commercial Medicine in America*. New Jersey: Rutgers University Press) (**alienation; feminism**).

COUNSELLING   Generically, the process of helping an individual understand their situation, plan for the future, or come to grips with a life event. Credentialled professionals who specialize, for example, in marital counselling, drug counselling or grief counselling usually provide such a service. In the Foucauldian tradition the seemingly 'neutral' process of helping an individual cope is analysed as an operation of power as individuals internalize the 'correct' reaction to life events (**abnormal; Foucault; psy-professions; talking therapies; technologies of the self**).

COURTESY STIGMA   People who associate with stigmatized groups often experience **stigma** themselves because of this association. This may be 'felt', that is, the individual assumes that because they are associated with the stigmatized group, for example, people with serious ongoing mental illness (**SOMI**), that they themselves are thought less of, or it may be 'enacted', that is, a response by 'normal' individuals which diminishes the identity of those associated with stigmatized groups who then experience rejection and discrimination (Scambler, G. and Hopkins, A. (1986) 'Being epileptic: coming to terms with stigma', *Sociology of Health and Illness*, 8: 26–43).

CREAM-SKIMMING   A term in the health insurance industry where the insurer identifies and targets individuals with low health risks, successfully pressuring them to take out policies they do not need, thereby maximizing premiums and reducing payouts.

CREDENTIALISM   Originating in the nineteenth century as a way of demarcating an occupation from competitors, the possession by an individual of a certificate, diploma or degree which is necessary to gain access to the occupation. Credentialism refers specifically to situations where the knowledge, practice or skill to perform a job does not change but the entry qualifications rise. It systematically excludes women, the poor and the powerless from specific occupations when they do not have the time or resources to pursue the qualification (Berg, J. (1972) *Education and Jobs: The Great Training Robbery*. New York: Praeger) (**Apothecaries Act; occupational closure; professionalization**).

CREUTZFELD JAKOB DISEASE   A disease of the brain caused by eating meat that has been infected by bovine spongiform encephalopathy. As a consequence of the

deregulation of the cattle industry in Britain, under **neoliberal** principles, cattle were allowed to be fed with meat rendered from sheep infected with scrapie, corrupting the food chain and infecting humans (Gore, S. (1996) 'Bovine Creuzfeldt-Jakob disease? Failures of epidemiology must be remedied', *British Medical Journal*, 312: 791–3).

CRITICAL THEORY   A response to economic determinism in Marxism, the Frankfurt School – associated with the names of Horkheimer, Adorno, Marcuse and Fromm – blended aspects of Freudian psychology, a rejection of positivism, and a focus on **ideology** and culture as sources of inequality. In a study of prejudice and ethnocentrism, for example, *The Authoritarian Personality* ((1950) Adorno, T. et al., New York: Harper and Row) a personality type was identified that was characterized by excessive conformity, the source of which was unequal power systems, especially in the patriarchal family (Held, D. (1990) *Introduction to Critical Theory: Horkheimer to Habermas*. Cambridge: Polity Press) (**cultural hegemony; Frankfurt School**).

CRUDE (MORTALITY/MORBIDITY) RATE   The number of new cases or deaths due to a disease divided by the total population that could be affected, without considering age or other factors. It is usually expressed as a rate per 100,000 persons per year.

CUBA   Despite a severe lack of resources Cuba's key health indicators – infant mortality, and life expectancy at birth – are similar to those of the United States and the industrialized world. The Cuban government takes financial and administrative responsibility for the healthcare needs of all its citizens, providing free preventive, curative and rehabilitation services. Because of its lack of resources the focus of government policy is on preventive public health, with strong community involvement. Its success is taken to indicate that high-tech Western medical interventions are not necessary to sustain the healthiness of a population and that publicly organized healthcare is more efficient than market based systems (Feinsilver, J. (1993) *Healing the Masses: Cuban Health Politics at Home and Abroad*. California: University of California Press) (**Chile**).

CULTURAL CAPITAL   The stock of knowledge that allows individuals and groups to operate effectively in the social system, accessing for example, the healthcare services. The French sociologist Pierre Bourdieu argued that in contemporary society we show who we are in consumption patterns, and these operate as hierarchies of inequality, that is, as forms of cultural capital. Those groups who have been most successful at developing their taste, and imposing their definition of 'good taste' on other groups, are those with high cultural capital. For Bourdieu inequality is not only economic but also cultural and psychological, with poorer groups' concepts of good taste gauged as second best. Bourdieu's work can be applied to social representations of the body in his concept of **habitus** (Bourdieu, P. (1984) *Distinction: A Social Critique of the Judgement of Taste*. Cambridge, MA: Harvard University Press) (**habitus**; **Mauss**).

CULTURE BOUND SYNDROMES   Patterns of aberrant behaviour specific to cultural groups. These groups consider these behaviours to be illnesses. Over 200 have been identified. The debate is whether they should be explained in terms of the categories of Western psychiatry, or anthropologically, as the outcome of the social organization of the group. There is some evidence that some Western diseases – such as **depression** and **schizophrenia** – are culture bound syndromes (Simons, R. and Hughes, C. (1986) *Culture Bound Syndromes: Folk Illnesses of Psychiatric and Anthropological Interest*. Boston: D. Reidel) (**disease**).

CULTURAL DETERMINISM   The argument that human beings are the product of their culture, rather than their biology. The impetus for the argument, which can be located in the work of Frans Boaz (1858–1942), was against racialist and evolutionist theories that asserted a hierarchy of racial types in the human population (Boas, F. (1940) *Race, Language and Culture*. New York: Macmillan) (**biological determinism**).

CULTURAL HEGEMONY   In Marxism the argument that the ruling class maintains its dominance not only through economic power but also through the control of cultural institutions such as education and the media which shape people's perception of reality so that they coincide with the interests of the ruling class. Medicine in this context presents a view of sickness and disease – that it is an individual's responsibility, that 'cure' requires the consumption of drugs and technology – that is congruent with a capitalist economic system. The term was developed by Italian Marxist, Antonio Gramsci (1891–1937) (Waitzkin, H. (1991) 'A critical theory of medical discourse', *Journal of Health and Social Behaviour*, 30: 220–39) (**critical theory; ideology; Marxist approaches**).

CYBERANATOMIES   With new medical technologies, based around the internet and the web, patients and body parts can be screened and digitalized for transfer around the globe from screen to screen, thus dissolving the body and the patient as a self (Moore, L. and Clarke, A. (2001) 'The traffic in cyberanatomies', *Body and Society*,

7 (1): 57–94) (**biotechnology; body; cyborgs; information and communication technologies; medical technology; social construction of technology; telemedicine**).

CYBERCULTURE   (information and communication technologies; internetinformed patient; self-help groups).

CYBORGS   The mixture of human and machine where biology and technology become inextricably linked. Haraway has argued that the new biotechnologies have unseated old Western dualisms such as mind/body, self/other and male/female so that there are no certainties about nature, the body or self left. Her work, underpinned by socialist-feminism, is particularly concerned with the ways that the new biotechnologies are used to construct race, gender and human relations. (Haraway, D. (1991) *Simians, Cyborgs and Women*. London: Free Association Books) (**biotechnology; body; cyberanatomies; medical technology; socialist feminism**).

D

DEATH There are a range of medical definitions of death. 1 the cessation of vital signs of pulse and breathing; 2 loss of the body's coordinating system, i.e. lower brain stem death; 3 cerebral cortex (i.e. higher brain) death. These competing medical definitions have meant that death has been a site of extensive public and professional debate especially as it relates to a distinction with **coma** and of the role of life support systems. The nearest to an accepted definition has four characteristics: 1 unreceptivity and unresponsiveness; 2 no movements or breathing; 3 no reflexes; 4 flat electro-encephalogram (Veatch, R. (1972) *Brain Death: Welcome Definition or Dangerous Judgement*, Hastings Center Report, 2). In health studies analyses of death are based on the assumption that death is not an instantaneous individual event but a complex social process reflecting social organization. This argument was first developed by Hertz (Hertz, R. (1905–6) *La Representation Collective de la Mort*. L'Année Sociologique; Hertz, R. (1960) *Death and the Right Hand: A Contribution to the Study of the Collective Representations of Death*. London: Cohen and West). Historically it has been shown that the way societies deal with death changes. Pope Ariès argues that we can chart the following changes in Western responses: 1 death used to involve the whole community; 2 the dying used to be in a position of power; 3 death has become hidden; 4 death has been transformed from a religious event into a disease under the control of the medical profession; 5 death has become dirty and disgusting, and an affront to modern medicine; 6 death has been removed from society, stripped of much of its public ceremonial aspects and hidden away (Ariès, P. (1974) *Western Attitudes Towards Death from the Middle Ages to the Present*. Baltimore: Johns Hopkins University Press). At an institutional level dying is a social process in which 1 the doctor decides when the transition to death has taken place; 2 announces it to others after certifying that it has occurred; 3 co-ordinates the process of dying so that everyone behaves in conformity with the rules (Sudnow, D. (1967) *Passing On: The Social Organization of Dying*. Englewood Cliffs: Prentice Hall). At the individual level E. Kubler-Ross has argued that a dying person goes through five stages: 1 Denial; 2 Anger; 3 Bargaining; 4 Depression; 5 Acceptance (Kubler-Ross, E. (1969) *On Death and Dying*. New York: Macmillan) (**bereavement; coma; death certificate; do not resuscitate; dying trajectories;**

hospice movement; **persistent vegetative state**; **social death**).

DEATH CERTIFICATE   The legal certificate of the cause of death signed by a legally qualified medical practitioner. Sociologists have demonstrated that non-medical factors play a role in the labelling of the cause of death, particularly where negative moral evaluation is a factor. Hence in Catholic countries, part of the reason for low suicide rates may be the reticence of medical practitioner's to use the label (Atkinson, J. (1978) *Discovering Suicide*. London: Macmillan). Also of interest because it can be shown to represent a **medicalization** of an event which may have alternative explanations. One example is the medical certification of death as caused by 'bruising and oedema of the brain associated with fractures of the skull'. The alternative political account of the cause of death (the context was Northern Ireland) was 'injuries caused by a rubber bullet' (Prior, L. (1989) *The Social Organization of Death*. London: Macmillan).

DECISION RULES   Guidelines developed by expert panels to aid physicians in their decision making processes, particularly in the context of ordering tests or radiography with an aim to reducing unnecessary expenditure. Examples include the Ottawa ankle rules for ordering radiography and the Pittsburgh evaluation of knee injuries.

DECONSTRUCTION   Based on the work of French theorist Jacques Derrida (1930–2004) a method of critically analysing texts to reveal the hidden structures and assumptions that underpin them. Thus, for example, the discourse of medicine can be deconstructed to show how it is fundamentally based on, for example, military metaphors (Arrigo, B. (1999) 'Martial metaphors and medical justice: implications for law, crime and deviance', *Journal of Political and Military Sociology*, 27 (2): 307–322) (**content analysis; discourse analysis**).

DEFENSIVE MEDICINE   In the context of rising litigation the tendency for doctors to protect themselves by ordering tests for all likely diagnoses of a patient's illness. The motivation is not medical but socio-legal. The rise of defensive medicine is one of the sources of the huge costs of modern medicine.

DEGRADATION CEREMONIES   Rituals of social exclusion in which the social persona of an individual is diminished as they enter a stigmatised social role, such as that of insane or deviant. Degradation may be both physical, as in having to wear specific clothing, such as hospital gowns, and psychological, when the person's name is replaced by a number or a disease label, for example, mad (Braithwaite, J. and Mugford, S. (1994) 'Conditions of successful reintegration ceremonies: dealing with juvenile offenders', *British Journal of Criminology*, 34 (2): 139–71). (**depersonalization; Goffman; moral career; stigma; total institution**).

DEINSTITUTIONALIZATION   The movement of individuals from an institutional setting to a community setting, usually referring to the mental health system. It is now used more generically to refer to the set of policies under **neoliberalism** to move services – aged care, disability care and hospital services – into the community or the home. Deinstitutionalization was heralded as a humane breakthrough in the treatment of the mentally ill, but in the absence of resources, has largely left them to fend for themselves, or put responsibility for them back on to their families (**asylums; care in the community; hospital at home; revolving door syndrome**).

DELPHI TECHNIQUE   A group decision making procedure, designed to generate consensus, where there are contested issues or strong and rival opinions, as when a group of experts disagrees about what is at issue (**nominal group process**).

DEMOGRAPHIC ENTRAPMENT   The situation where a community cannot be supported at the ecological level, cannot migrate, and economically has insufficient exports to pay for food and medicines. The health consequences are starvation and early death, as in Rwanda (McMichael, A., Guillebaud, J. and King, M. (1999) 'Contrasting views on human population growth', *British Medical Journal*, 319: 931–32) (**epidemiological polarization; epidemiological transition**).

DEMOGRAPHIC   TRANSITION   (**epidemiological transition**).

DENTISTRY   Medical specialists who deal with the teeth. They are unique among the healthcare occupations in their independence from medical control, having the right to carry out surgery, and to prescribe and administer drugs.

DEPENDENCY   Reliance on drugs or alcohol to manage social life (**addiction**).

DEPENDENCY RATIO   A summary statistical measure that compares the proportion of children (0–15) or aged (65+) to the working age population (15–64) multiplied by 100. It is used to estimate the level of caregiving in the population, but also open to considerable controversy in interpretation (**ageing; intergenerational conflict**).

DEPERSONALIZATION   The stripping of identity, the deprivation of legal rights, the loss of credibility, the loss of privacy and the loss of the right to initiate social interactions with staff of patients in mental hospitals, also referred to as mortification by **Erving Goffman** in *Asylums*. At the general level it refers to the experience of being inducted into any total institution, from the army or monastery, to prison or hospital, where the individual's previous identity is dismantled and replaced with a new one (Rosenham, D. (1973) 'On Being Sane in Insane Places', *Science*, 179: 250–8) (**degradation ceremony; moral career; total institution**).

DEPRESSION   A sense of hopelessness, which has been shown to be the product, not of the individual (as suggested by medicine and psychiatry), but of the quality of social relationships. For example, lack of social support for lower working class women has been shown to make them susceptible to depression. Women are more likely to be diagnosed as depressed than men, and to be prescribed anti-depressants and **tranquillizers**. Depression is also associated with economic stress, and whether or not the individual experiences a sense of control over their life events (Brown, G. and Harris, T. (1978) *Social Origins of Depression*. London: Tavistock) (**locus of control**; **mental illness**; **social support**; **stress**).

DEPROFESSIONALIZATION   An umbrella term to capture changes in the relationship of medicine to the market, the state, technological change and the growth of an empowered consumer movement each of which has contributed to a decline of **medical dominance**. The argument is that the medical profession has lost its autonomy in that it is now answerable to state health authorities on the one hand, and capitalist investors into the medical market on the other; that it has lost its aura of arcane knowledge with the increasingly 'routine' and technical aspects of its work; and that it has lost prestige in the face of an informed consumer movement which questions its authority and is turning increasingly to **complementary** and **alternative** medicines to treat themselves (Haug, M. (1988) 'A Re-examination of the hypotheses of physician deprofessionalisation', *Milbank Quarterly*, 66 (Supp 2): 48–56) (**internet-informed**

patient; McDonaldization/McDoctor; medical dominance; proletarianization; substantive rationality).

DEREGULATION   The actions of neoliberal governments to loosen state control over the provision of health and welfare services, based on the claims that the market will provide the best protection for the consumer, the best distribution of resources and promote economic growth and efficiency. There is no empirical evidence to support these claims, and the deregulation policies have been shown to significantly reduce access to, the quality of, and the planning for health and welfare services (Collyer, F. and White, K. (1997) 'Enter the market: competition, regulation and hospital funding in Australia', *Australian and New Zealand Journal of Sociology*, 33 (3): 344–63) (**corporatization**; **neoliberalism**; **privatization**).

DE SAUSSURE, FERDINAND (1857–1913) Swiss linguist, and author of *Course in General Linguistics*, who argued that language is a system of signs in which terms are related to each other, rather than related to an externally existing object. This laid the basis for the 'linguistic turn' in the social sciences where the argument was made that since reality could only be known through language, and since language was conventional, then the labels applied to an object, for example, a bodily state as diseased, represented the successful construction of the phenomenon, in this case, by the medical profession (**conventionalism**; **discourse**; **power/knowledge**).

DESCARTES,   RENÉ   (1596–1650)
Seventeenth-century French philosopher. In an attempt to firmly ground knowledge, he argued, the philosopher must first of all give up belief in everything he thinks he knows. However, he recognized in this process that one thing could not be doubted, that he was thinking. Hence his famous credo 'Cogito ergo sum': 'I think therefore I am' (**Cartesian**).

DESKILLING   The subdivision of tasks into smaller tasks, with the aim of reducing wages, and increasing productivity. It may also take the form of redefining tasks so that a lower paid occupation takes them over, for example moving nursing responsibilities down the hierarchy from registered nurses to enrolled nurses. Technological artifacts may also be redefined as suitable for a lower occupation, as in the passage of the stethoscope from the doctor to the nurse, where its use is no longer defined as a status symbol or as an aspect of arcane knowledge.

DEVIANCE   The breaking of rules and expectations of social life. Whether or not an action is defined as deviance is a product of social and political factors and not something inherent in the act. Many contested diseases are regarded by powerful groups as deviant acts of individuals trying to avoid their social responsibilities, a phenomenon **Parsons** called motivated deviance. Alternatively, people expressing these concerns may be acting in the only way open to them, in the face of structural strains around their social roles and demands placed on them (**chronic fatigue**

syndrome; drapetomania; norms; post traumatic stress disorder; repetitive strain injury; sick role**).

DIABETES   Examined sociologically in a number of ways. In the first the chronic experience of diabetes is shown to empower the person to make a positive adaptation to a chronic illness, and as a consequence of their knowledge, based on experience, allows for an equal partnership with the medical practitioner, or even a rejection of the medical account of their condition (Drummond, N. and Mason, C. (1990) 'Diabetes in a social context: just a different way of life in the age of reason', in S. Cunningham-Burley and N. McKeganey (eds), *Readings in Medical Sociology*. London: Routledge). A second way is to examine how individuals respond to and manage the stigma of being labelled 'diabetic' in everyday life. (Rajaram, S. (1997) 'Experience of hypoglycemia among insulin dependent diabetics and its impact on the family', *Sociology of Health and Illness*, 19 (3): 281–301). At a more macro level, diabetes and its consequences is shown to be a product of class related factors, with mortality rates from diabetes twice as high in the lowest socio-economic groups as those in the highest socio-economic groups. (Chaturvedi, N., Jarrett, J., Shipley, M. and J. Fuller (1998) 'Socioeconomic gradient in morbidity and mortality in people with diabetes', *British Medical Journal*, 316: 100–5) (**chronic illness; stigma**).

DIAGNOSIS   The definition of a condition as a disease by a legally qualified medical practitioner. In the history of medicine how this process is accomplished has changed from what the patient tells the doctor (bedside medicine), to what the doctor tells the patient (hospital medicine), to what the tests tell the doctor (laboratory medicine). From a sociological perspective what gets diagnosed as a disease is as much the product of the social, economic and political environment as it is a product of biology (**bedside medicine**; ***Birth of the Clinic, The***; **consultation**; **disease**; **medicalization**).

DIAGNOSIS RELATED GROUPS (DRG) Part of the new public management the organization of payments to hospitals based on the classification of diagnosis and their medical and surgical treatment, thus allowing for the quantification of every aspect of care provided. Since each diagnostic group is funded at a specific price, variations in patient responses to treatment have to be largely overlooked in the interests of meeting budget (**casemix**; **clinical pathways**; **new public management**).

DIAGNOSTIC AND STATISTICAL MANUAL (DSM) The handbook of the **American Psychiatric Association**, now in its fourth revised edition. It was first published in 1952 and set out the criteria by which to diagnose mental illness. The DSM-III (1973) revolution moved psychiatry firmly away from psychoanalytic explanations and towards biological and neurological accounts of **mental illness**. The move caused a furore in American psychiatry and illustrates the political nature of

psychiatric classification (Bayer, R. and Spitzer, R. (1985) 'Neurosis, psychodynamics, and DSM III', *Archives of General Psychiatry*, 42: 187–96) (**anti- psychiatry**; **homosexuality**; **mental illness**; **post traumatic stress disorder**).

DIAGNOSTIC LIMBO Individuals who experience a decline in functioning but are not diagnosed with a disease. For example, multiple sclerosis may not be diagnosed for two years after the onset of symptoms. These individuals present to many doctors in search of an explanation of their condition, but have them dismissed. Alternatively, the presentation of symptoms by individuals for which there is no settled medical explanation, as in chronic fatigue syndrome or premenstrual tension (Corbin, J. and Strauss, A. (1988) *Unending Work and Care: Managing Chronic Illness at Home*. San Francisco: Jossey-Bass) (**abnormal illness behaviour**).

DIAGNOSTIC SHOCK The impact on an individual, who otherwise thought of themselves as well, of the diagnosis of a disease, as for example, of a cancer or of AIDS. With no preceding symptoms such a diagnosis puts the individual into the patient role without prior adjustment, and threatens their sense of identity as they redefine themselves in terms of the illness (Sourkes, R. (1982) *The Deepening Shade*. Pittsburgh: Pittsburgh University Press) (**abnormal illness behaviour**).

DIALECTICAL BEHAVIOUR THERAPY A therapeutic technique for addressing the problems (particularly of women) with a diagnosis of borderline personality disorder. These individuals self-harm and are difficult to keep in therapy and treat. Dialectical behaviour therapy adopts traditional techniques such as individual and group therapy as well as less traditional increases in access to the therapist after hours by the client (Linehan, M. (1993) *Cognitive Behavioural Treatment of Borderline Personality Disorder.* New York: Guilford Press).

DIET It is estimated that poor diet is responsible for 15 per cent of all deaths in Western countries. In a sociological approach diet is not considered a lifestyle choice. Income level defines access to the range of foods available, providing the individual with limited scope for choice within that range. Choice is also limited by the social distribution of food. What are regarded as good dietary choices – unprocessed whole grains and raw sugar for example – are more likely to be available in higher social status areas and cost more than processed foodstuffs. (Blane, D., Bartley, M. and Davey Smith, G. (1997) 'Disease aetiology and materialist explanations of socioeconomic mortality differentials', *European Journal of Public Health*, 7: 385–91) (**health determinants; lifestyle choices; lifestyle factors; malnutrition; materialist analyses**).

DISABILITY While usually thought of as a biological given, disability is as much about social factors: access to buildings and transport, and of the attitudes of others in the workplace that have a marked impact on the participation of the disabled in social and economic life. The basis for a social model of disability was laid in the 1970s by the Union of Physically Impaired Against Segregation (UPIAS). In *The Fundamental Principles of Disability* (1976: 114) they rejected medical and individualized notions of disability, defining disability as: 'the disadvantage or restriction of activity caused by a contemporary organization which takes no or little account of people who have physical impairments and thus excludes them from participation in the mainstream of social activities'. Building on this the World Health Organization distinguished between impairment, the biological deficit, disability, the degree of loss of functioning, and handicap the social problems consequent upon being labelled as disabled (**(dis)ablism; handicap; International Classification of Impairments, Disabilities and Handicaps; labelling theory; spoilt identity; stigma**).

DISABILITY ADJUSTED LIFE YEARS (DALYS) A measure of a population's health, the total amount of healthy life lost, to all causes, either from premature mortality or from some degree of disability during a period of time (**burden of disease; quality adjusted life years**).

DISABILITY FREE LIFE EXPECTANCY (DFLE) The measure of how long an individual will live without disability. The emphasis is not on life expectancy, but the quality of life without activity limitations.

(DIS)ABLISM Disabled people suffer not only because of their condition, but also because of the reactions of others, resulting in (dis)ablism, that is, institutionalized discrimination that results in a poorer social life, lack of access to public spaces, less participation in the educational system, and less participation in the workforce (Barnes, C. (1994) *Disabled People in Britain and Discrimination: A Case for Anti-Discrimination Legislation.* London: C. Hurst and Co) (**disability; handicap**).

DISCIPLINARY POWER   In Foucault's work the ways in which modern institutions – schools, hospitals, medical practices, prisons and asylums for example – exercise coercive power to discipline and regulate the behaviour of individuals. The emphasis is less on these institutions wielding power overtly, but rather on the ways in which we internalize their definitions of normal behaviour. At the level of the society, Foucault distinguishes disciplinary power from the sovereign power of the premodern period, in which power was centralized in the king, and its limits determined by his ability to enforce his will. Thus disciplinary power is far more effective at bringing about social order, not least because its workings go unnoticed (**anatomo-politics; biopolitics; biopower; carceral society; Foucault; governmentality; psy-professions; power/knowledge; surveillance; technologies of the self**).

DISCOURSE   In Foucault's work the group of statements that constitute a field of study. For example the discourse of medicine is built around the concepts of disease. Disease does not in itself exist, but rather is held in existence by the words

that make it. Professional discourses shape and determine what can be said about a condition, who has the right to treat it, and how it will be treated. In *The Birth of the Clinic* (1973) Foucault documented the development of the discourse of professional medicine in the eighteenth and nineteenth centuries (**de Saussure; psy-professions; power/knowledge; technologies of the self**).

DISCOURSE ANALYSIS   The assessment of validity claims in a body of knowledge. Discourse analysts emphasize the ways in which apparently 'neutral' knowledge claims – such as that of scientific medical knowledge – carry implicit assumptions based on class, gender and ethnicity. In this approach there is no such thing as an impartial or objective knowledge since all knowledge is grounded in specific economic, gendered and historical moments (**content analysis**).

DISEASE   In medicine, the malfunctioning of the body as a consequence of infection by a germ or virus, or the departure from normal functioning of an organ. In this usage diseases present themselves unproblematically as facts within the context of a natural science methodology and are purely physiological occurrences. This definition is systematically challenged in the health studies literature, which emphasizes the interplay between politics, economics and social factors such as gender, and the construction of a condition as a disease. Sociologists distinguish between disease, the label applied to a condition by the medical profession; illness, the subjective experience of bodily states of an individual; and sickness, the successfully entry into the **sick role** . Thus there is no simple one-way determination from biology to the social state of being sick (**abnormal; bedside medicine; clinical iceberg; discourse; disease, social model; germ theory; health; normal; social gradient of disease**).

DISEASE IDENTITY DEPENDENCY   One consequence of **chronic illness** and the attempts by individuals to come to terms with it by forming self-help groups, in which the disease state and the diseased self become central to their self-definition. Other responses may be to 'set the situation right', by coming to grips with the illness, and ongoing inability to cope, or the pursuit of a cure (Crossley, M. (1998) 'Sick role or empowerment – the Ambiguities of Life with an HIV positive diagnoses', *Sociology of Health and Illness*, 20: 507–31) (**liminality; narrative accounts of illness**).

DISEASE MANAGEMENT SYSTEMS   US programmes to tackle specific diseases, such as asthma, diabetes, and congestive cardiac failure, run by private companies with the aim of bringing healthcare costs down. Drug companies involved, whose main aim is to sell more drugs, target high-risk patients by monitoring prescription patterns to identify patients with chronic disease, bringing their products to the patient's attention, so that the patient can then inform their doctor about them, thus increasing the pressure to prescribe them.

This strategy is called 'direct to consumer advertising' (Bodenheimer, T. (1999) 'Disease management – promises and pitfalls', *The New England Journal of Medicine* 340 (15): 1202–6).

DISEASES OF AFFLUENCE   A term used in the mid-twentieth century to describe the development of chronic illness such as diabetes and the non-infectious diseases such as cancer, heart attacks and stroke. The argument was that these conditions were a product of the successful control of the diseases of the nineteenth century – infectious diseases and epidemics – and of the development of sedentary lifestyles, inappropriate diet, smoking and drinking patterns of individuals. Notwithstanding the investment of billions of dollars into the cause and treatment of these conditions failure to bring them under control demonstrates the limitations of the medical model with its focus on the on the body and the individual independently, of the social factors which induce and maintain individuals' **lifestyle** and **lifestyle choices** (McKinlay, J. and McKinlay, S. (1989) 'A review of the evidence concerning the impact of medical measures on the decline of mortality in the United States in the twentieth century', *International Journal of Health Services*, 19: 181–208) (**diseases of poverty; health determinants; lifestyle choices; lifestyle factors**).

DISEASES OF POVERTY   The demonstration that social inequality produces patterns of disease in which the poor and those with low social status suffer more and die sooner than those at the top of the social system (**social gradient of disease**). Widely held to have been significantly ameliorated with the development of the **welfare state** and national health insurance systems after World War II. However with the development of **neoliberalism** there has been a resurgence of the infectious diseases of the nineteenth century. As a consequence of lack of controls over water supplies and the contamination of water supplies by sewage there have been outbreaks of epidemic cholera in the Americas, and in more developed countries the burden of disease is increasingly falling on the poor as inequality systematically widens (Pan American Health Organization (1994) *Health Conditions in the Americas.* Washington, DC: PAHO) (**health determinants**; **poverty**; **social inequality**; **socio-economic status**).

DISEASE, SOCIAL MODEL Rather than focusing on individual diseases and individual bodies, health research and health policy should be directed to the economic, political and cultural institutions that produce disease. Peter Davis has proposed classifications of disease based on the economic, social, cultural and political determinants of ill-health and disease. In the economic sphere, the institution of the labour market, inside the economic framework of capitalism, results in profit being placed before safety, and systematically produces industrial deaths and accidents. He points to the social shaping of disease, through the institutions of family and kinship, working themselves out in the

context of urbanization and social mobility, as sources of hypertension and mental illness. Cultural factors of beliefs, practices and lifestyles, manifest in different consumption patterns, especially of diet and alcohol, are key factors in obesity, bowel cancer and lung cancer. At the political level are those diseases that are a product of the structures of power and the different participation rates of different groups in an unequal society, which result in diseases due to problems of access to services and equity in the distribution of services (Davis, P. (1994) 'A socio-cultural critique of transition theory', in J. Spicer, A. Trlin and J. Walton (eds), *Social Dimensions of Health and Disease.* Palmerston North: Dunmore Press) (**health determinants**; **lifestyle choices**; **lifestyle factors**; **social inequality**).

DISEMBODIMENT A term used to critique **biomedicine**, that it deals with the patient's disease as if it had an independent existence from the patient's body, that is, it is reductionist in its account of human sickness and **disease**. In another usage, an epistemological argument made by **feminists**, critiquing the claim by Western science that knowledge does not carry within it implicit assumptions based on the normality of the male body, while simultaneously constructing women's bodies as the source of unreliable knowledge (Lawrence, C. and Shapin, S. (1998) (eds), *Science Incarnate: Historical Embodiments of Natural Knowledge.* Chicago: University of Chicago Press). The developments in **biotechnology** have led some theorists to speculate that the 'natural' human body has been dissolved as we come more and more to represent **cyborgs** (**biologistic**; **reductionism**).

DISENGAGEMENT THEORY Based on the work of Cumming and Henry the argument that successful ageing involves a gradual withdrawal from social roles in anticipation of death (Cumming, E. and Henry, W. (1961) *Growing Old: The Process of Disengagement*. New York: Basic Books). By contrast activity theory, with more support from the empirical evidence, argues that continued social involvement has positive psychological benefits for the aged and that they can continue to make a useful contribution to society (Searle, M., Mahon, M., Iso-Ahola, J. and Sdrolias, S. (1995) 'Enhancing a sense of independence and psychological well-being among the elderly: a field experiment', *Journal of Leisure Research*, 27 (2): 107–24) (**ageing; ageism**).

DIX, DOROTHEA (1802–87) American campaigner for mental health reform, particularly the separation of the criminal from the insane, and for the development of separate institutions for each. Her work led to the establishment of state mental hospitals. In 1861 she was appointed Superintendent for Nurses in the Union Army. Like **Nightingale** in England, she developed nursing as well as reinforced traditional feminine stereotypes of the nurse's role (Dix, D. (1999) *Asylum, Prison and Poorhouse*, edited by D. Lighter, Illinois: Southern Illinois University Press) (**Bedlam**).

DOCILE BODY In Foucault's sociology of health the claim that the power relations of modern societies are experienced not only through institutional structures but at the level of the body. Thus we actively seek to construct and maintain our bodies as normal, constantly monitoring for example their weight and shape, by dieting and going to the gym (Crawford, R. (2000) 'The ritual of health promotion', in S. Williams (ed.), *Health, Medicine and Society*. London: Routledge). In **Foucauldian-feminism** the emphasis is on the way that patriarchal society produces women's bodies as docile. Women's movements and bodily representations are restricted by cultural mores of modesty; and the routines of women's daily lives are made up of make-up and beauty practices which constitute her body in the ideal of femininity. Out of these practices the woman's body is produced, 'a practiced and subjected body' (Bartsky, S. (1988) 'Foucault, femininity and the modernization of patriarchal power', in I. Diamond and L. Quinby (eds), *Feminism and Foucault: Reflections on Resistance*. Boston: Northeastern University Press) (**bodyism; citizenship; fitness; new public health; self-care; somatic norms; technologies of the self**).

DOCTOR/NURSE GAME Given the subordinate position of nursing to medicine, and the patriarchal relations of the two occupations, nurses have to be seen to defer to doctors in public, though in carrying out their tasks have greater autonomy than their formal position would suggest. The public display of compliance, with the behind the scenes reality of nursing autonomy, is called the doctor/nurse game. Studies of doctor–nurse interactions are grounded in **symbolic interactionism** demonstrating the ways in which formal rules are negotiated in practice, and that organizational practices and relationships are more fluid than they seem (Hughes, D. (1988) 'When nurse knows best: some aspects of nurse–doctor interaction in a casualty department', *Sociology of Health and Illness*, 10 (1): 1–22) (**medical dominance; Strauss**).

DOCTOR–PATIENT RELATIONSHIP Rather than just being the delivery of a technical service, the encounter with the medical practitioner can be conceptualized in terms of types of interaction that change over the course of an illness, and depending on the symptoms. Thus it may take the form of activity (doctor) passivity (patient) in the context of intensive care; guidance-cooperation, where the treatment is for an acute illness; and mutual participation in terms of managing ongoing illness. (Szasz, T. and Hollender, M. (1956) 'A contribution to the philosophy of medicine: the basic models of the doctor-patient relationship', *Archives of Internal Medicine*, 97: 589–92). The relationship has also been conceptualized in terms of consensus, conflict, negotiation, and with the rise of **consumerism** as a contractual relationship (Bury, M. (1997) *Health and Illness in a Changing Society*. London: Routledge) (**compliance; consultation; medical dominance; Parsons; sick role**).

DOCTORS In everyday usage those members of the medial profession legally qualified to diagnose disease and to prescribe drugs, though in fact the title is reserved for those holding a doctorate, that is the postgraduate degree of Doctor of Philosophy, from a university. Some other occupations with undergraduate training (such as dentistry and veterinary science in Australia) are also allowed by law to title their practitioners 'doctor'.

DOCUMENTARY ANALYSIS The examination of materials ranging from personal photographs, diaries and letters to public materials such as newspapers, works of fiction and archives in libraries. The documents can be analysed, for example, to provide insight into the personal world of sickness and disease, professional relationships between medical and paramedical practitioners, or the construction of public health campaigns (Markova, I. and Farr, R. (1995) (eds), *Representations of Health, Illness and Handicap*. Chur: Harwood Publishers).

DOMESTIC VIOLENCE Internationally, one of the major causes of women's disability and death. In the United States, domestic violence is responsible for 40 per cent of the female homicide rate and up to 2 million women are beaten every year. In some cultures forms of domestic violence, leading to death, are institutionalized: bride burning in India, when the bride's dowry is regarded as too small, and honour killing in Arab countries in which a women's male relatives will kill her for alleged sexual impropriety (Lane, S. and Cibula, D. (2000) 'Gender and health', in G. Albrecht, R. Fitzpatrick and S. Scrimshaw (eds),

Handbook of Social Studies in Health and Medicine. London: Sage) (**gender linked health risks; sexual harassment; somatization**).

DONOR INSEMINATION　Sperm from a male donor is placed in the woman's cervix, fallopian tubes or uterus to enhance the likelihood of pregnancy. The donor may be the woman's partner or an anonymous man. For some feminists and lesbians it allows women the freedom to have a child without having sex or a relationship with a man. Other feminists, though, point out that in the case of surrogate mother arrangements it may result in women being represented as breeding machines and as 'wombs for hire' (Ardittie, R., Klein, R. and Minden, S. (1984) *Test-tube Women: What Future for Motherhood?* Boston: Pandora Press) (**new reproductive technologies**).

DO NOT RESUSCITATE (DNR)　An advanced care directive directing medical staff not to attempt resuscitation, usually in situations where the patient has suffered neurological damage, due to accident or medical procedures, or, again, due to accident or medical procedures, will be dependent on life-sustaining technology, as for example, when in a coma (**advanced care directives; coma; death; euthanasia; iatrogenesis; persistent vegetative state; physician assisted suicide**).

DOUBLE-BLIND TRIAL　Most commonly used in the trial of a new drug to test its efficacy. Neither the patient nor the doctor

knows if a new drug is being used, or if an already existing drug is being administered and taken, or if a placebo, an inert substance, is being administered. The aim is to prevent bias in the assessment of the new drug produced by knowledge of its use, which is the **placebo effect**. (**evidence-based medicine; Thomas theorem**).

DRAMATURGY　(**Goffman**).

DRAPETOMANIA　The diagnoses of a disease suffered by American plantation Negroes in the nineteenth century, the tendency to run away from their master. Used by historical sociologists of disease to demonstrate the social, political and ethnic shaping of disease. Running away from the plantation owner becomes a disease because of the specific social and political circumstances of a racist society in which whites dominated and subjugated Negroes in an economic system of slavery. Its existence was both a product of that society and helped to reinforce the power relations of that society. The treatment of the condition also reflected the ethos of the time. The nineteenth century was a period in which professional medicine was developing on the basis of a claim to technical and scientific skills. It was replacing the Church as the institution delegated the task of admonishing wayward individuals and bringing them back into the realms of normal society. So rather than explain the activities of the Negroes in religious terms – that they were possessed – and call in the priests, the white plantation owners called in the doctors. And the doctors, as skilled practitioners of a technical and scientific practice, diagnosed the condition as a disease and prescribed a remedy: the surgical removal of both big toes, thereby making running a physical impossibility. It is a good example of the ways in which the classification of disease reflects social, cultural and ethnic, as well as economic factors in the ways in which some actions are diagnosed as disease (Engelhardt, H. (1981) 'The disease of masturbation: values and the concept of disease', in A. Caplan, H. Engelhardt and J. McCartney (eds), *Concepts of Health and Disease*. Reading, MA: Addison Wesley) (**agoraphobia; anorexia nervosa; learning disabilities; medicalization; miners' nystagmus; repetitive strain injury; social control**).

DRIFT HYPOTHESES (social drift hypothesis).

DRUG ADDICTION (addict).

DRUG THERAPY Chemical and biological substances administered to prevent or cure disease. The focus of much sociological research is on examining the interface between the objectives of the drug companies to maximize their income and the needs of the population to have access to well tested products (Davis, P. (1997) *Managing Medicines: Public Policy and Therapeutic Drug*. Buckingham: Open University Press).

DUALISM The division of the social world into binary opposites, such as reason and emotion, or body and mind, male and

female, privileging one over the other. In feminist analyses, the argument is made that these dualisms are used to link women with nature, intuition and irrational emotionalism, and to construct them as determined by the biological fact of reproduction and of being at the mercy of their hormones. Men, on the other hand, are constructed as rational, objective and as a part of culture. **Radical feminists** accept a fundamental difference between men and women, arguing that because women are closer to nature they 'know' in different and better ways than men (**standpoint epistemology**). Their approach has given rise to considerable debate over whether or not they have conceded too much to patriarchal assumptions, since it accepts that the differences between men and women are as much biological as political (Jagger, A. (1983) *Feminist Politics and Human Nature*. New Jersey: Rowman and Allanheld) (**ecofeminism; essentialism; feminism; post structuralism; sexism**).

DUKE HEALTH PROFILE (DUKE) Originally the Duke-UNC Health Profile (DUHP) a questionnaire, developed at Duke University and the North Carolina School of Public Health, to measure self-reported health related quality of life and functional health status (Parkerson, G. (1999) *Users Guide for Duke Health Measures*. Duke University Medical Center: Department of Community and Family Medicine) (**health status assessment**).

DURKHEIM, ÉMILE (1858–1917) A French sociologist who in a series of works sought to establish sociology as a scientific endeavour. He argued that sociology was the study of objectively existing social facts, which preceded the existence of any individual, and were external to and coerced individuals. Language, legal and monetary systems are good examples: we are born into them, use them, comply with them, and when we die they continue on for the next generation. In his work on suicide he distinguished sociology from psychology as well as attempting to answer a public health problem: how is suicide distributed through society and why does it form the patterns that it does? He argued that the level of social integration in a society determined suicide rates. Too much led to altruistic suicide, while too little to egotistic and fatalistic suicide rates. His work has been criticized for over emphasizing the role of social structures (**structural functionalism**) and for overlooking both the role of the individual and the individual's perception of the situation (**anomie**; **Kant**; **positivism**; **qualitative research**; **social pathology**; **suicide**; **Weber**).

DYING TRAJECTORIES Whereas dying appears to be a straightforward biological event, **participant observers** in US hospitals demonstrated that in fact it was a carefully orchestrated social event. In particular Glaser and Strauss (1961, *Time for Dying*. Chicago: Aldine) demonstrated that both hospital staff and family members constructed accounts of the dying process to make sense of it. Thus death could be 'lingering', the 'expected quick death' or the 'unexpected quick death'. Each trajectory has implications for staff and relatives of how to handle the situation. Thus the expected quick death is unexceptional for staff, but inexplicable to relatives. The unexpected quick death is disruptive for all and requires considerable negotiation to be brought into line. The lingering death stretches everybody's resources and may result in **social death** as staff and relatives become worn out (**bereavement**; **Chicago School of Sociology**; **death**; **grounded theory**; **microsociological**).

DYSLEXIA A learning disability involving reading, writing and spelling. From a sociological perspective the condition is of interest as individuals manage the **stigma** of being identified as dyslexic, experience discrimination and provide accounts of their situation (Booth, T. (1996) 'Sounds of still voices: issues in the use of narrative methods with people who have learning difficulties', in L. Barton (ed.), *Disability and Society: Emerging Issues and Insights*. London: Longman) (**learning disabilities**; **medicalization**).

E

EATING DISORDERS (anorexia nervosa; binge-purging; bulimia; obesity).

ECO-FEMINISM A position in feminism that argues that women, as a consequence of their biology, or their psychology, but in either case, their unique characteristics, are closer to nature and, therefore, in a better position to protect nature from **patriarchal** exploitation. In terms of illness and disease it implies that women will be healers and carers of people who suffer, rather than seeking technological cures for the diseases of patients (**dualism; essentialism; patriarchal medicine; standpoint epistemology**).

ECOLOGICAL MODEL In **epidemiology** the study of the interaction between the environment and populations of hosts and parasites. Historical epidemiologists of the plague, such as **Zinsser**, have argued that the relationship is mediated by social structures such as ethnicity and religion, which act to protect groups from the impact of epidemics. It also refers to the relationship between humans and the biosphere, a relationship that is seriously out of balance, with the **World Health Organization** estimating that current resource usage by Western

societies needs to be reduced by four-fifths. The consequence if this is not achieved will be ecological disaster (World Health Organization Commission on Health and the Environment. (1992) *Our Planet, Our Health*. Geneva: WHO).

ELIAS, NORBERT (1897–1990) German sociologist who argued against **Weber** that the developmental process in the West is a progressive, liberalizing and humanizing one. Elias also argued that the history of medicine is not the history of the application of rational scientific insights: rather it is the record of cultural, political and economic changes in European societies. He analysed the developments of concerns with health and hygiene as reflecting a broader social movement that reflects the increased 'delicacy of feeling' between individuals. Health and the maintenance of personal hygiene, is a reflection of this change. Further, health becomes the symbol of correct social relationships because, with the democratization of European society and the individualization of personality structures, it becomes a field of practice open to all (Elias, N. (1978) *The Civilizing Process*. (2 Volumes). Oxford: Basil Blackwell). Foucault's work challenges Elias: **Foucault** points to the same developments but argues that they represent the development of a **disciplinary power** in which individuals internalize the correct norms of behaviour, as a consequence of the state's requirement for a docile population (**bodyism**; **docile body**; **fitness**; **new public health**; **somatization**; **technologies of the self**).

EMBODIMENT   A sociological term that draws attention to the lived experience of the body as opposed to the **mechanistic** and **biologistic** understanding in biomedicine. It is an attempt to overcome the mind–body dualism of our **Cartesian** heritage, which privileged the rational mind over the emotional body (**body**; **body politics**; **Cartesian**; **mind–body dualism**; **mind–body relationship**).

EMOTION WORK   (**affect management**).

EMOTIONS   An area of growing interest in health studies. Are emotions susceptible to sociological explanation or are they part of the biological and physiological substratum of human existence? **Parsons** had pointed to the requirement that medical professionals control their emotional involvement in dealings with their patients with his concept of affective neutrality and the role of emotions to social interaction was central to the work of **Erving Goffman**. Current understandings locate emotions as an outcome of social interaction. (Kemper, T. (1981) 'Social constructionist and positivist approaches to the sociology of emotions', *American Journal of*

Sociology, 87: 337–62) (**affect management**; **homicide**).

EMPIRICAL   A method of investigation emphasizing direct observation and experimentation to test hypotheses (**empiricism**).

EMPIRICISM   The proposition that knowledge has to be based on the observation of the empirical facts provided to us by our sensory organs. In this approach, the only worthwhile knowledge is based on the methods of the natural sciences, which will allow us to observe an objectively existing reality. This approach to what counts as knowledge underlies the **medical model** of **disease**. In Durkheim's **positivist** sociology, social reality is argued to be a fact, amenable to study using scientific methods. Empiricism and positivist sociology are challenged by Kantian approaches to knowledge that emphasize the role of the human mind in constructing reality, which Kant argued is a priori structured to sort and organize the infinite amount of sensory data that exists. Sociologists influenced by Kant, particularly **Max Weber**, argue that our knowledge of the social world is a social accomplishment, a product of social, cultural and linguistic factors, and that the social sciences must use their own interpretative methods to explain and understand (rather than predict and control) human action. In the sociology of health this leads to a focus on the meanings and constructions of sickness and disease rather than taking them to be part of an objectively existing nature (**Chicago School of Sociology;** **Kant; scienticism; social construction/ constructionism; verstehen**).

EMPOWERMENT   Widely held to be the outcome of **consumer participation** empowerment has been defined as: 'An intentional, ongoing, process centred in the local community, involving mutual respect, critical reflection, caring, group participation, through which people lacking an equal share of valued resources gain greater access to and control over those resources' (Cornell Empowerment Group. (1989) 'Empowerment and Family Support', *Network Bulletin*, 1 (2): 1–23). Alternatively it may be seen as an aspect of **neoliberalism** constructing individuals as responsible for themselves as they operate in the healthcare market; an ideological statement (**ideology**) of how communities can help themselves; or a **blame the victim** approach in social policy (**community; market; social capital**).

EMPLOYMENT   The experience of working conditions has been demonstrated to significantly affect people's health. In particular the experience of low status, high strain jobs with little control over the work process is significantly linked to a wide range of physical ailments, including cardiovascular illness, depression, and angina, as well as poorer self-rated health (Marmot, M., Bosma, H., Hemingway, H., Brunner, E. and Stansfeld, S. (1997) 'Contribution of job control and other risk factors to social variations in coronary heart disease incidence', *The Lancet*, 350 (9073):

235–9) (**alienation; occupation and health; occupational disease; unemployment; Whitehall Studies**).

ENCROACHMENT   In the sociology of the professions the process by which para-professional groups extend their areas of practice into areas previously controlled by a dominant profession. For example, the attempts of pharmacists in hospitals to develop the specialist occupation of clinical pharmacy, to take precedence in the decision to deliver drugs, over a doctor's prescription; or the development of the nurse-practitioner who can diagnose diseases and prescribe drugs (Eaton, G. and Webb, B. (1979) 'Boundary encroachment: pharmacists in the clinical setting', *Sociology of Health and Illness*, 1 (1): 69–89) (**medical dominance; professionalization; social closure; social usurpation**).

ENGELS, FREDERICK (1820–95)   author of *The Condition of the Working Class in England* (orig. 1848) Moscow Progress Publishers (1973), one of the most important foundations for social explanations of sickness and disease. Engels advanced three central arguments about the cause of disease in industrial capitalist societies. The first was that what people suffer from is not the product of their own individual makeup. This contrasts with the prevailing view in the nineteenth century, and in the twentieth century of medicine and psychology, which focus solely on the individual. He develops his argument using examples. **Accident proneness** is the product of industrial organization and not a psychological characteristic of individuals. It is the product of management techniques where workers have to work at a forced pace, independently of the risks they put themselves at. His analysis of alcoholism locates it, not in the psychodynamics of the individual, but in the miseries of industrial cities. Living in slums, malnourished, at risk of sudden death, and living an impoverished life turned people to drink. Hence the starting point of Engels' account of disease was social organization and not an approach that focused on and blamed the individual. Second, and continuing from this point, Engels argued steadfastly for a social explanation of individual circumstances, rejecting explanations that pointed to divine providence as the source of an inevitable inequality. Third, Engels argued that sickness and disease are primarily the product of social conditions and not inevitable biological occurrences. Not only do working conditions cause orthopaedic disorders, but also tuberculosis, typhoid and syphilis are the product of working conditions and living standards. For Engels the industrial revolution and the private ownership of property resulted in 'social murder' (**sanitation; social history of medicine; social medicine**).

ENLIGHTENMENT, THE   An inter-related series of political, philosophical, and social changes occurring in eighteenth-century Europe as reason, science and empirical experience replaced divine revelation and the authority of the Church as the basis of human knowledge. While eighteenth-century medicine was far from uniform, in

general there was hope that the application of mathematics and the methods of the natural sciences would produce a new scientific medicine. In this context, there were ongoing disputes between those who conceptualized the body as machine-like (**mechanistic**) and those who insisted that the human being was more than just matter (**vitalism**). While anatomy and physiology continued to develop at the theoretical level they had little impact on clinical practice or on the health of the population (Porter, R. (1997) *The Greatest Benefit to Mankind*. London: Harper Collins) (**Cartesian**).

ENVIRONMENTAL PROTECTION AGENCY US Federal agency charged with regulating the impact of industrialization on the people's health. Because it is largely dependent for information about hazards provided by the companies they are supposed to oversee, it is limited in its impact. Most problems come to its attention after the fact and it has little preventative impact, on either pollution in the environment or the workplace (**acid rain; life scapes; occupational disease; popular epidemiology**).

ENVIRONMENTAL RISK FACTORS   Both the impact of the natural environment (pointed to by Hippocrates around 400BC when he linked malaria to living near swamps) and the effect of the social and political environment on health. In the social sciences the emphasis in explaining disease is on those social and political factors over which individuals have no control and that produces and distributes disease (**ecological model**; **health determinants**; **hygiene**; **materialist analyses**; **social history of medicine**).

EPIDEMIC The appearance of the same disease in a large number of people at the same time, such as the Black Death in the fourteenth century or the Spanish Flu epidemic of the 1920s. While epidemics appear to sweep over entire populations, the evidence is that their impact is mediated by social variables, such as poverty and ethnicity. Thus the impact of even highly infectious agents has to do as much with social organization as with the power of nature. By corollary the solution to infectious disease is social and political reform, not medical intervention at the individual level (Zinsser, H. *Rats, Lice and History*. Boston, MA: Little Brown) (**ecological model**; **epidemiological transition**; **Virchow**; **Zinsser**).

EPIDEMIOLOGICAL POLARIZATION The consequence of introducing market economies for healthcare into underdeveloped countries is to exacerbate the difference in health, nutrition and mortality rates of the rich and poor. This divides the population into a small group at the top who can afford access to healthcare services on the market and the bulk of the population who cannot. The introduction of **privatization** goes hand in hand with the deregulation of the public health system thereby reversing any gains that may have been made in health status of the population over the twentieth century

(Frenk, J. and Gonzalez-Block, M. (1992) 'Corporatism and health care: a comparison of Sweden and Mexico', *Health Policy*, 21: 167–80) (**Chile**; **Cuba**; **epidemiological transition**).

EPIDEMIOLOGICAL TRANSITION A term coined to describe long-term changes in the patterns of morbidity and mortality in the West. The long-term shift is from pandemics of infectious disease to degenerative diseases in three phases: the age of pestilence and famine; the age of receding pandemics; and the age of man-made diseases. The main demographic features of this transition are: a decline in mortality levels; and an increase in life expectancy. The main impact of the transition is on children, who now survive infancy and on women who now survive childbirth. While the transition operates at a population level there are significant class and ethnic differentials in its impact within populations. Under conditions of **demographic entrapment** no transition occurs (Omran, A. (1971) 'The epidemiological transition: a theory of the epidemiology of population change', *Milbank Memorial Fund Quarterly*, 49: 509–38) (**health transition**).

EPIDEMIOLOGY Literally, the study of the people's health, more commonly, the study of patterns of disease in a population. There is a debate within epidemiology between clinical and social epidemiologists about the aims and methods of research. Clinical epidemiologists focus on the refinement of statistical measures of disease patterns, reporting their findings in highly abstract mathematical terms. In this tradition epidemiology seeks to be a pure, natural science that will feed into the treatment of individuals by identifying individual **risk factors** in their behaviour. Social epidemiologists argue that research should be on those societal factors that place individuals at risk of disease and that research should focus on developing more refined social variables – of ethnicity, class, education, income or housing for example – as mediators of an individual's health, leading to social and political policies that will enhance the health of the population (Beaglehole, R. and Bonita, R. (1997) *Public Health at the Crossroads*. Cambridge: Cambridge University Press) (**case control studies; causal inference; clinical epidemiology; Leeds Declaration; new public health; popular epidemiology**).

EPILEPSY   A disorder of the brain resulting in chronic uncontrollable seizures or fits. Sociologists study it in the context of 'becoming epileptic'; of family responses to a member who has epilepsy; of the person's experience of dealing with their doctor; and of the impact of the **social stigma** of epilepsy on their ability to get a job. In short, there is a great deal more to epilepsy than the diagnoses of a biological disorder (Schneider, J. and Conrad, P. (1985) *Having Epilepsy: The Experience and Control of Illness*. Philadelphia, PA: Temple University Press) (**chronic illness**).

EPISTEMES   Associated with Foucault's work: the basic concepts underlying the thought of a period, for example, the belief in rationality, truth and objectivity in Western scientific thinking. Epistemes give rise to discourses, that is, ways of thinking and talking about the world, such as the categories of sane/insane, or diseased/healthy (**Foucault**).

EPISTEMOLOGICAL BREAK   The radical transformation in fields of scientific thought, in which one **paradigm** replaces another. The implication is that there is no cumulative development in scientific knowledge. Developed in the context of medicine and biology by **Georges Canguilhelm** and in Foucault's history of medicine, especially *The Birth of the Clinic*. Prior to Foucault, **Ludwig Fleck** developed a similar history of medicine, analysing the transitions in 'thought styles' between one medical period and the next (**social history of medicine; Stern; Whig histories of medicine**).

EPISTEMOLOGY   The branch of philosophy that enquires into the nature of knowledge, and especially of how to distinguish it from belief or faith. The debate in health social studies is what constitutes knowledge of a condition or disease. **Biologistic** accounts argue that **disease** is an objectively existing condition, to be approached using the methods of the natural sciences. Sociologists emphasize the ways in which disease is socially produced and constructed. Interactionists examine the ways in which individuals and groups interpret and make sense of their condition (**Chicago School of Sociology**; **medical model**; **sociology of scientific knowledge**).

ESSENTIALISM   The belief or claim that there are fundamental characteristics to some groups of human beings that makes them different from others. This belief is usually grounded in an appeal to biological differences as central to identity. It may be self-ascribed by a group, as in **radical feminist** approaches which assert the fundamental role of a woman's ability to give birth as essential to her identity, or ascribed to a group, as in labelling a group as being of a different 'race' (**dualism**; **eco-feminism**; **ethnicity**).

ETHICS, MEDICAL   In general the study of the merits, risks and social impact of the activities of the medical profession. This includes topics such as **death** and dying and issues such as **euthanasia**, **mercy killing** and **physician assisted suicide**; reproductive health issues, such as **new reproductive technologies**, **abortion**, **cloning**, **genetic screening** and **eugenics**; issues to do with the carrying out of medical research such as the **Nuremberg Code**; and issues regarding the accessibility, distribution and utilization of medical care. Medical ethics also refers to the principles that should guide medical conduct. These are: beneficence, that is, to act in the best interest of the patient; to do no harm; to respect the patient's autonomy

in deciding on their treatment; to treat all patients with dignity; and to be truthful about a patient's condition and treatment. At a structural level, there are many barriers to acting ethically, not the least of which is that a practitioner's income depends on their treatment recommendations, leading to over treatment, over prescribing, and to over referral for tests. That is there is a **perverse incentive** for them to act unethically (Lewins, F. (1996) *Bioethics for Health Professionals: An Introduction and Critical Approach*. Melbourne: Macmillan) (**Belmont Report**; **bioethics**; **Helsinki Declaration**; **Nuremberg Code**; **Tuskegee syphilis experiment**).

ETHNIC GROUPS   Positively or negatively valued status identities based on a shared culture, language or place of origin. Negatively valued low status groups face severe economic discrimination, at the basic level of access to loans, and to the basic underpinnings of participation in economic life, such as healthcare and health insurance, adequate schooling and access to the legal system. This flows over to the explicit outcomes of lower wages, and participation in the informal sector of the economy with its increased exposure to health hazards at work. In a vicious causal circle the outcome is segregated residential areas, increased exposure to the hazards of industrial ghettos and slums, poisoning, environmental hazards, and the corollaries of addictive and violent behaviour. These political and economic inequalities are added to by a general disparagement and denigration of cultural values and health belief systems, and a stereotypical representation of ethnic groups as responsible for their own problems (Kreiger, N. (1993) 'Racism, sexism, and social class', *American Journal of Preventive Medicine*, 9 (Suppl.): 82–122) (**blame the victim; ethnicity; race**).

ETHNICITY   In some cases the self-ascribed cultural and linguistic characteristics of a group claiming a common origin (**essentialism**). In others the pejorative labelling of minority groups by more powerful groups. It may thus have positive or negative political outcomes depending on the power relations of the group involved. Ethnic minority groups generally have poorer health and higher mortality rates, though there are significant variations. However the explanation for this has caused considerable debate as researchers attempt to separate out the relative impact of socio-economic variables and ethnicity. It now appears to be the case that ethnicity contributes in its own right to poorer health, because over and above being members of the working class, members of low status groups suffer persistent discrimination and racial harassment (Nazroo, J. (2001) *Ethnicity, Class and Health*. London: Policy Studies Institute) (**ethnic groups; race**).

ETHNOGRAPHIC STUDIES   Qualitative research in which the researcher participates in the social world of those being studied for a prolonged period of time, either overtly or covertly, with the aim of explaining and understanding the participants' actions. The process contrasts with positivist research, with its aim of conducting research to facilitate predicting and controlling social actions of others. Ethnography developed out of symbolic interactionism, and as a research method, aims to show how people go about creating and making meaning and sense of their social interactions. The concern is with the culture of the group, that is, its shared meanings and symbols. Ethnographic studies were given prominence by the **Chicago School of Sociology** and led to participant observation studies in hospitals (**dying trajectories**), asylums, and old people's homes. Ethnography is open to a number of criticisms: it may be purely descriptive; it may take the presentation of the group's perspective at face value, missing tensions and contradictions in the group; and because it tends to focus on a specific setting, misses the links between the group and the wider society, especially in terms of power relations (Hammersley, M. and Atkinson, P. (1995) *Ethnography: Principles in Practice*. London: Routledge) (**ethnomethodology; Goffman; hermeneutics; participant observation; phenomenology**).

ETHNOGRAPHY   The observation of a social setting by a researcher, commonly used in anthropology, but also sociology (**ethnographic studies**).

ETHNOMETHODOLOGY   Literally folk (ethno) methods (methodology) for making sense of the world. Ethnomethodologists study the way people make sense of their daily life, not as a set of structures imposed on them, but as a creative set of interactions.

The contrast is with structuralist accounts of social life, which see individuals as being produced and formed by social institutions. In medical settings, using conversational analysis, ethnomethodologists show how patients negotiate with doctors to define the condition under examination, rather than just being passive recipients of the doctor's definition of the situation (Silverman, D. (1987) *Communication and Medical Practice*. London: Sage) (**Thomas theorem; structure–agency debate; Chicago School of Sociology; conversation analysis; ethnographic studies; microsociological**).

ETIOLOGY   The study of the causes of **disease**. Medical theories emphasize biological, individualistic and **lifestyle** explanations. By contrast sociological approaches emphasize the role of political, economic, and cultural factors in the production and distribution of illness and disease. Within sociology, arguments about the cause of disease will vary depending on the theoretical focus adopted: Marxists point to the centrality of class; feminists to the role of patriarchy; and for Foucauldians it is the role of the state through the helping professions, defining certain actions as **abnormal**, that produces disease categories (**psy-professions**). What unifies all the approaches, and the combinations of them (e.g. **Marxist-feminism**) are the arguments that disease is socially produced and distributed and that medicine performs a social control function at the same time as it reinforces patterns of **inequality** in society (**biologistic;**

disease, social model; health determinants; Marxist approaches; patriarchal medicine).

EUGENICS   From the Greek, meaning 'well-born'. The claim is that the characteristics of different social groups are based in their shared genes and that by systematically controlling the reproduction of the group the genetic characteristic can be eliminated, if negatively valued, or enhanced if positively evaluated. In its most common form it is the claim that entire subordinate groups in the population have a different genetic structure from the elite. It was most fully realized during World War II in Hitler's attempt to eradicate 'Jewish' genes, as well as 'homosexual' genes, 'gypsy' genes and 'retarded' genes so as to protect the 'Aryan' genes of the Germans. However eugenics is not a peculiarly Nazi aberration, forming the basis of British psychology at the end of the nineteenth century and educational practices in the twentieth century. In the USA it was used in the 1920s and 1930s to justify the forcible sterilization of tens of thousands of Eastern-European immigrants on Ellis Island (Chorover, S. (1979) *From Genesis to Genocide*. Cambridge, MA: MIT Press) (**heredity; IQ controversy; social Darwinism**).

EUTHANASIA   Literally meaning a 'good death', the decision to intentionally allow a person to die when it is considered that there is no chance of them having a viable life, as for example, following brain death. It may be passive, in the decision not to treat an individual, or active, in the deliberate administration of drugs to induce death. **Physician assisted suicide** is the collaboration between the doctor and the patient to terminate life (**coma**; **death**; **do not resuscitate**; **ethics, medical**; **mercy killing**).

EVALUATION   The appraisal of a healthcare policy or medical intervention to determine their impact. In the positivistic tradition, with its emphasis on natural science models the focus is on value free, quantitative measurement. Critics argue that evaluation is inherently political, always involves value judgements, and cannot aspire to claims of objectivity (Guba, E. and Lincoln, Y. (1989) *Fourth Generation Evaluation*. London: Sage). The need for evaluation arises from the fact that many medical technologies and practices have either never been evaluated or are known to have no demonstrated efficacy (**Cochrane Centre**; **evidence-based medicine**; **health related quality of life**; **health technology assessment**; **National Institute of Clinical Evidence**).

EVIDENCE-BASED MEDICINE (EBM)   A recent development in medicine arguing that only those medical interventions that have been proven to work should be used (**evaluation**). The argument is against the use of clinical wisdom handed down from generation to generation of practitioners, and to try and ensure that medical practitioners continue their education after graduating. What constitutes evidence is the results of randomized controlled trials, preferably **double-blind**. Because of its

positivistic methodology it has been criticized by those arguing, from within the medical profession, that clinical skill (the art of medicine) is part of medical practice and forms the backbone of medical autonomy and is not open to this form of evaluation, and from those outside, that it rules out unprofitable interventions, such as public health initiatives, or alternative medical practices which are not funded for trials. Sociologists argue that the development of evidence-based medicine can be seen as the defensive reaction of a profession under challenge as it attempts to consolidate its claim to be a science, while providing a vehicle for increased standing in the medical community for epidemiologists (Willis, E. and White, K. (2003) 'Evidence-based medicine, the medical profession and health policy', in V. Lin and B. Gibson (eds), *Evidence-Based Health Policy*. Melbourne: Oxford University Press) (**casemix**; **clinical trial**; **Cochrane Centre**; **health technology assessment**; **medical dominance**; **National Institute of Clinical Evidence**).

EXPERIMENTAL MEDICINE   An experiment is the controlled manipulation of conditions in the attempt to arrive at certain knowledge (**empiricism**). Claude Bernard (1813–1878) in his *Introduction to the Study of Experimental Medicine* (1865) argued that the experimental method was the way to develop knowledge of health and disease. He was arguing against the practice of medicine which involved the passive observation of gross anatomical consequences of disease. The development of experimental medicine, and of the germ theory of disease, deflected attention from social and environmental factors (**sanitation**; **social medicine**) as the cause of disease, reduced disease to a biological event, and individualized treatment, based on drugs and technology. This **biomedical model** is the target of health social studies (**bedside medicine**; **causal inference**; **empiricism**; **positivism**; **reductionism**).

F

FAMILY   In Christian cultures the married man and woman and their biological offspring. This family structure is good for the mental health of men and bad for the mental health of women, who have the primary care role for all its members, and increasingly, for aged parents and parents-in-law. The family, usually the women in it, is the first contact in the **lay referral system** and to the extent that it is working well, a source of **social support**. It is also the site of the hidden healthcare system, in which women provide the majority of care (**domestic violence; gender; gender linked health risks; gendered health; gender roles; health services, hidden**).

FAMILY PLANNING   The act, through natural or artificial methods of contraception, of limiting and spacing the number of children a couple wishes to have. The ability to restrict the number of children, and to decide when to have them, has significantly changed the social and economic role of women in Western societies, as well as reducing infant and maternal mortality. Family planning clinics provide information on contraception, sexually transmitted diseases and abortion (**assisted reproductive technologies; childbirth;**

gender linked health risks; marital status; reproduction).

FAMILY THERAPY COUNSELLING   involving not just the individual but the social unit they live in. It may involve helping the family come to grips with a patient's illness, or alternatively, treating the family as the source of one of its member's problems. Feminist family therapists argue that gender roles and socialization mean that women are disempowered in family relationships (Goodrich, T. et al. (1988) *Feminist Family Therapy*. New York: Norton and Company) (**gender; gender linked health risks; gendered health**).

FARR, WILLIAM (1807–83)   Statistician and medical practitioner, one of the founders of epidemiology and a leading member of the public health movement. He was one of the pioneers of the use of statistics to examine public health, arguing that statistics were the basis for a programme of economic, environmental and social reform. His system of vital statistics was the basis for establishing the first international classification of disease

(Susser, M. and Adelstein, A. (1987) 'The work of William Farr', in M. Susser (ed.), *Epidemiology, Health and Society*. New York: Oxford University Press) (**Chadwick**; **Graunt**; **hygiene**; **Petty**; **sanitation**; **Simon**; **social history of medicine**; **social medicine**; **Vilerme**; **Virchow**).

FEE-FOR-SERVICE   The payment for services provided by the doctor, paid by the patient, even if they are subsequently reimbursed through a health insurance system. This method of payment leads to **supplier induced demand**. It also results in doctors over-ordering tests or procedures. In the face of spiralling costs governments in the USA and the UK have attempted to make doctors more responsible for the costs they produce in the health system (**capitation**; **Jarvis' law**; **managed care**; **market**; **perverse incentives**).

FEMALE GENITAL MUTILATION (FGM)   A range of traditional surgeries, conducted primarily in Africa, in some parts of the Middle East and on some Asian women, that removes all or part of the external genitalia. The procedures take two forms. In reduction a total or partial clitoridectomy is performed sometimes in association with removal of the labia minora. In covering operations the clitoris, the labia minora and parts of the labia majora are removed and the wound held together so that the scar grows closed. A small object is placed in the wound to leave an aperture for the flow of urine and menstrual blood. The health consequences are devastating. The mutilation is practised without

anesthesia and results in hemorrhaging, shock, infection and pain. Pelvic inflammatory disease results from chronic infection; infertility from the blockage of the fallopian tubes by scar tissue; and the process contributes to the high rate of maternal mortality in the Sudan and Somalia. The procedure is justified on traditional and religious grounds, the control of women's sex drive, or for the increased pleasure of men (Toubia, N. (1994) 'Female circumcision as a public health issue', *New England Journal of Medicine*, 331: 712–16) (**circumcision (female)**).

FEMALE HEALTH   (**domestic violence**; **feminism**; **gender**; **gender linked health risks**; **gendered health**; **family**; **patriarchy**; **patriarchal medicine**; **sexism**).

FEMINISM   In general, feminist health sociologists argue that medicine and **patriarchy** control women by defining passivity, dependence and submission as appropriate feminine traits (**sexism**). Women's illnesses are both a consequence of, and a response to patriarchal society. In feminist analyses medicine is shown to define women by their biology and their reproductive capacity: menses, pregnancy and menopause. When defined as medical problems, which can only be resolved with medical solutions, women lose control of fundamental aspects of their experience – fertility, sexuality, menopause and ageing. In patriarchal medicine women's bodies are defined in contrast to the 'good', 'healthy' male body and found wanting. Hence women are constructed by definition as inferior, sicker and more at risk of biological disorder than men. In performing this analysis patriarchal medicine moves from social categories, of mother, house worker, and carer, to biological categories of menstruating, pregnant and menopausal, and combines by sleight of hand the two, obscuring the social basis of women's problems. However feminism is neither unitary, nor internally coherent as a social theory, with the different theoretical bases of its various strands – liberal, radical Marxist and Foucauldian – which has implications for the analyses of medicine and explanations of health and disease in contemporary society. The general concepts of feminism have also been criticized by postmodern feminists who see the positing of patriarchy as the sole explanation of women's position as part of modernist social theory. The confidence of asserting that patriarchy did or does something to women, that there is an all-pervasive male gaze, that power is centralized in the patriarchal institutions of the state have all undergone significant challenges. So too has the idea that womanhood, or the feminine, is a universal and intrinsic characteristic of women. Rather the fluidity of the concept and of the variability in the practices of what it is to be a woman have been held up by poststructuralists and postmodernists, as well as activists from non-European, non-middle class and non-academic backgrounds (Anthias, F. and Yuval-Davies, N. (1993) 'Contextualising feminism: gender, ethnic and class divisions', *Feminist Review*, 15: 62–75) (**clinical drug trials; dualism; eco-feminism; Foucauldian-feminism; liberal feminism;**

Marxist feminism; memory work; patriarchal medicine; postmodernity; radical feminism; sexism).

FERTILITY   The ability to produce offspring. The fertility rate is the ratio of live births in an area to the population of that area expressed per 1,000 population per year. The control of women's fertility has been central to patriarchy under capitalism, and the focus of the feminist critique of medicine (**feminism; new reproductive technologies; patriarchal medicine**).

FIELD-BASED RESEARCH   The entry into a specific social organization (such as a hospital) so as to understand its working in detail, using a variety of qualitative research methods such as interviewing and participant observation. The aim is to understand the social setting from the perspective of the participants (**Chicago School of Sociology; ethnography**).

FINRRAGE   Feminist International Network New Reproductive Technologies and Genetic Engineering. A meeting of feminist activists at a conference in Lund, Sweden in 1985, who rejected the **new reproductive technologies** as a form of **eugenics** and of social control of women's reproductive capacities. (Raymond, J. (1993) *Women as Wombs. Reproductive Technologies and the Battle Over Women's Freedom*. San Francisco: Harper Collins).

FITNESS   Generally being in good physical condition. Of interest sociologically given the commercialization of fitness, the pursuit of fitness as a lifestyle, and the increasing moral approbation in the **new public health** for those who do not produce and maintain themselves as fit, and therefore as socially responsible, bodies (Maguire, J. (2002) 'Body lessons: fitness publishing and the cultural production of the fitness consumer', *International Review of the Sociology of Sport*, 37 (3/4): 449–64) (**bodyism; healthism; morality and medicine**).

FLECK, LUDWIG (1896–1961) The author of *The Genesis and Development of a Scientific Fact* (orig. 1935; in English 1979, University of Chicago Press), one of the most important early formulations of the sociology of knowledge approach to the study of medicine. In a series of case studies – the history of syphilis, the development of anatomical drawings, and the development of the Wasserman Reaction as a test for syphilis – he argued that while medical knowledge is assumed to be objective, scientific knowledge of an independent biological reality, it could be shown to be the product of specific historical, cultural, political and economic factors. As a medical specialist in the area of blood disorders he worked on the establishment of the Wasserman Reaction and provided the first account of how scientists produce their findings in the laboratory, in a process in which scientific artefacts, the researchers and the broader political and economic environment all interact to produce the scientific fact. This approach has been developed in contemporary sociology of science in **actor-network theory**. Fleck argued that scientific theories existed to restrict scientific practitioners to specific areas and problems of research, acting as a world view, which he labelled 'thought collectives'. Thomas Kuhn developed his work into the more familiar concept of **paradigm (Bachelard; Canguihelm; sociology of scientific knowledge; Stern; thought styles**).

FLEXNER REPORT Abraham Flexner (1866–1959) revolutionized the structure of American medical training. On the basis of his report medical training became part of the university system, and based in the natural sciences, sharply demarcating it from 'quackery'. It also eliminated over half of the proprietary medical schools then existing in America (Flexner, A. (1910, 1972) *Medical Education in the United States and Canada*. NY: Arno Press). The fact that his report was funded by the American philanthropic foundation, the Carnegie Foundation, and others such as Rockefeller Foundation donated $US 66 million to nine medical schools conforming to the findings of the report – and effectively locating health care in expensive, technologically based hospital treatments – has lead to some analysts pointing to the interface between capitalism and the development of scientific medicine (Brown, R. (1979) *Rockefeller Medicine Men: Medicine and Capitalism in America*. Berkeley: University of California Press) (**Apothecaries Act; ideology; medical dominance**).

FOCUS GROUPS　　A form of **interview** and method of data collection involving individuals discussing a topic with the researcher acting as moderator. Focus groups are often used to clarify issues or problems and to establish agendas for future research (**Delphi technique; non-probability sampling**).

FOLK HEALING　　Traditional forms of healing practices, for example, curanderismo in Mexico, based on religious, magical and herbal interventions. Knowledge is handed down by oral tradition over generations to the wise men or woman practitioners. In developed Western societies folk healing is embedded in **lay cultures, lay referral systems** and **lay knowledge** (**indigenous healing**).

FOOD AND DRUG ADMINISTRATION (FDA)
The American drug regulatory body that allows the marketing of a new drug. Its Congressional mandate is to protect the public from unsafe drugs (**diet; malnutrition; pharmaceutical companies**).

FORMAL RATIONALITY　　The pursuit of a set of goals following rules, regulations and laws independently of their impact, as in, the bureaucratic administration of the healthcare system. As developed by Max Weber, the spread of rationalization, meant the increasing routinization of social life, the development of bureaucratic forms of control, and a loss of meaning. In medicine it has been agued that the development of routinized forms of treatment has meant the loss of the clinical art of medicine and led to deprofessionalization. The contrast is with **substantive rationality** (Ritzer, G. and Walczak, D. (1988) 'Rationalisation and the deprofessionalisation of physicians', *Social Forces*, 67 (1): 1–21) (**bureaucracy; Frankfurt School; (McDonaldization/McDoctor); medical dominance; proletarianization; Weber**).

FOUCAULT, MICHEL (1926–84)　　One of the most influential social theorists of the late twentieth century who in a series of books on the prison (1977, *Discipline and Punish*, Harmondsworth: Penguin), the asylum (1967, *Madness and Civilization*, London: Tavistock) and the hospital (1973, *The Birth of the Clinic*, London: Routledge) among others, challenged liberal views of a progressive development of a more humane treatment of the criminal, the deviant and the sick. Foucault's central argument is that modern medicine is a manifestation of an administered society in which the centralization of information is essential for social planning. In a synthesis of classical social theory, Foucault agues that modern society is one in which there is the application of scientific principles (**rationalization**) to an increasingly 'thing' like body (**alienation**) in specialized institutions (**bureaucratization**) in the interests of restoring the individual to normal functioning. The origins of this development are in the **demographic transition** of the eighteenth and nineteenth centuries. With the increase in population new forms of knowledge about people developed. This new knowledge was of individuals as objects to be counted and monitored (**surveillance**) to predict and control their behaviour, and to provide the state with information to control them. Thus Foucault's neologism, power/knowledge: the new academic disciplines of psychology, psychiatry, and medicine, and the social sciences, were also 'disciplines' in the sense of prescribing how people should act and behave, the lifestyles they should adopt, and in establishing norms of behaviour, which as disciplines they could enforce. Knowledge, whether of the biological or the social, is never disinterested but is linked to forms of social control, and establishes the 'scientific' criteria by which we distinguish the sane from the insane, the sick from the well, and the deviant from the normal (**abnormal**; **Bachelard**; **biopolitics**; **biopower**; **Canguihelm, discourse**; **psy-professions**; **surveillance**; **technologies of the self**).

FOUCAULDIAN-FEMINISM   The attempt to link Foucault's analysis of the body and power with feminist analysis of the subordination and control of women. The **body** is the focus of professional monitoring by doctors, the site at which we internalize social norms of correct appearance and dressage. Foucault's view of power as an ever-present yet diffuse aspect of social relationships allows feminists to provide an account of how women incorporate as well as resist patriarchal images of the body. Screening programmes for women – particularly for **breast cancer** – are a good illustration. Mass screening enshrines the examination of the individual woman's body linked to population based disease statistics (**surveillance medicine**). In what would appear to **liberal feminists** to be a discourse of empowerment, taking into account women's desire to know about and control their bodies, mass public health campaigns have been initiated. However it also presents women with a double bind: by definition it renders women frail and potentially always sick, yet simultaneously they are autonomous and active agents responsible for monitoring their own health. Thus screening programmes have subverted feminism, incorporating some of its central points – autonomy, self-responsibility and control of the body – into a self-monitoring incorporation by women into state administrative structures and the norms of medical surveillance. Tensions between the two theories are also large. Foucault nowhere refers to gendered bodies, and operates with a masculinized model of the body. Additionally there are problems in the theory of power: where Foucault sees dispersed power fields, feminists see organized patriarchal power (Diamond, I. and Quinby, L. (1988) *Feminism and Foucault: Reflections on Resistance*. Boston: Northeastern University Press).

FRAMES   A concept in the sociology of Erving Goffman to describe 'the principles of organization which govern social events and the actor's subjective involvement in them' (Goffman, E. (1974) *Frame Analysis: An Essay on the Organization of Experience*. New York: Harper and Row). The frame provides the context within which to understand a social interaction. Thus in a gynecological examination the frame is of a medical encounter rather than of a sexual act (Henslin, J. and Biggs, M. (1985) 'The sociology of the vaginal examination', in J. Henslin (ed.), *Down to Earth Sociology*. New York: Free Press) (**Chicago School of Sociology; Goffman; microsociological**).

FRAMINGHAM STUDY A study of the community of Framingham, a suburb of Boston, Massachusetts, begun in 1948 and involving over 10,000 individuals. The study has established the importance of **social networks** in maintaining people's health and as a protective factor in a wide range of diseases, in particular, coronary heart disease (**cohort studies; health determinants; social networks analysis; social support**).

FRANK, JOHANN PETER (1745–1821) Author of *System einer vollstandigen medicinischen* (1779–1826) (System of a complete medical police), Frank argued that the health of the population was tied to the strength of the nation and was to be aligned with the law and administered by the state. His work was the basis for social reform movements in the nineteenth century, based on his statement that poverty was the 'most powerful mother of disease' (Frank, J. P. (orig. 1790; 1961) 'The people's misery: mother of diseases: an address in

1790', *Bulletin of the History of Medicine*, 35: 81–100) (**medical police; sanitation; social medicine; Villerme; Virchow**).

FRANKFURT SCHOOL So named because the Institute for Social Research was established there in 1923 and with rise of Nazism, moved to the USA. Its most influential members were Theodore Adorno, Herbert Marcuse and Max Horkheimer. While not having a direct impact on health sociology, two of their main themes flavour the orientation of the discipline: the argument that culture also shapes and represses individuals (in contrast to a Marxist analysis that the economy is dominant); and that the pursuit of rationality destroys the essence of human beings as technical rationality replaces values in our orientation to the world (**best-care practices; cultural hegemony; formal rationality; ideology; Weber**).

FREUD, SIGMUND (1856–1939) Austrian psychologist, physiologist and medical practitioner, and author of over twenty books, including *The Interpretation of Dreams* (1900), *The Psychopathology of Everyday Life* (1901) and *Three Essays on Sexuality* (1905). Freud developed theories of psychosexual development (the oral, anal and genital stages); the structure of the mind (superego, ego and id); and of the role of the unconscious in explaining everyday actions. The id comprises the instinctual sexual drives, the superego the conscience, and the ego is the outcome of the relationship of these two. When there is conflict between what the person wants and what they know is wrong (e.g. sexual relations with the parent of the opposite sex) then defence mechanisms (repression, sublimation, fixation, and regression) come into play to resolve the conflict and keep it from consciousness. There has been considerable debate over all aspects of Freud's thought (Frosh, S. (1984) *The Politics of Psychoanalysis: A Philosophical Critique.* Berkeley: University of California Press) (**anxiety; psychoanalysis; talking therapies**).

FUNCTIONALISM Theories of society that argue that sets of interlocking social institutions, such as the family, the school system, the legal system and so on, interact with each other to produce and maintain the social system. In conservative approaches the emphasis is on social stability and the reproduction of society (**Parsons**). In critical or Marxist approaches the emphasis is on the reproduction of the social system, as well as inherent conflicts between different social institutions that lead to social change. Sociologists in the **microsociological** tradition reject the account of social reality as

stable and external to individuals, arguing that it is the result of ongoing social interaction. In health studies both approaches have made important contributions to our understandings of the healthcare system as part of either wider societal relations, or to the ways in which individuals negotiate social life (**negotiated order; structural functionalism; symbolic interactionism**).

FUNCTIONING AND WELL BEING PROFILE (FWBP) A 149 item health research instrument developed by the Rand Corporation. Its focus on the individual rather than on a disease allows for comparison of the different experience of disease amongst individuals and of individuals with a disease with the general population (Brazier, J. et al. (1992) 'Validating the SF-36 health survey questionnaire: new outcome measure for primary care', *British Medical Journal*, 305: 160–64) (**health status assessment**).

FUNNELLING In qualitative interviewing, the process of refining the discussion from generalities to specifics (**interviews**).

G

GADAMER, HANS (1900–2002) A German philosopher in the **hermeneutical** tradition, Gadamer argued in *Truth and Method* (1975, New York: Seabury Press) that there could be no objective scientific knowledge, since experience and culture shape and form us. He has been influential as a source in the interpretative, qualitative tradition in sociology, with its emphasis how people make sense of and construct their world (**Chicago School of Sociology; Heidegger; Husserl; interactionist sociology; Kant; Schutz; sociology; verstehen; Weber**).

GALEN (c129AD–216?) Claudius Galenus, a Roman physician and philosopher, who synthesized Greek and Roman medical knowledge and practice into a system which was to dominate Europe for 1,500 years. Galen argued that disease was caused by an imbalance of the four **humours** that made up the body: blood, phlegm, black bile and yellow bile. Balance was restored through dieting, purging, and blood letting (**Hippocrates**).

GAMBLING A good example of **medicalization**. First, there has to be something about the behaviour that makes it problematic to powerful groups and to broadly accepted cultural beliefs about the right way to live life. Gambling, in nineteenth-century America was at odds with the Puritan culture of the capitalist work ethic. It undermined the idea that one should work hard and save. So in the first place, there is a broad cultural definition of the behaviour as deviant. Second there is a process of 'prospecting', of making the 'medical discovery' of the problem. Thus in 1943 Edmund Bergler published the first paper in a medical journal which discussed the neurotic gambler as a medical problem. In sociological analysis this is 'staking a claim' to the topic as a medical topic. However, because the behaviour has struck a general chord as a problem in the culture, other interest groups will be forming at the same time. Third, then, there is likely to be a 'contest' between medical definitions and non-medical definitions and interests in the behaviour. So while Bergler published the first medical book on the topic in 1957, at the same time Gamblers Anonymous, a self-help, non-medically based group was formed. This leads in turn, fourth, to 'claims making' between the groups. Is gambling a problem of the psyche, of compulsive behaviour, of weak willed people, is it genetically inherited, or a biologically based malfunction of the brain? At this stage the medicalization process may stop – the competition from lay, legal or religious groups for control of the problem may be too strong and medicine withdraws from the competition. Alternatively, and fourth, the medical turf may be 'secured' and legitimacy of the medical definition of the problem advanced. This usually happens with the successful setting up of a hospital treatment programme, followed by a legislative enactment that the condition is a medical problem, in need of medical treatment, as occurred in the gambling example in Maryland in 1978, with the establishment of the first hospital based therapy team. With this development we have the institutionalization of the claim that the behaviour is a medical problem, for which medical solutions must be found. The final stage of the process is the recognition by the rest of the medical community that this indeed is a medical problem. In the case of gambling this occurred in 1980, when the American Association of Psychiatrists included a new entry in their handbook, *The Diagnostic and Statistical Manual*, of the disease of pathological gambling (Conrad, P. and Schneider, J. (1980) *Deviance and Medicalization: From Badness to Sickness*. St Louis: C. V. Mosby) (**alcoholism; repetitive strain injury**).

GATEKEEPING The role that the general practitioner plays in managing a patient's access to specialists, radiology and pathology tests (**corporatization**). In research a gatekeeper is one who controls institutional access to the site, denying or facilitating the research programme.

GAZE, CLINICAL (clinical gaze).

GENDER Sociologists distinguish between sex, the biology of being male or female and gender, the social roles ascribed to men and women. Gender, that is masculine and feminine social roles, has a significant impact on health. Women are 'sicker' and men die earlier. Young men in particular are vulnerable as they attempt the transition into adulthood dying at twice the rate of young women from accidents, violence and suicide (**hegemonic masculinity**). Women appear to be sicker because they are more diagnosed as sick and because of the **medicalization** of their reproductive functions. The social role of mother and housekeeper means that women do a double shift of paid and unpaid work which impacts on their health. Gender differences in health are not as large as they were with more women in the workforce and the higher incidence of smoking in women, though there are still marked differences in the diagnoses of psychiatric illness among women (Annandale, E. and Hunt, K. (2000) (eds), *Gender Inequalities in Health*. Buckingham: Open University Press) (**marital status; men's health; sexism; sex role socialization; tranquillizers**).

GENDER LINKED HEALTH RISKS Western medicine assumes that what distinguishes the health of men and women is their different biology. For sociologists and feminists it is the different risks that their social roles expose them to that is at issue. Women are at greater risk of **iatrogenesis** because of the medicalization of reproduction (**childbirth**); of suffering through screening programmes; of the social roles of mother and housewife (**gender**); and because they are socialized to present complaints to the doctor. Men, in conforming to the idea of masculinity self-medicate with alcohol and drugs, do not report symptoms, and delay treatment. Consequently they die sooner of preventable diseases than women (**domestic violence; family; hegemonic masculinity; housing and health; male stoicism; marital status; men's health; sexual harassment**).

GENDERED HEALTH　　The patterning of sickness and disease as a consequence of the different social roles of men and women (**gender; hegemonic masculinity; male stoicism; marital status; men's health; sexism**).

GENDER ROLES　　The culturally and historically specific characteristics ascribed to the categories of masculine and feminine social roles (**gender; sexism**).

GENEALOGY　　In Foucault's work, the study of the formation of the **discourses** that shape and form us. The contrast is with orthodox history which presents an enlightened now, progressing out of a dark past, leading to an ever better future (**Foucault; Whig histories of medicine**).

GENEISM　　The claim that what human beings do is a consequence of the biochemical properties that make them up, and that these biochemical properties in turn are made up of the genes that constitute them (**reductionism**). Thus human activity is reducible to genes, and genes cause human society to take the shape that it does, rather than social, political, economic or cultural factors. Genetic explanations, with their veneer of scientificity, and appearance as objective 'facts', displace social explanations and deny them validity. Their 'scientific basis' is used to close down debates about economic, social or political causes of individuals' health and disease (Willis, E. (1998) 'Public health private genes: the social consequences of genetic biotechnologies', *Critical Public Health*, 8: 13–9) (**genetic determinism; heredity; human genome project; IQ controversy; scienticism**).

GENERAL PRACTICE PHYSICIAN (GP) Medical practitioners located in the community who provide medical services to ambulatory patients. In 1952 The Royal College of General Practitioners was established to maintain and develop the standing of general practice, particularly to defend it from the view within medicine, that the general undergraduate medical degree was to enable individuals to go on to specialist training, and that those who did not could only do 'general' practice. In the 1990s with the ongoing specialization and differentiation in the health practitioner market, the rise of the consumer movement and the **feminist** movement, there have been continuing challenges to general practice. It has been postulated that it is experiencing **deprofessionalization** and there is a general decline in **medical dominance**. The entry of capitalist investors into general practices in Australia has seen the **proletarianization** of general practitioners (White, K. (2000) 'The state, the market and general practice: the Australian case', *International Journal of Health Services*, 30 (2): 285–308) (**consumerism; corporatization; market**).

GENETIC DETERMINISM   The claim that genes produce our psychological and physical characteristics. It is often used to justify the hierarchical inequalities of modern societies. Genetic explanations of disease are based on the assumption that social life needs to be explained in terms of the characteristics and behaviours of individuals (**reductionism**). These behaviours in turn are properties of the individual's brain. The behaviour can be quantified and individuals can then be ranked in terms of how much or how little of the characteristic they have. A normal range is constructed, with abnormal individuals identified and seen as in need of medical care. The behaviour is then held to be a property of the brain, with a specific location in the brain, and the product of specific biochemical processes. Some biochemical processes may be caused by the environment; others are immutably a product of the brain. Thus an equation of hereditability can be drawn up. Dealing with the abnormal conditions involves tracking down the 'genes' responsible for them, and then through eugenics, trying to eliminate them (**eugenics; genetic reductionism; geneticization; human genome project; IQ controversy**).

GENETIC DISORDERS   While up to sixty diseases have a known genetic basis this at most increases the probability of the individual getting the disease since complex interchanges with the environment will determine whether or not the disease will develop (Yates, J. (1996) 'Medical genetics', *British Medical Journal*, 312: 1021–5). Sociologists emphasize that it is more coherent to talk of a genetic vulnerability to environmental risks which predispose individuals to disease. The risks are socially, politically, and economically 'shaped', not genetically 'produced' (**genetic determinism; new genetics**).

GENETIC MANIPULATION   Following the invention of recombinant DNA technology, the laboratory based technique that allowed for the copying of DNA and the isolation of the specific functions of specific genes.

GENETIC REDUCTIONISM   The privileging of genetic explanations for human characteristics and attributes at the expense of social explanations (**genetic determinism; geneticization; new genetics**).

GENETIC SCREENING   The targeting of individuals held to be at risk of passing on a genetic disorder (**eugenics**). Public resistance to screening for disorders is a notable instance of lay resistance to claimed scientific advances. Sociologists have documented the ways in which individuals assess the increased risks of social outcomes if they test for genetic risks: that they may be labelled part of a genetic underclass; denied insurance; restricted in their work; and made targets of compulsory genetic counselling (Richards, M. (1993) 'The new genetics: some issues for social scientists', *Sociology of Health and Illness*, 15: 567–86) (**genetic determinism; heredity**).

GENETIC TESTING   A process to identify inherited congenital diseases. As with **genetic screening** there has been considerable public resistance to testing programmes, not least because, while a probable cause may be identified, there is still no probable cure.

GENETICIZATION   The explanation of individual difference, disorders, behaviours or conditions as caused by abnormal genes. In the popular press these range from alcoholism, to obesity, learning problems, homosexuality, and divorce, to list just a few. Rejected in health social studies as a form of **reductionist** explanation, based on unsupported 'scientific' claims, this explanation allows for the labelling and monitoring of groups in the population who are perceived as deviant. It also masks as 'natural' and unchangeable characteristics of individuals that are social in origin. The interface between patriarchal medicine and genetics has been shown in the stigmatization of mothers for their fetus' abnormalities (Lippman, A. (1993) 'Prenatal genetic testing and geneticization: mother matters for all', *Fetal Diagnosis and Therapy*, 8 (suppl): 175–88) (**geneism; IQ controversy; new genetics; race**).

GERM THEORY   Nineteenth-century theory of disease as caused by micro-organisms, that is, germs or bacteria. The first use of the term is in 1870, by the British physician Jabez Hogg, in the *Medical Times and Gazette* of London. The appeal of the germ theory was that, in industrialized capitalist societies, it had few implications for state intervention in society and individualized the cause of disease. The germ theory located the potential cures of disease in a search for drugs and technologies in the newly established bacteriological laboratories. It was opposed by the sanitarians who pointed to cleaning the streets, housing conditions, protecting the purity of water and controlling the production and sale of foodstuffs as the key to improving the population's health (Tesh, S. (1982) 'Political ideology and public health in the nineteenth century', *International Journal of Health Services*, 12: 321–42) (**Chadwick; Engels; Farr; infectious disease; miasma; social history of medicine; social medicine; Whig histories of medicine**).

GERONTOLOGY   An interdisciplinary branch of medicine, involving biology, psychology, psychiatry and social science dealing with the aged. It is primarily biologistic and psychological focusing on the body of the aged and the individual experience of ageing at the expense of the wider social factors that unequally structure the ageing process (**ageing; triple jeopardy**).

GIFT RELATIONSHIP   In pre-modern societies, without a formal economy, the French sociologist **Marcel Mauss** argued in

The Gift (orig. 1925; translated into English 1954) that the exchange of gifts, often of enormous value, was a moral transaction that established and maintained social relationships between individuals and groups. His insight was used by **Richard Titmuss** in his analysis of the American blood bank system, based largely on money and in which human blood was treated as a commodity and the British system, which was based on voluntary donorship and altruism. The British system was safer (the US had four times higher hepatitis infection rate from infected blood) and more efficient. Titmuss argued that social relationships built on altruism, voluntarism, and the gift were better than those based on the exchange of commodities for profit and self-interest (Titmuss, R. (1971) *The Gift Relationship: from Blood to Social Policy*. New York: Pantheon) (**organ donation**).

GLOBAL BURDEN OF DISEASE, PART OF (GBD) In 1996 the World Health Organization, in association with Harvard School of Public Health and the World Bank published *The Global Burden of Disease: A Comprehensive Assessment of Mortality and Disability from Diseases, Injuries and Risk Factors.* It developed the concept of **disability adjusted life years**, and defined the burden of disease as the gap between current health status and an ideal situation where everyone lives into old age free of disease and disability (**burden of disease**).

GOFFMAN, ERVING (1922–82) Canadian sociologist in the **symbolic interactionist** tradition, whose work focuses on how people manage their selves and present and sustain them in everyday life. He developed a metaphor of social life as a stage, calling his approach to sociology dramaturgy. The focus of this sociology is on the ways in which participants negotiate their social roles (1959, *The Presentation of Self in Everyday Life*. New York: Anchor Books). His most important books in health sociology were *Asylums: Essays on the Social Situation of Mental Patients and Other Inmates* (1961, New York: Anchor) in which he documented the ways in which inhabitants in **total institutions** resist the degradation and **stigma** it imposes on them; and *Stigma: Notes on the Management of Spoiled Identity* (1963, New York: Simon and Schuster) in which he examines how individuals whose identity has been negatively labelled pass themselves as normal (**Chicago School of Sociology; courtesy stigma; degradation ceremonies; depersonalization; frames; microsociological; spoilt identity**).

GOVERNMENTALITY Foucault's word for the process of producing individuals in modern society. Through the work of the **psy-professions** and the workings of **power/knowledge** contemporary citizens monitor and administer themselves. The historical contrast is with centralized power under a monarch who manages the population with the overt use of force (**anatomo-politics; biopower; bodyism; disciplinary power; fitness; Foucault; morality and medicine**).

GRAUNT, JOHN (1620–74) Pioneer of the use of statistics to demonstrate patterns of disease and death. His *Natural and Political Observations ... Upon the Bills of Mortality* (1662) established that rural living was healthier than urban living, that there was an excess of male births, and that there were seasonal changes in mortality (**Chadwick**; **Engels**; **Farr**; **Petty**; **Snow**; **social history of medicine**; **social medicine**; **Villerme**; **Virchow**).

GROUNDED THEORY   The argument that sociological research should be based on an intensive observation of real social situations, rather than making a priori theoretical assumptions about what is happening. The contrast is with **Talcott Parsons'** theory-building enterprise. For example, Parsons theorized the **doctor–patient** relationship in terms of the requirements of the social system, whereas grounded theorists actually observing doctor–patient interactions found that they did not conform to Parsons' model. The tradition has been particularly important for participant observation studies of hospitals and asylums, and of the social organization of death (**dying trajectories**) (Glaser, B. and Strauss, A. (1967) *The Discovery of Grounded Theory: Strategies for Qualitative Research.* Chicago: Aldine) (**Chicago School of Sociology**; **interactionist sociology**; **microsociological**; **participant observation**; **symbolic interactionism**).

GROUP   INTERVIEWS   (focus groups; interviews).

H

HABITUS A concept in the work of French sociologist Pierre Bourdieu (1930–2002) describing settled, **class** specific ways of representing the body. Bourdieu argued that the body is a form of physical capital that enhances or limits access to scarce social resources and marks the individual's social location. For example, the well-shaped and well-maintained body is used to show to others that we discipline and control ourselves and that we are worthy, if not superior members of society. (Bourdieu, P. (1990) 'Structures, habitus, practices and "belief and the body"', in *Pierre Bourdieu: The Logic of Practice*. Tr. R. Nice. Cambridge: Polity Press) (**bodyism; body politics; cultural capital; fitness; Mauss; morality and medicine; self-care; somatic norms; technologies of the self**).

HANDICAP The World Health Organization distinguishes impairment, the impact on the body of disease or accident; disability, the resulting impact on functioning and activity levels; and handicap, the resulting social disadvantage as a consequence of discrimination. The social treatment of the impaired or disabled – whether of ostracism, discrimination or stigmatization – outweighs the impact of the biological condition (**disability; (dis)ablism; international classification of impairments, disabilities and handicaps; stigma**).

HARVEY, WILLIAM (1578–1657) British medical practitioner, the first to demonstrate the circulation of the blood and to overthrow the Galenic system of medicine, moving medicine onto a footing with the natural sciences, based on observation and dissection. It is worth noting that Harvey's model of the body was still based on vitalism – he did not conceptualize the body as machine like – and at this philosophical level did not transcend Aristotelian epistemology (Porter, R. (1997) *The Greatest Benefit to Mankind*. London: Harper Collins) (**Galen; mechanistic**).

HAWTHORNE EXPERIMENTS A series of experiments carried out at the Hawthorne plant of the Western Electric Company, Chicago, in the mid-1920s and 1930s. In one of these, the illumination experiment, lighting conditions were varied between an experimental group and a control group of workers. Production went up in the experimental group (whose lighting was dimmed down to the equivalent of moonlight!) as it did in the control group. The study demonstrated that when people have attention paid to them they perform better. In health social studies a similar effect has been demonstrated. Groups of patients who are fully informed about their forthcoming surgery, meet the operating staff beforehand, and are debriefed afterwards, require fewer drugs for pain relief after surgery and are discharged earlier from hospital than those who experience normal hospital procedures (Egbert, L., Battit, G., Welch, C. and Bartlett, M. (1964) 'Reduction of post-operative pain by encouragement and instruction of patients', *New England Journal of Medicine*, 270: 825–27) **(Thomas theorem)**.

HEALTH   Defined by the World Health Organization (WHO) as 'not merely the absence of disease and infirmity but complete physical, mental and social well-being' (World Health Organization (1978) *Primary Health Care*. Geneva). The earliest definition is attributed to Pericles in the fifth century BC: 'Health is that state of moral, mental and physical well-being which enables a person to face any crisis in life with the utmost grace and facility'. The WHO definition has been criticized for its idealism and lack of attention to the patterns of inequality in society that produce and distribute sickness and disease. Conservative sociologists have defined health as the ability to carry out social roles and emphasized the interplay of medical professionals and would-be patients in bringing about social stability by monitoring entry to the **sick role** Marxists, on the

other hand, show how health is defined in terms not of how people might feel but of their capacity to undertake paid labour. In this perspective medicine does not function to cure and heal but to rehabilitate the individual without changing the social structures, particularly class relationships that produce and unequally distribute disease. (Kelman, S. (1975) 'The social nature of the definition problem in health', *International Journal of Health Services*, 5: 625–42) **(class; disease; ideology; Parsons)**.

HEALTH BELIEF MODEL   Originally a psychological model of health-seeking behaviour which emphasized that the individual's own perceived susceptibility to disease, perception of the severity of the illness, and the perceived costs and benefits of seeking medical assistance had the power to predict individuals' health behaviour. The model was later modified and new variables were added to investigate the relations between health beliefs and other aspects of health-related behaviour such as help seeking, compliance, and health-protective behaviour (Becker, M. (1974) (ed.), *The Health Belief Model and Personal Health Behaviour.* New Jersey. Charles B. Slack) **(lay culture; lay referral system)**.

HEALTHCARE SYSTEMS   The way in which the delivery of healthcare is achieved varies according to the political and economic framework of different societies. In the USA, individuals, responsible for themselves, negotiate their healthcare needs on the market, where doctors sell their products on a **fee-for-service** basis. **Welfare states** are based on the assumption that for some goods – like health or education – there is a societal responsibility based on the rights of **citizenship** for the state to manage these sectors. These societies, Australia, Canada and England for example, have a blend of market and state involvement, where a national insurance system guarantees everyone access to healthcare, provided by private medical practitioners. Socialist societies, for example **Cuba** or in the past **Chile** provided a fully nationalized health system, providing universal healthcare coverage by state employed health officials. The least effective and most expensive form of healthcare delivery is the free market, fee-for-service model (**comparative health systems; corporatization; market; perverse incentives**).

HEALTH DETERMINANTS　　In **biomedicine** health determinants are aspects of **biological hazards**, to be treated with drugs and technology. In health social studies the emphasis is on the impact of the social environment on people's health and illness. The World Health Organization (1998) in its *Social Determinant of Health: The Solid Facts* (Regional Office for Europe: WHO) identified the ten known determinants of ill-health and disease: the **social gradient** of inequality, the impact of **stress**, early life exposures to social insults such as poverty, homelessness and hunger, **social exclusion**, the impact of the work environment, the impact of **unemployment**, the presence or absence of **social support**, addiction induced by social

circumstances, access to quality food and transport services. Health policy that addresses the social basis of illness and disease will do far more for the population's health than biomedical interventions (**Black Report; diet; health information systems; life course analysis; materialist analyses; occupation and health; social inequality**).

HEALTH INEQUALITIES　　The socially patterned experience of poorer health based on **class** position though also intersecting with **gendered health issues** and **ethnicity**. Studies have found marked differences in health experiences with those at the bottom of the social system having a much higher mortality rate than those at the top, independently of **lifestyle** factors. This is not restricted to specific diseases but applies to the majority of diseases. People in the lower classes suffer more from chronic illness. Their children weigh less at birth, and they are shorter. There are also marked inequalities in access to preventative services. National and international patterns of growing inequalities of wealth and income in the West mean that inequalities of health are also widening (Wilkinson, R. (1996) *Unhealthy Societies: The Afflictions of Inequality.* London: Routledge) (**Black Report; health determinants; inequality; neo-Marxism; social gradient of disease; Whitehall Studies**).

HEALTH INFORMATION SYSTEMS　　The collection of data about individuals and populations to facilitate the delivery of health services. In a biomedically dominated health system the important data is considered to be that which is about individuals, their bodies, and their unique chances of falling sick or becoming diseased. In a health social science approach the important information would relate to the known social and political determinants of sickness and disease that exist independently of the individual. These include household income at the time of birth (a measure of the impact of poverty); the structure of the community they live in – whether physically in terms of patterns of industrialization, or socially, in terms of urban isolation and lack of access to transport. Thus the first approach produces a medical record – with the policy implication of intervention at the individual level – while the second produces a record of health determinants with policy implications at the level of social, political and economic structures (**health determinants**).

HEALTH INSURANCE The payment of monies in advance so that in the event of sickness, disease or disability the insured will have access to medical services and treatment. Health insurance systems vary across Western societies from Britain and the Scandinavian countries which have state managed national, health insurance systems to the USA where only a minimal national insurance system is in place and a greater reliance is placed on the private market, with Australia falling between the two. Private health insurance in a **fee-for-service** market is the best predictor of high health-care costs with poor healthcare returns, as in the USA (Scott, C. (2001) *Public and Private Roles in Health Care Systems*. Buckingham:

Open University Press) (**health maintenance organizations**; **market**; **medicare**; **Medicaid**; **perverse incentives**; **preferred provider organizations**; **uninsured**).

HEALTHISM The increasing responsibility that individuals must take under **neo-liberal** social health policies for themselves, evaluating risks to which they are alerted by experts, and as 'responsible' citizens they react to. A lack of care for the self is socially read as a lack of responsibility to both self and society. The problem for individuals is that there is no way of evaluating the blizzard of risks that experts tell them they are exposed to. They are then always in a state of uncertainty about their health which requires constant monitoring (Peterson, A. (1996) 'Risk and the regulated self: the discourse of health promotion as politics of uncertainty', *Australian and New Zealand Journal of Sociology*, 32 (2): 44–57) (**citizenship**; **fitness**; **health promotion**; **new public health**; **psy-professions**; **risk**; **risk factor epidemiology**; **risk society**; **technologies of the self**).

HEALTH MAINTENANCE ORGANIZATIONS (HMOS) A form of health insurance, originally in the USA, in which subscribers pay monthly dues to an organization for treatment when they need it. The Kaiser Foundation Health Plan started in 1942, and by the mid-1990s the Kaiser Permanente programme, employed 2,500 doctors, operated fifty-eight clinics and twenty-three hospitals. HMOs have around one-third less the hospitalization levels and surgical procedures than in the private fee-for-service market showing that payment methods are one of the strongest predictors of doctors' treatment decisions. HMO-employed doctors participate in a profit-sharing agreement, which reduces unnecessary tests and procedures, as well as unnecessary hospitalization and thus have no incentive to over-treat (**fee-for-service; perverse incentives; supplier induced demand**).

HEALTH PERCEPTIONS QUESTIONNAIRE (HPQ) A questionnaire that is self-administered asking questions about general health (rather than specific conditions) and answered in terms of excellent, good, fair or poor. On the basis of the answers respondents can be assessed on six subscales: 1 past health; 2 present health; 3 future health; 4 health related worries and concerns; 5 resistance or susceptibility to illness; and 6 the tendency to view illness as part of life (Ware, J. (1976) 'Scales for measuring general health perceptions', *Health Services Research*, 11: 396–415) (**health status assessment**).

HEALTH PROMOTION At a general level the provision of information to enhance health. In the past public health promotion under the **welfare state** emphasized interventions in the social and political environment. Under the new **public health** the focus has moved to individuals, the **risks** they take and **lifestyle** interventions. This new focus is used to justify reduced government expenditure on public health promotion sheeting home

responsibility for healthcare initiatives to individuals (Crawford, R. (2000) 'The ritual of health promotion', in S. Williams (ed.), *Health, Medicine and Society: Key Theories, Future Agendas*. London: Routledge) (**blame the victim; bodyism; citizenship; healthism; new public health**).

HEALTH RELATED QUALITY OF LIFE (HRQL) An attempt to measure either through qualitative or quantitative research a person's physical functioning, health and sense of well being. The most useful application of the concept has been in trials of drugs where, for example, three different drugs will have the same clinical outcome, but different **side effects** on patients. HRQL research allows for the documentation of these side effects in a way that a clinical assessment of the drugs does not (Croog, S. et al. (1986) 'The effects of antihypertensive therapy on quality of life', *The New England Journal of Medicine*, 314: 1657–64) (**evaluation; health status assessment; quality of life; sickness impact profile**).

HEALTH SERVICES The provision of social and medical support to those in need. In the past a distinction was made between primary health care, provided on a one to one basis by a medical practitioner to a patient; secondary health care, the provision of services by hospitals and clinics; and tertiary healthcare, the provision of specialist services and specialized care. To these have to be added, with the rise of **neoliberalism care in the community** and **home health care** (**health services, hidden; hospital at home; informal care**).

HEALTH SERVICES EVALUATION The evaluation of the structure, process and outcome of health services. Structures include facilities, staffing levels funding principles and equipment. Processes relate to the actual practice of healthcare professionals in a health setting, while outcomes are measured in statistics such as hospital separation rates or mortality statistics. Evaluation is much more difficult where what is at issue is disability, suffering or pain (Donabedian, A. (1966) 'Evaluating the quality of medical care', *Milbank Memorial Fund Quarterly*, 44: 169–79) (**casemix; Cochrane; Cochrane Centre; health technology assessment; National Institute of Clinical Evidence; randomized control trials**).

HEALTH SERVICES, HIDDEN The provision of healthcare by lay persons in the home and outside of the formal healthcare system. The bulk of healthcare in modern societies is carried out in the domestic economy, usually by women. The public health sector could not function without the hidden economy of the free provision of care for the aged and those with chronic illness and disability (Levin, L. and Idler, E. (1981) *The Hidden Health Care System: Mediating Structures and Medicine.* Cambridge, MA: Ballinger) (**health services; hospital at home; informal care**).

HEALTH STATUS A generic term for the health of an individual or group in terms of physical and emotional well being. It can be assessed either through the administration of self-reporting questionnaires or at the population level by reference to variables such as infant and maternal mortality. In health insurance health status refers to an individual's history of claims making, receipt of healthcare services, their medical history and **genetic** background (**health status assessment; Karnofsky's performance status scale; sickness impact profile**).

HEALTH STATUS ASSESSMENT Research tools to measure functional, emotional and subjective aspects of a patient's well being. These may be generic, examining a wide range of health related states, disease specific, defined by the pathology of the condition, or preference based, providing a measure of the patient's perceptions, and resulting in a measure of quality adjusted life years. Health status assessment is strong on correlations and weak on explanations of health and illness. (McHorney, C. (2000) 'Concepts and measurement of health status and health related quality of life', in G. Albrecht, R. Fitzpatrick and S. Scrimshaw (eds), *Handbook of Social Studies in Health and Medicine.* London: Sage) (**health perceptions questionnaire; health related quality of life; Karnofsky's performance status scale; quality adjusted life years; sickness impact profile**).

HEALTH SYSTEMS AGENCIES (HSAS) An attempt to facilitate consumer involvement in health services at grass roots level, in the USA and established in 1974. Their impact was negligible and they were abandoned in the 1980s. In Britain a similar imitative was the establishment of Community Health Councils (1974), which have not challenged traditional health services or professionals (White, D. (2000) 'Consumer and community participation: a reassessment of process, impact, and value', in G. Albrecht, R. Fitzpatrick and S. Scrimshaw (eds), *Handbook of Social Studies in Health and Medicine*. London: Sage) (**consumer participation**).

HEALTH TECHNOLOGY ASSESSMENT (HTA) The projective modelling, under controlled conditions, of how a health technology will behave if introduced into healthcare practices. A state based initiative in the UK, it is predicated on two assumptions: that clinical judgement on the part of the medical users of current technologies is not sufficient to demonstrate their usefulness; and of the uncertainty of the usefulness of many common medical technologies (**casemix**; **Cochrane Centre**; **evidence-based medicine**; **health services evaluation**; **medical technology**; **National Institute of Clinical Evidence**).

HEALTH TRANSITION An extension of the theory of **epidemiological transition** arguing that we have now moved into a fourth stage of the relationship between modern societies and disease. These changes relate to changes in life expectancy, with male life expectancy catching up with females; the reduction of some degenerative diseases; and a greater postulated role for **lifestyle factors** as the source of disease. The fundamental reliance of this 'new' transition theory on

individual behaviour means that it excludes the social, political and environmental factors at the core of the production and distribution of disease (Rogers, R. and Hackenberg, R. (1987) 'Extending epidemiologic transition theory: a new stage', *Social Biology*, 34: 234–43).

HEALTHY CITIES PROJECT The World Health Organization's attempt to implement the policies of the **Ottawa Charter** in community based health enhancing initiatives, which take a multi-sectoral approach to health, that is, involving not just the public health department, but also say, the department of roads and transport. While supposedly based on community activity the project was a top-down driven initiative and met with mixed results.

HEALTHY YEARS EQUIVALENT (HALE) The number of years an individual can expect to live without loss of quality of life from sickness or disease (**burden of disease**).

HEGEMONIC MASCULINITY Recent arguments in **gender** studies suggest that being masculine can be bad for your health (**gendered health risks**). This is especially the case in terms of hegemonic masculinity, the dominant discourse of what it is to be male – the white, Anglo-Saxon Protestant form of rational, domineering, aggressive and exploitative male. While hegemonic masculinity significantly benefits dominant male groups, it also produces the high death rates of 15–25-year-old men as they make the transition out of adolescence into adulthood, adopting hazardous lifestyles resulting in violent death, drug abuse and suicide (Connell, R. (1995) *Masculinities*. St Leonards, NSW: Allen and Unwin) (**gender linked health risks**; **male stoicism**).

HEIDEGGER, MARTIN (1899–1976) Exponent of a position in philosophy known as **phenomenology**. His work has influenced the social sciences because, like Weber, he emphasizes the ways in which objects are constituted in interaction rather than self-evidently existing and that it is the meaning attributed to them that makes them significant. He also distinguished between the methods of the natural sciences, which looked at phenomena from the outside, and the human sciences which seek to examine from the inside, capturing the meaning of the situation for the individual or group (**Chicago School of Sociology**; **Gadamer**; **Husserl**; **Kant**; **microsociological**; **Schutz**; **verstehen**).

HELP-SEEKING BEHAVIOUR A major research programme of health social sciences literature has been to document the triggers to accessing medical treatment, or on the other hand, the failure to access health services when sick. The history of this research focus reflects the evolution from a **sociology in medicine** to a **sociology of medicine**. Early approaches focused on the psychological characteristics of individuals who failed to utilize health services, over utilized health services, or failed to comply with medical directives. Later approaches document the sense-making of individuals

as social agents who interpret and construct the meaning of their physical symptoms in ways that do not fit the medical model (**clinical iceberg**; **lay culture**; **lay referral system**).

HELSINKI DECLARATION Recommendations for the ethical conduct of medical research involving human beings, adopted at the eighteenth World Medical Assembly, Helsinki, in 1964. Specifically the declaration distinguishes between research that aims at the better diagnosis of disease or treatment for disease, and research that is carried out for purely scientific reasons with no necessary diagnostic or therapeutic value for the patient. In the latter case the dominant motive in conducting research must be the protection of the life and health of the patient. The declaration, it should be noted, does not bind medical researchers to ethical research (World Medical Organization (1996) 'Declaration of Helsinki', *British Medical Journal*, 313 (7070): 1448–9) (**Belmont Report**; **ethics, medical**; **Nuremberg Code**; **Tuskegee syphilis experiment**).

HEREDITY In biology the passing down to offspring of certain physical characteristics coded in **genes**, for example, eye colour. In Social Darwinism the claim that social characteristics are inherited and that through eugenics, that is selective breeding, these characteristics can be modified. Social Darwinism provided the backdrop for the foundation of British psychology in the work of Francis Galton (1822–1911) and Karl Pearson (1857–1936), and in the twentieth century Cyril Burt (1883–1971). Their argument was that the position of individuals in society reflected their innate abilities, and that those at the bottom should be prevented from reproducing. Theories of heredity were hotly contested by the sanitationists who argued that malnutrition, homelessness, or drunkenness, for example, were the product of the development of industrial capitalism, and not signs of genetic inferiority among the working class (**Engels; eugenics; genetic determinism; IQ controversy; social medicine**).

HERMENEUTICS/HERMENEUTIC CIRCLE
Originally the study of sacred texts which located them in the context of their historical period. Currently an approach to understanding which moves from the whole to the part, then to the whole again. The approach has been influential in qualitative health research with its emphasis on the construction of meaning by social agents (**Gadamer; Heidegger; Husserl; social constructionism**).

HIPPOCRATES   (c.460–c.377BC) Greek physician, from the school of Cos, and the founder of public health. The group of works associated with his name, the *Corpus Hippocraticum*, emphasize the role of the environment in the production and distribution of disease, as in *Air, Places and Waters*. The Hippocratic school of medicine, as synthesized by Galen (130–201AD), dominated Western medicine for over 1,000 years (**humoural theory**). The Hippocratic oath, which binds a doctor to do no harm, has been drawn upon by medicine in its professionalization process, to locate itself at the origins of Western civilization (Hippocrates (1939) *The Genuine Works of Hippocrates.* Tr. F. Adams. Baltimore: Williams and Wilkins) (**Belmont Report; Helsinki Declaration; hygiene; Nuremberg Code**).

HISPANIC AMERICANS   A generic term for non-blacks in the USA, of Latin American descent. While the category confuses ethnic groups with very different health problems – for example, Mexican women are at the lowest risk of hypertension, while Central American women are at higher risk and Cuban and Puerto Rican women are at the highest risk – it is nevertheless the case, that as a group, these peoples are at higher risk of hypertension, tuberculosis, alcoholism and so on (Williams, D. and Collins, C. (1995) 'US socioeconomic and racial differences in health: patterns and explanations', *Annual Review of Sociology*, 21: 349–86) (**African Americans; American Indians; Canadian Inuits**).

HITE REPORT   Shere Hite, author of *The Hite Report: A Nationwide Study on Female Sexuality* (1968, 1989, 2000) claimed that women are far more dissatisfied with their relationships than public perception, or their partners, would expect. Their partners do not emotionally satisfy 84 per cent of them, with 95 per cent reporting emotional and psychological harassment. Within five years of marriage 70 per cent of women are having extramarital affairs, while within two years of marriage 87 per cent of women are no longer in love. Her work did much to fuel the women's liberation movement of the 1960s and 1970s, contributing to expectation of women to have the right to enjoy sexual satisfaction (pointing out that 70 per cent of women do not achieve orgasm through intercourse though they achieve it easily by masturbation). She rejects the physiological approach to sexuality shared by both Kinsey and Masters and Johnson and emphasizes the meaningfulness of a sexual relationship. Her work has been criticized since only a **self-selected sample** responded to her questionnaires (**Kinsey**; **Masters and Johnson**).

HIV   (Human Immunodeficiency Virus) (**AIDS**).

HOLISM   Explanations of social life that focus on the social whole, rather than on the individual components that make it up. Émile Durkheim argued that society was a reality in its own right, and could not be studied by reference to the actions of individuals (**suicide**). In philosophy the argument is that since constituent parts function differently within the whole organism, organic wholes must be studied in their unity. Holism in health studies rejects reductionist and mechanistic explanations of the experience of sickness and disease as a consequence of the breakdown of parts of the body. Rather it locates the experience of disease in the totality of the individual's social relationships (**social support**) and the causes of disease in the

organization of society, particularly, in **class** relationships, **gender** relationships, and **ethnicity** (**mechanistic**; **reductionism**; **vitalism**).

HOLISTIC MEDICINE   Approaches to treating disease that focus on the whole individual rather than just the individual's biological parts. Holism is usually associated with **alternative medicine** (**mechanistic**; **reductionism**; **vitalism**).

HOME HEALTHCARE   (**care in the community**; **health services, hidden**; **hospital at home**; **informal care**).

HOMEOPATHY   A medical system founded by the German physician Samuel Hahnemann (1755–1843). He rejected **allopathic** medicine for its lack of a holistic approach to the patient and emphasized exercise, diet and clean air as the basis of a healthy life. His system was based on two principles: the law of similars, or that like cures like; and the law of infitesimals, that is, the smaller the dose the more effective the medicine. In some countries (for example the United Kingdom) homeopaths are recognized medical practitioners and are reimbursed by state health insurance systems (Coulter, H. (1984) 'Homeopathy', in J. Salmon (ed.), *Alternative Medicines: Popular and Policy Perspectives*. New York: Tavistock) (**complemetary/alternative medicine**; **holism**).

HOMICIDE   The unlawful taking of another human being's life. Usually explained as the exceptional act of an individual, sociologists have demonstrated that violent crime rates, including homicide rates, are closely linked to income inequality, and further that the motivation in crimes of violence against people is that the assailants felt that they were not respected. In this approach emotional experiences are linked to low social status and are central to a loop that incorporates violence, inequality and mortality. In most cases the perpetrator and the victim are known to each other (Wilkinson, R., Kawachi, I. and Kennedy, B. (1998) 'Mortality, the social environment, crime and violence,' *Sociology of Health and Illness*, 20: 578–97) (**domestic violence**).

HOMOSEXUALITY   Attraction to and sexual activity with a person of the same sex. The reconceptualization of homosexuality from a sin to a psychological and mental disorder through the nineteenth and twentieth centuries provides a good example of **medicalization** of what is regarded as a deviant identity. Homosexuality also provides an example of how medical concepts of disease can be normative statements of how to act. It was listed in the first *Diagnostic and Statistical Manual* of the American Psychiatric Association as a sociopathic personality disturbance and as a form of sexual deviation. In 1973 DSM III declassified it as a mental illness, replacing it with 'sexual orientation disturbance', that is a condition affecting individuals unhappy with their gay orientation (Weeks, J. (1986) *Sexuality and its Discontents*. London: Routledge and Kegan Paul). Feminists argue that in a patriarchal society sex is

by definition violent and for the gratification of men, and that lesbianism (attraction between women) is a political statement and the only viable form of satisfactory relationships for women (Greer, G. (1971) *The Female Eunuch*. London: Paladin) (**morality and medicine**).

HORMONE REPLACEMENT THERAPY (HRT)
With the cessation of menses (**menopause**) oestrogen levels in women fall, and are linked to increased likelihood of broken bones and heart disease. Feminists reject this construction of women as part of the process of **medicalization** and as reflecting norms of appropriate feminine roles in Western society, particularly that they remain sexually available for men. Other analysts draw attention to the strong economic interests in medicalizing the ageing, mainly female, population as a source of enormous profit through the consumption of drugs (Greer, G. (1991) *The Change: Women, Ageing and the Menopause*. Auckland: Harnish Mailton).

HOSPICE MOVEMENT   The trend towards the development of specialized institutions for the dying. Pioneered by Cicely Saunders who founded St Christopher's Hospice in London in 1967, the hospice movement marks a significant reconstruction of death from the 1970s onwards. It is a reaction to the prolongation of life by modern medical interventions, the bureaucratization of death in the hospital, and in a secular society, the problem of the meaning of death. Rather than being hidden away (**death**) we are in the process of re-constructing the dying process, whereby we talk about it, rearrange it, legislate it, and give it a new meaning: 1 Talk about it, as witnessed in the growth of death counselling where we are inveighed not just to 'talk', not just to 'intellectualize', but participate in 'authentic' talk. 2 The hospice movement rearranges death to escape the bureaucracy of the hospital and to escape the control of medical definitions, to escape 'cure' and re-arrange the structure of care for the dying by creating a special space, a 'dying place' which emphasizes 'comfort' 'serenity' and 'happiness'. 3 Death is now legislated for, to allow the dying person to make choices, such as living wills or 'do not treat' orders, and 4 In terms of meaning the post-1970s discourses on death have a number of characteristics. The implicit belief in immortality, the growth of the near death experience and the development of the idea that death is pleasant, are all aspects of a humanistic (rather than religious) rejection of secularism and materialism. The new discourse of death reflects a belief in progress, personal or societal, and that there is a solution to all problems: 1 the dying process is an occasion for self-improvement and personal 'growth'; 2 the dying process and grief is an occasion for self-improvement and 'personality' growth for the family; 3 death can be 'serene' and 'pleasurable'; and 4 that this has to be 'achieved' – it is not just given in the process of dying. This achievement is worked for and expressed since it is only through 'expression' of the dying process that opportunities for growth occur (Lofland, L. (1976) (ed.), *Towards a Sociology of*

Death and Dying. London: Sage) (**death**; **bereavement**).

HOSPITAL AT HOME   Under the impact of cost saving initiatives (**neoliberalism**) patients are more and more discharged from hospital early, or now have day surgery, for conditions that in the past would have been treated in the hospital. This has pushed the burden of care back into the home and on to women. Minimally 15 per cent of working age women in Britain are caring for the sick, the disabled or elderly often with enormous impact on their own health and well being (Opie, A. (1991) *Caring Alone: Looking After the Confused Elderly at Home*. Auckland: Oxford University Press) (**care in the community**; **deinstitutionalization**; **health services, hidden**; **informal care**).

HOSPITALS   An institution for the care of the sick, developing in the West out of medieval religious institutions. These institutions were undifferentiated in the sense of providing care to travellers, the poor and the sick. It is with the development of industrial capitalism and the **germ theory** of disease that they evolved into specialist institutions in which professional medical practitioners dealt with the sick (**bedside medicine**). Sociologists have examined them in the context of **Weber's** theory of **bureaucracy**, pointing to the conflict between the values of the medical practitioners and the administrators. In a **symbolic interactionist** tradition they have been studied in terms of the micro organization of order and practice within **total institutions**.

Under the impact of **neoliberalism**, the development of the **hospital at home** and **informal care** their centrality for the delivery of primary healthcare is changing (Armstrong, D. (1988) 'Decline of the hospital: reconstructing institutional dangers', *Sociology of Health and Illness*, 20 (4): 445–57).

HOUSING AND HEALTH   Housing conditions have been demonstrated to have a significant impact on health and disease rates. For example, there is a twelve-fold difference in accidental deaths due to falls in the homes of the poor that are caused by overcrowded and unsafe conditions (Blane, D., Bartley, M., and Davey Smith, G. (1997) 'Disease aetiology and materialist explanations of socioeconomic mortality differentials', *European Journal of Public Health*, 7: 385–91). Feminist sociologists have conceptualized the home as a workplace, demonstrating its impact on women's health. Women home workers have high rates of cancer, possibly due to the unregulated toxic materials in the 'cottage industry' that is domestic work. Of the 6,245 deaths in home accidents in 1971, 35.3 per cent happened to men, while 64.7 per cent happened to women. Half of all accidents in the home happen to women, with men accounting for only 21 per cent (Broom, D. (1986) 'Occupational health of houseworkers', *Australian Feminist Studies*, 2: 15–33) (**gender linked health risks; health determinants**).

HUGHES, EVERETT (1897–1983)   Professor of Sociology at the University of Chicago,

Hughes was influential in operationalizing **symbolic interactionism** in extensive field work based on **ethnographic** research. He directed the study carried out by Howard Becker *Boys in White* (1961, Chicago: University of Chicago Press) which showed that, contrary to the public face of medical education, medicine is like any other occupation, socializing its practitioners – who are boys dressing up – into its codes of practice. The tone of the book reflects the transition to a **sociology of medicine** approach, especially when contrasted with the 1957 publication of Merton's *The Student Physician: Studies in the Sociology of Medical Education* (Cambridge MA: Harvard University Press), which presented medical training as a esoteric practice (**Chicago School of Sociology; microsociological**).

HUMAN GENOME PROJECT   The attempt to isolate, identify and code the 50,000–100,000 genes and several billion nucleotide bases believed to make up the human genome. The claim is that specific genes will be identified and linked to specific diseases and ultimately allow for gene therapy, the elimination of unwanted genes. While the costs are enormous (the US government is investing over \$US200 million a year) the profit lies in patenting specific genes. Given the enormous complexity of gene interactions, and of genes with the environment the dream is not likely to be fulfilled (Willis, E. (1998) 'The Human Genome Project: A Sociology of Medical Technology', in J. Germov (ed.), *Second*

Opinion: An Introduction to Health Sociology. Melbourne: Oxford University Press) (**geneism; genetic determinism; reductionism**).

HUMANISTIC SOCIOLOGY   The development of a sociology, in the 1960s in the USA, that emphasized the role of the human subject in creating, managing and maintaining social reality. In health sociology the notable examples are Goffman's *The Presentation of Self in Everyday Life* (1959, New York: Doubleday), *Asylums* (1961, New York: Anchor) and *Stigma* (1963, New Jersey: Prentice-Hall). Humanistic sociology was based on **symbolic interactionism** and was a reaction to the **structural functionalism** of **Talcott Parsons** which had emphasized the ways in which individuals conform to the social roles provided to them by the social system (**Chicago School of Sociology; Goffman; grounded theory; role**).

HUMAN POPULATION LABORATORY (HPL) The first systematic attempt at measuring the physical, mental and social health of a general population. Methodologically these studies developed the role of the social survey – particularly lengthy questionnaires conducted by mail – as a robust source of information about health status (Belloc, N., Breslow, L., and Hochstein, J. (1971) 'Measurement of physical health in a general population', *American Journal of Epidemiology*, 93: 328–36) (**health status assessment**).

HUMAN RIGHTS AND HEALTH   Article 25 of the Universal Declaration of Human Rights, adopted and proclaimed by the General Assembly of the United Nations, on December 10, 1948 states: 'Everyone has the right to a standard of living adequate for the health and well-being of himself and of his family, including food, clothing, housing and medical care and necessary services; and the right to security in the event of unemployment, sickness, disability, old age or other lack of livelihood in circumstances beyond his control'. These sentiments underpinned the **welfare state** and the right of every citizen (**citizenship**) to have access to health services. Since the late 1970s, with the rise of **neoliberalism** in Western industrialized democracy these rights have been wound back, and health become more of an individual's responsibility and a commodity for sale on the market (**lifestyle; risk**).

HUMOURAL   THEORY   Developed in Ancient Greece and associated with **Hippocrates** and **Galen** an explanation of the cause of disease based on the existence of the four humours of the body: blood (hot, moist); phlegm (cold, moist); black bile (cold, dry); and yellow bile (hot, dry). These in turn had four qualities – hot, cold, wet, and dry and interacted with the four elements of the environment – earth, water, air and fire. Treatment involved identifying the constitutional character of the patient which was produced out of the interaction between the humours and the environment – sanguine, phlegmatic, choleric or melancholic – and then to restoring balance between the humours through bleeding, dieting, or purging.

HUSSERL, EDMUND (1859–1938) A philosopher and proponent of **phenomenology** an interpretative epistemological position rejecting the natural sciences as of any value for knowledge of individuals. Human action is inherently intentional and conscious and needs to be understood from the 'inside', rather than observed from the 'outside'. The philosophical position has provided support for interactionist health social studies, through its development by **Alfred Schutz**. Researchers in the qualitative tradition distinguish themselves from **positivist**, **behaviourist** and **biomedical** approaches to the study of social events (**Gadamer; Heidegger; hermeneutics/hermeneutic circle; Husserl; Schutz; verstehen**).

HYDROTHERAPY (HYDROPATHY) In Hippocratic medicine water was one of the elements, imbued with the ability to cure diseases. The use of hot springs and mineralized water to cure or assuage illness has been documented throughout history. Hydrotherapy flourished in the nineteenth century, as an alternative to **allopathy** with the popularization of spas throughout Europe. In the US, again in reaction to allopathic medicine's 'heroic' interventions – bloodletting, purging, blistering and vomiting – hydrotherapy was an attractive option (**complementary/ alternative medicine; Hippocrates**).

HYGIENE In general, adherence to rules of correct behaviour around the body, its excrement, urine and in many cultures, menstrual blood. Originally these were taboos grounded in a religious view of the world and with the development of the **germ theory** took on the guise of scientific prescriptions of how to behave. In the history of medicine the Hygienists were a group of European nineteenth-century medical reformers who advocated urban reform as a cure for disease (**Asclepius; medical police; social medicine; Villerme**).

HYPERACTIVITY The postulation by the medical profession of a biological disease characterized by inattentiveness and inappropriate social interactions. This is despite the absence of any known biological underpinning of the 'disease'. Sociologists use it as an example of **medicalization**, in which social norms are enforced by using medical categories to label and treat deviant individuals (**attention deficit disorders; autism spectrum disorders; learning disorders; morality and medicine**).

HYPNOSIS The induction of a trance-like state in a person, making them suggestible to the promptings of the hypnotist, popularized in the nineteenth century by Anton Mesmer (hence the alternative usage of mesmerism). Proponents claim that under hypnosis the body can be induced to cure itself, not to experience pain, and provide access to the unconscious when blended with psychoanalysis (**Freud**).

HYPOCHONDRIASIS An all encompassing concern for one's physical health, or the attribution of serious physical consequences to simple physical processes such as sweating or heart rate. Hypochondriacs resist reassurance that there is nothing wrong, doctor shopping – visiting many medical practitioners – until they find one who will support their interpretation of their condition. Conditions that are medically disputed, such as **chronic fatigue syndrome**, may result in the person being labelled a hypochondriac (**abnormal illness behaviour; diagnostic limbo**).

HYSTERIA A disease of women in the nineteenth century (though far older historical references to it exist). As the nineteenth century developed, it produced enormous social upheaval and women experienced new options for joining the workforce as school teaching, nursing and voluntary reform work developed. Men, on the other hand were concerned to constrain women in their traditional roles within the household. In this a medical system developed that insisted emphatically on the differences between men and women. It was argued that in men the brain predominated, and in women it was the nervous and reproductive systems, and in particular the ovaries and the uterus. Women who went, or attempted to go to work, put themselves at risk of of hysteria by denying the biological imperative of reproduction. Furthermore, education would lead to sickness, since the brain and the ovaries could not develop simultaneously. Hence the disease of hysteria worked on a number of levels. It allowed men to classify women who attempted to participate in the workforce as diseased. In turn this provided an active and hostile role for women to respond to male attempts to control them (Turner, B. S. (1984) *The Body and Society: Explorations in Social Theory.* London: Sage) (**agoraphobia; anorexia nervosa; drapetomania; masturbatory insanity**).

IATROGENIC/IATROGENESIS   From the Greek, meaning 'physician caused'. Ivan Illich demonstrated the ways in which modern medicine actually causes sickness and disease, a process for which he coined the word 'iatrogenesis'. Clinical iatrogenesis is the damage done to the patient by the practices of medical practitioners. Social iatrogenesis is when the healthcare system actually supports those features of industrialized capitalist societies that cause disease and death. Structural iatrogenesis is the increasing dependence of the population on professional healthcare for what used to be 'normal' experiences of the human condition, especially suffering and death (Illich, I. (1975) *Limits to Medicine: Medical Nemesis*. Harmondsworth: Penguin).

IDEALISM   In social theory a term used to describe those approaches to studying society that emphasize language, discourse and culture as the driving forces of social life. **Ethnomethodology, symbolic interactionism** and **phenomenological sociology** all emphasize the micro level of social life and the ways in which individuals produce reality. They tend, from a materialist perspective, to overlook the role of power – patriarchal, economic (**class**) and

political – in setting the agenda of what can be negotiated and over which individuals and groups may have little or no input (**health determinants; materialism; phenomenology**).

IDEAL TYPE   In Weberian (**Weber**) sociology an analytic device to construct models of social phenomena by highlighting their central characteristics. For example Weber constructed an ideal type of the characteristics of a **bureaucracy**, which while it will never be found in its pure form, allows the sociologist to identify approximations to it in society.

IDEOLOGY   In common-sense usage, a set of beliefs about society held by a specific group. In the Marxist tradition the systematic distortion of people's views of society in the interests of the ruling class. In Marxist analysis of contemporary medicine the argument is that it performs three ideological functions. First, by providing, however inadequately, healthcare, it legitimates the status quo, acting as an agent of social control by rendering what are basically social problems to an individualistic level. Second, in its equation of hospital care and the consumption of drugs as healthcare it reproduces the capitalist mode of production. Third, it reproduces the capitalist class structure both in the organization of health workers and in the consumption patterns it generates (Navarro, V. (1976) *Medicine Under Capitalism.* New York: Prodist) (**critical theory; cultural hegemony; Frankfurt School; Marxist approaches**).

IDENTITY   Our sense of self can be understood sociologically from two perspectives, one at the micro level, the other at the macro level of social relationships. In the tradition of **Goffman** and **microsociological** approaches our identity is the successful management of our role performances. It is constantly adjusted and manipulated as we go through various status positions, of doctor, patient or nurse for example. From a macrosociological perspective our identity is the inscription of social structures on our bodies and in our psyches. Foucault, for example, argues that our identity as individuals is produced and sustained by the **power/knowledge** of the **psy-professions** and by the way we use **technologies of the self** to produce ourselves. The two approaches alert us to the fact that our identity is socially produced, but they are also largely irreconcilable. Our identity is specifically shaped in our experience of illness, especially **chronic illness** and in the diagnoses of terminal illness (**hospice movement**) (**diagnostic limbo; diagnostic shock; idealism; liminality; materialism; Mead**).

ILLNESS BEHAVIOUR   The actions of an individual experiencing ill-health symptoms. The experience of illness is not a direct result of biological reality, but rather differentially experienced by individuals, usually along class, gender and ethnic lines. The decision to approach a doctor is shaped by the individual's knowledge of the frequency with which the condition occurs in the population; the familiarity of the symptoms; the predictability of the outcome; and the perception of the threat of the illness. The experience of illness, and of pain is also culturally shaped. (Mechanic, D. and Volkhart, E. (1961) 'Stress, illness behaviour and the sick role', *American Sociological Review*, 1: 86–94) (**abnormal illness behaviour; clinical iceberg; lay referral system; sick role; symptom iceberg**).

INCIDENCE   The number of new cases of disease, or the number of new events (e.g. cancer) in a defined population within a specified period of time, usually expressed as a rate per 100,000 (**prevalence**).

INDIGENOUS COMMUNITY (**indigenous peoples**).

INDIGENOUS HEALING   Native, folk and popular practices for health and healing, for example Mexican Americans curanderos, Inuit shamans, or Haitian voodoo healers. These are often thought to be characteristic of non-Western, pre-modern societies. However, in Western societies the persistence of such practices is reflected in alternative and **complementary** medical practices. It has been argued that these practices reflect resistance to the **scienticism** – the separation of the body from the mind, and of the person from the experience of disease – in Western medicine. (Singer, M. and H. Baer (1995) *Critical Medical Anthropology.* New York: Baywood). Belief in spiritual healing is also widespread in developed Western societies, either in some form of Christianity such as Christian Science, or adopted from Eastern traditions (McGuire, M. (1988) *Ritual Healing in Suburban America.* Rutgers: Rutgers University Press) (**clinical iceberg; folk healing; lay referral system**).

INDIGENOUS PEOPLES The inhabitants of Australia, New Zealand, Canada and North America at the time of colonization by the British. Being an indigenous person is a marker for poorer health status and shorter life span in all cases and their condition has been captured in the idea that they constitute a third world in the first. Common to all indigenous cultures are a distrust of Western medical practices (combined with a rejection of their medical practices by Westerners); poor levels of funding for healthcare; a problem of attracting medical practitioners to their communities; and poor transportation and remote living conditions (Young, E. A. (1995) *Third World in the First: The Development of Indigenous Peoples.* London: Routledge) (**Aboriginal Health Services; American Indians; Canadian Inuit; New Zealand Maori**).

INDIVIDUALISM Theories of social life that argue that only individuals exist, and that only individual actions should be studied. In epidemiology risk factor analysis that emphasize **lifestyles** as the source of disease focuses only on individuals and neglects the social environment that produces them. In sociology such approaches are referred to as microsociological, usually in American developments such as **symbolic interactionists, ethnomethodology** and **phenomenology** (**clinical epidemiology; healthism; holism; reductionism**).

INDIVIDUALIST HEALTH PROMOTION The targeting of individuals' lifestyles and risk 'choices' as part of the **new public health** in which individuals are solely responsible for their health or illness status. Driven by the development of **neoliberalism**, the decline of the **welfare state** and the erosion of the idea that **citizenship** is the basis for access to universal healthcare, it legitimates the withdrawal of government funding from the health area (Beaglehole, R. and Bonita, R. (1997) *Public Health at the Crossroads.* Cambridge: Cambridge University Press) (**healthism; lifestyle choices; lifestyle factors**).

INDUCTION In the philosophy of knowledge, an approach that argues that truth is dependent on the collection of empirical data. We can never ultimately know the truth since disconfirming discoveries are always possible. The contrast is with deductive reasoning, in which on the basis of true premises, we can reach logical conclusions. Most sociological research in health studies is of the inductive kind (**causal influence; Popper**).

INDUSTRIAL DISEASE   Disease caused by working in a specific industry (such as asbestosis in the asbestos industry) or more generally the impact of capitalist work structures on employees. Whether or not a condition is a disease that is caused by the work environment is one that will be hotly contested by the employers and championed by the unions (**repetitive strain injury**). Members of the medical profession are enrolled by the employers, denying the reality of the condition or the employer's responsibility for it, and arguing that innate characteristics of the individual made them vulnerable to the condition (**alienation; blame the victim; brown lung disease; employment; occupation and health; Occupational Health and Safety Administration**).

INEQUALITIES IN HEALTH   The existence of inequalities of health (both between the first world and the third world, and within the first world) are the product of inequalities of wealth and income. The more unequal a society is the worse the health inequalities are. As the developed Western societies are becoming more unequal so to is the health gap between the richest and the poorest and the healthy and the sick (Wilkinson, R. (1996) *Unhealthy Societies: The Afflictions of Inequality*. London: Routledge) (**Black Report; class; inequality; poverty; social gradient of disease; Whitehall Studies**).

INEQUALITY   The unequal distribution of material and social resources in society. In the sociology of health it is now accepted that inequality in and of itself is a factor in producing ill health and disease. Countries with the shallowest gradient between the rich and the poor (e.g. Japan) have the best health indicators while those with steep gradients between the rich and the poor (e.g. the USA) have the worst health indicators. The experience of poverty, homelessness and unemployment – socio-economic inequality – result in social exclusion, a lack of social networks and low levels of social support resulting in low self-esteem leading to greater vulnerability to disease and early death (Wilkinson, R. (1996) *Unhealthy Societies: The Afflictions of Inequality*. London: Routledge) (**Black Report; class; diseases of affluence; diseases of poverty; health determinants; poverty; social gradient of disease; social inequality; Whitehall Studies**).

INFANT MORTALITY RATE   The number of live-born babies dying prior to the 364th completed day of life per 1,000 live births. The infant mortality rate is regarded as vital sign of the health of a society, reflecting as it does the care given to expectant mothers and their newborn. The single best intervention that any government can make to improve the health of its population is the provision of universal, free care for mothers-to-be and new-born infants (Shi, L. (1994) 'Primary care, speciality care and life chances', *International Journal of Health Services*, 24: 431–58).

INFECTIOUS DISEASE   Diseases attributed to the presence of a germ and spread by contact between individuals. From 1870 onwards, with the development of bacteriology, the dominant explanation for disease became one that focused on the role of germs in causing sickness. This led to the decline of **social medicine** and other approaches emphasizing the role of the social and political environment as the causes of disease. Germs and not poverty were held to be the cause of sickness and disease. As **McKeown** has shown the impact of scientific medicine was negligible in comparison with social reform (**Chadwick**; **contagionism**; **germ theory**; **hygiene**; **miasma**; **Snow**; **social history of medicine**; **social medicine**; **Whig histories of medicine**).

INFORMAL CARE   Unpaid care provided usually in the home and usually by woman to the sick and elderly. The **deinstitutionalization** of the mentally ill and the development of the **hospital at home** have contributed markedly to the demands placed on the informal sector and consequently women, to provide care at no cost to the state. In Australia, for example, unpaid labour in the provision of welfare services during 1997–98 was conservatively estimated at AUS$24.5 billion which was more than double the federal government's direct monetary expenditure of AUS$10.9 billion (Greig, A., Lewins, F., and White, K. (2003) *Inequality in Australia.* Cambridge: Cambridge University Press) (**care in the community**; **health services, hidden**; **neoliberalism**; **targeted health services**).

INFORMATION AND COMMUNICATION TECHNOLOGIES (ICTS)   A range of technological developments whose impact on medicine is still being examined. These may range from forms of medical care which take place using electronic mediators such as the world wide web, or the internet, to telemedicine, where a surgeon in another country can operate on a patient's body. They also include new forms of surveillance of both the patient – lifetime electronic smart cards with their entire medical history encoded – and of the doctor's diagnostic and prescribing habits, electronically gathered by state agencies. Their impact on both patients – perhaps empowered by internet knowledge, or using the web to access support groups – and on doctors – greater oversight of their practices – is currently a developing area of research (**cyberanatomies**; **internet-informed patient**; **support groups, online**; **telemedicine**).

INFORMED CONSENT   The agreement of the patient to undergo a medical or surgical procedure following the provision of information about the risks by the medical practitioner. Under the Helsinki Declaration it is a requirement of the ethical practice of medicine that informed consent, preferably in writing, be given. It can be argued that because of the imbalance of knowledge and power between the medical practitioner and the patient that informed consent can never be properly given and that it functions to protect doctors from legal action (Corrigan, O. (2003) 'Empty ethics: the problem with informed consent', *Sociology of Health and Illness*, 25 (7): 768–86)

(Belmont Report; ethics, medical; Helsinki Declaration; Nuremberg Code).

INSANITY   The diagnoses of a disorder of the mind by a psychiatrist. Up until the early 1950s the underlying factors were based on the work of Freud. Following the development of psychopharmaceuticals – mood altering drugs – the play of unconscious factors was replaced by a focus on organic features of the brain (**American Psychiatric Association; antipsychiatry; asylums; Bedlam; mental illness; post traumatic stress disorder**).

INSTITUTIONALIZATION   The development of styles of behaviour, in order to survive in an institution, such as a prison, asylum, hospital or the army, which then make the individual incapable of surviving and operating in the ordinary world. Such behaviours, for example, could be excessive deference, loss of autonomy, loss of a sense of self and the inability to initiate a conversation. In **total institutions**, as examined by **Goffman**, the individual's personality is deliberately broken down so that they are re-made as the institution would like them (**degradation ceremonies**).

INSULIN COMA THERAPY   A pharmoconvulsive therapy (that is, the administration of a drug to induce a seizure), the administration of sufficient insulin to a psychiatric patient to induce shock and coma, by reducing blood sugar levels. The treatment was introduced by

Ukrainian psychiatrist Manfred Sakel in 1927. The claim was that it was an effective treatment of affective disorders and schizophrenia. It was replaced in the 1950s and 1960s with electroconvulsive therapy. Forms of 'shock' treatment have been central to the practice of psychiatry since the nineteenth century, based on the claim by psychiatrists that, despite not understanding why they do, they do work (Fink, M. (1984) 'Meduna and the origins of convulsive therapy', *American Journal of Psychiatry*, 141 (9): 1034–41) (**antipsychiatry; Bedlam; Diagnostic and Statistical Manual; mental illness; Pinel; psychotherapeutics; Tuke**).

INTELLIGENCE TESTS (IQ TESTS)   A range of psychological tests – the Stanford-Binet and the Wechsler among them – supposedly capable of measuring an individual's innate verbal, mathematical and spatial skill. IQ tests have been subjected to major criticism, especially for being culturally and class bound (and thereby automatically guaranteeing that ethnic minorities and the poorly educated will fare less well on them), and for the presumption that intelligence is a stable personality factor independent of social relationships. Their chief proponent in Britain, Cyril Burt, was found to have fraudulently reported his findings to sustain his conviction that the British class structure reflected real innate abilities of individuals, and that the class hierarchy was both natural and inevitable (**Binet; IQ controversy**).

INTENTIONAL INJURY   Causes of disease and or death that are purposely inflicted on oneself or others. The term includes **suicide** and **homicide**. Most intentional injury occurs within the family (**domestic violence**).

INTERACTIONIST SOCIOLOGY   Approaches in sociology which emphasize the active negotiation of meaning by individuals in the conduct of their life. These approaches include grounded theory, phenomenological approaches and symbolic interactionism. They are based on the works of the American philosopher, **G. H. Mead** who developed a theory of the self as the outcome of interactions with others, and in a constant process of being shaped, developed and exchanged, as the individual dealt with others in their environment (**Chicago School of Sociology**; **dying trajectories**; **Goffman**; **grounded theory**; **microsociological**; **phenomenology**; **qualitative research**; **symbolic interactionism**).

INTERGENERATIONAL CONFLICT   The argument that the increasingly aged population in the Western world will lead to a blow out in welfare and healthcare costs, advanced in the World Bank document *Averting the Old Age Crisis* (1994), is fuelling resentment between the old and the young and leading to a breakdown in 'inter-generational trust'. However sociologists argue that this economic prediction is based on ageist assumptions and that the old and elderly are in fact healthier and more self-supporting than assumed (Mullen, P. (2000) *The Imaginary Time*

Bomb: Why an Ageing Population is not a Social Problem. London: Tauris) (**ageing**; **ageism**).

INTERNATIONAL CLASSIFICATION OF DISEASE   The World Health Organization's organization of diseases, based on a bio-medical model and understanding of sickness and ill-health. From the perspective of anthropologists it excludes the culturally variable ways that those in other cultures conceptualize disease, and from a sociological perspective, the ways in which different groups within Western societies make sense of and negotiate disease (**anthropology of health**; **lay referral systems**).

INTERNATIONAL CLASSIFICATION OF IMPAIRMENTS, DISABILITIES AND HANDICAPS (ICIDH)   First published in 1980 the ICIDH made clear the distinctions between: impairment, the structural or functional abnormality caused by injury or disease; disability, the limitation the individual faces in the conduct of daily life; and handicap, the social disadvantage that impaired and disabled individuals experience. Critics argued that while such a model was an improvement on the medical model, it still left the source of the problem in and with the individual rather than the social environment that created the disability and handicap. Reflecting this, the title of the World Health Organization's 1997 publication on this topic is *International Classification of Impairments, Activities and Participation* (**disability**; **(dis)abilism**; **handicap**).

INTERNATIONAL CLINICAL EPIDEMIOLOGY NETWORK (INCLEN) An international initiative to develop public health workforces – trained in interdisciplinary contexts – in underdeveloped countries, and to provide scientific and financial support (White, K. L. (1991) *Healing the Schism: Epidemiology, Medicine and the Public's Health*. New York: Springer).

INTERNET-INFORMED PATIENT Considerable speculation, but little empirical research, fuels discussions on the impact of the internet on healthcare. It may be a source of empowerment, increasing the patient's sense of control over their disease, and allowing them to challenge **medical dominance**. It has been suggested that by empowering patients the internet has contributed to a loss of control of medical information by the medical profession, and contributes to their **deprofessionalization** and **proletarianization** (Hardey, M. (2001) 'E-health: the internet and the transformation of patients into consumers and producers of health knowledge', *Information, Communication and Society*, 4 (3): 388–405) (**information and communication technologies; support groups, online**).

INTERVIEWS A standard form of research in the social sciences, asking people questions and listening to their answers. Interviews range from the structured, to the semi-structured, to the unstructured. This is also a continuum, moving from the structured in which the interviewer controls the entire interaction,

through to the unstructured which takes more the form of a conversation. This continuum corresponds to a quantitative style of interview (the administration of a survey) at one end through to a qualitative free-wheeling interaction at the other. Interviews can provide factual information, information on what people do or do not do, and ask about beliefs, aspirations experiences, and feelings. Unstructured interviews can provide extremely rich and complex information. Practical problems include getting accurate and truthful responses to closed questions (e.g. How often? How many?) or alternatively full and sincere answers to open ended questions (How do you feel about x?) (Silverman, D. (1993) *Interpreting Qualitative Data: Methods for Analysing Talk, Text and Interaction*. London: Sage) (**focus groups; questionnaires**).

INVERSE CARE LAW Those most in need of healthcare can least afford it, while those with least need can most afford it. Private, **fee-for-service** medical practitioners are also likely to establish themselves where people can most afford them, hence producing regional imbalances where those most in need cannot access services either. (Tudor-Hart, J. (1971) 'The inverse care law', *The Lancet*, 1: 405–12) (**Jarvis' law**).

IN VITRO FERTILIZATION (IVF) The fertilization of the woman's egg outside her body. The eggs are mixed with male sperm in a glass dish (in popular culture, a test-tube) and when fertilized, implanted in the woman's womb (**assisted reproductive technologies; childbirth; donor insemination; new reproductive technologies**).

IQ CONTROVERSY   Francis Galton (1822–1911), a founder of British psychology, first proposed the idea of an individual, definable and heritable characteristic called 'mental ability'. He was certain that this intelligence was normally distributed, that it was inherited, and that it could be bred, by increasing the fertility of the able and preventing the unfit from breeding, that is, through eugenics. He believed that the class structure of Britain reflected natural abilities with the professional and middle classes at the top, and the unfit, the poor and the working class at the bottom. If the top bred more, and the bottom less, then society would be improved. Thus the origins of eugenics lie in British psychology rather than Hitler's Germany. Cyril Burt (1883–1971), following R. Fisher (1890–1962), argued that intelligence was virtually entirely hereditable and that environmental influences played little or no part in its development. His work was used to fix in place the British class structure through the administration of the 11-plus exam which sorted the population irredeemably into their class position. The fact that much of his research has been found to be fraudulent has had little impact on the belief in 'IQs'. In America, in the context of a backlash against the civil rights movement of the 1960s and finding affinities with **behaviourism** Arthur Jensen (1923–) and Hans Eysenk (1916–97) proposed deterministic accounts of the genetic contribution to intelligence as measured on tests of the Intelligence Quotient. They argued that the distribution of IQ as measured by IQ tests – on which American Negroes and working class people do poorly – reflected real differences among racial and class groups in society and that remedial intervention in schooling would have no impact on these individuals. Indeed, they argued that the introduction of 'head start' programmes in schools would falsely raise the expectations of Blacks and working class students thereby fostering resentment. The most recent contribution to this debate is the work of R. Hernstein and C. Murray (1994) in their book *The Bell Curve: Intelligence and Class Structure in American Life* (New York: Free Press). They claim that IQ tests are not biased against ethnic minorities and that measured intelligence differences are objective, scientific and heritable. The racial and class structure of American society is therefore grounded in biology, natural and unchangeable. Environmentalists reject this biological determinism, seeing individual characteristics as minimally a mix of heredity and environment, with environmental factors playing the larger part, and have pointed to the threat of a resurgence of eugenics in the context of the 'new genetics' (**behaviourism; Binet; eugenics; genetic determinism; heredity; intelligence tests; nature/nurture debate; new genetics; race**).

ISOLATION   The combination of social exclusion, a lack of **social support** and exposure to **stress** have been identified by the World Health Organization as key causes of disease and early mortality. These characteristics of individuals' social lives are, in turn, reflections of and shape their participation in the labour market. Thus issues of socio-economic status, social integration and health are all deeply intertwined, and for any given individual will form an interconnected mosaic that will determine how healthy they are in life, and when they will die. (Wilkinson, R. and Marmot, M. (1998) (eds), *Social Determinants of Health – The Solid Facts*. Geneva: World Health Organization) (**health determinants**; **inequalities in health**; **inequality**).

J

JARVIS' LAW   Named after the author of the 1852 paper 'On the supposed increase in insanity' (*American Journal of Insanity*, 8: 331–61). Jarvis found that the amount of mental illness diagnosed in a community is a consequence of the proximity to mental health facilities and does not reflect 'real' levels of mental illness. The nearer you live to an asylum the more likely you are to be diagnosed as mad. Rates of surgical procedures such as tonsillectomies and hysterectomies have also been shown to be the product of the number of specialists in the area (Sohler, K. and Thompson, J. (1970) 'Jarvis' law and the planning of mental health services', *Public Health Report*, 85: 503–10) (**fee-for-service; inverse care law; supplier induced demand**).

JOB STRAIN   The impact of one's job can be good or bad for one's health. In the 'demand-support-control model' researchers have shown that jobs with high demands and low decision-making produce emotional and physical ill-health. Furthermore, with low social support at work individuals are at increased risk of adopting poor **lifestyle choices** such as drinking and smoking. Job strain has been shown to be responsible for 10 per cent of heart attacks in the work place (Theorell, T. and Karasek, R. (1996) 'Current issues relating to psychosocial job-strain and cardiovascular disease research', *Journal of Occupational Health Psychology*, 1: 9–26) (**alienation; occupation and health; psychosocial risks**).

JOURNALLING   The keeping of a research diary by a field worker documenting their thought processes and reactions while conducting a study.

K

KANT, IMMANUEL (1724–1804) Important in the philosophy of social science, laying the foundation of non-positivist approaches to research. Kant argued against the empiricists that while knowledge is based on the senses, it is not given by them. Rather the knowing subject imposes meaning on the data. This argument underlies **social constructionism** and Weber's **verstehen** methodology. The alternative position in sociology is represented by **Émile Durkheim** who in his analysis of **suicide** argued that social facts are objective, external and constraining and impose themselves on the individual (**empiricism**; **positivism**).

KARNOFSKY'S PERFORMANCE STATUS SCALE An important early (1948) attempt to measure the impact on patients of palliative care in cancer. It recognized that overall functioning is not defined only by the pathology of the disease but also by psychological and social factors and that these have to be taken into account when assessing treatment and its likely outcomes (**health status assessment**; **sickness impact profile**).

KINSEY, ALFRED (1894–1956) A professor of zoology at Indiana University who in 1947 founded the Institute for Sex Research. In 1948 the Institute published *Sexual Behaviour in the Human Male* (Philadelphia: W. B. Saunders) and in 1953 *Sexual Behaviour in the Human Female* (Philadelphia: W. B. Saunders). Kinsey claimed to show that people were far more sexually active than public discourse of the time allowed, and that the overhangs of Victorian culture repressed the sex drive. His work, not surprisingly, given some of its claims in a homophobic culture, for example, that 37 per cent of all men have had homosexual sex to the point of orgasm, aroused controversy (**Hite Report**; **Masters and Johnson**).

KINSHIP A network of individuals related by blood or marriage. Of interest for sociologists examining the impact of kinship on people's **help seeking behaviour**. The evidence is mixed but large kinship networks appear to inhibit health seeking behaviour (**lay referral system**; **social networks analysis**).

KUHN, THOMAS (1922–) Author of *The Structure of Scientific Revolutions* (1962, Chicago: University of Chicago Press) and historian of science. Kuhn argued that each scientific period (for example, the Copernican, the Newtonian or the Einsteinian) adhered to a **paradigm** that set it puzzles to solve. Paradigms were not superseded by 'better' paradigms, rather the community of scientists lost interest in them when confronted with unsolvable puzzles or when too many inexplicable results were produced. Kuhn's **conventionalism** was very influential in the shaping of the social studies of science in England and the USA, though was not as radical as it seems to those working in the European tradition of the history and philosophy of science (**Bachelard; Canguihelm; Fleck; Popper; Whig histories of medicine**).

L

LABELLING THEORY Originally developed in the sociology of deviance, labelling theorists pointed to the way in which deviance was the product not of an act itself, but of the reactions of others to it. The 'primary deviance' was less important than the 'secondary deviance' of the individual's response to being labelled, for example, as mentally ill. In the sociology of health the theory has been widely used to explore how the 'master status' of being diseased, for example, as someone who has cancer, overwhelms all other aspects of the person's identity. Sociologists of mental illness have used labelling theory to highlight the contextual nature of what it is, and who it is, that gets labelled as mentally ill (Scheff, T. (1975) *Labeling Madness*. Englewood Cliffs, NJ: Prentice-Hall) (**antipsychiatry; learning disabilities; liminality; spoilt identity; stigma**).

LABORATORY MEDICINE The third stage in modern medicine, following bedside and hospital medicine in which the treatment of disease and the experience of it are reduced to the print-out of normal ranges returned after testing at the laboratory. In this stage both the doctor's charismatic power as a healer, and the patient's subjective experience of the condition are subjected to a scientific rationalization and rendered irrelevant (**bedside medicine; disease; normal**).

LAING, RONALD (1927–89) Author of *The Divided Self* (1980), *The Politics of Experience* (1968) and with Aaron Esterson of *Sanity, Madness and the Family* (1965, New York: Basic Books), a Scottish psychiatrist and leader of the **antipsychiatry** movement. Laing's argument was that to diagnose someone as mad was a form of **social control**, bringing under the jurisdiction of psychiatry individuals who did not conform to patterns of normal behaviour. Furthermore the actions of these individuals could be shown, not to be madness, but reasonable responses to intolerable situations, particularly in the context of family relationships.

LALONDE REPORT, CANADA The 1974 report by Marc Lalonde, the Canadian Minister of Health and Welfare, *A New Perspective on the Health of Canadians*, arguing that morbidity and mortality from chronic disease was preventable and calling for a re-orientation in health policy from bio-medicine to public health.

However public health was conceptualized mainly as targeting individuals' **lifestyle choices (new public health; Ottawa Charter).**

LATENCY MODEL   The impact over time of early markers of health and illness such as birth weight, mother's lifestyle behaviour or genetic factors. Sociologists agree that intrauterine and early life experiences are critical in shaping people's later health, but that these variables do not exist independently of social factors **(Barker hypothesis; life course analysis; Midtown Manhattan Study).**

LAY CULTURE   The ways in which individuals construct meanings about illness in contrast to the way in which the medical profession constructs diseases. Lay culture organizes the way in which individuals perceive their symptoms, and whether or not they will approach a medical professional (Zola, I. (1973) 'Pathways to the doctor: from person to patient', *Social Sciences and Medicine*, 7 (9): 677–89) **(clinical iceberg; help-seeking behaviour; lay referral system; pluralist approaches).**

LAY KNOWLEDGE   The perspective on an illness or disease that an individual has, often in contrast to the explanation provided by the medical model **(lay culture; lay participation; lay referral system).**

LAY PARTICIPATION   The activities of non-medical groups in the healthcare system. These may be self-help groups based around the experience of a disease, or **consumer** groups who see participation in the health sector as part of their democratic right (Popay, J. and Williams, G. (1996) 'Public health research and lay knowledge', *Social Science and Medicine*, 42: 759–68) **(disease identity dependency; lay culture; lay referral system).**

LAY REFERRAL SYSTEM   The experience of biological symptoms does not automatically trigger a visit to the doctor and up to one-third of the population will ignore them, self-medicate or consult friends and family about the meaning of the experience. This consultation with friends and family about the meaning of symptoms is called the lay referral system. It highlights the interpretive aspect of illness as individuals draw on their own and others' understanding to provide an account of the situation **(lay knowledge).** Individuals with large friendship networks consult the doctor more frequently than those with large family networks (Rogers, A., Hassell. K., and Nicolaas, G. (1999) *Demanding Patients? Analysing the Use of Primary Care.* Buckingham: Open University Press) **(clinical iceberg; illness behaviour; lay culture; self-help groups; sick role; symptom iceberg).**

LEARNED HELPLESSNESS   A concept in psychology, the response of an individual to circumstances, which are unpleasant, and for which there is no alternative but to adjust to them. For example, the impact of the work environment in which individuals have no control over the content or pace of their work (whether blue collar or white collar) has been demonstrated to be a significant predictor of a range of diseases, including cardiovascular disease. Thus learned helplessness is not only about how a person acts, but also about how their body reacts. In sociological studies learned helplessness is not a personality characteristic but a socially induced response to the environment (Karasek, R. and Theorell, T. (1990) *Healthy Work: Stress, Productivity and the Reconstruction of Working Life.* New York: Basic Books) (**alienation; employment; psychoneuroimmunology/ psychoneuroendocrinology**).

LEARNING DISABILITIES A range of conditions – dyslexia, attention deficit/ hyperactivity disorder, specific learning disorder – which have developed through the late twentieth century to explain children's inability to do well at school. Sociologists see them as the outcome of a number of specific social changes. With the development of the middle class, education became a prerequisite for non-manual jobs and second the success of one's children at school became a status symbol – an indication of one's worth as a parent. This double movement made education a site for dispute when the individual failed. Educational reformers argued that otherwise good students failed because of the 'factory' style system of educational production, with forced progress through grades based on age. Alternatively, it was argued that it was not the fault of any particular individual or of large classes, but of the biology of the individual student. Thus

the construction of learning disabilities as a class of 'diseases' meets a good deal of need in not blaming parents, the child or the educational system. Doctors may treat these 'diseases' and they are usually treated biochemically, but their origins are in the social structure and not in the biological individual (Erchak, G. and Rosenfeld, R. (1989) 'Learning disabilities, dyslexia, and the medicalization of the classroom', in J. Best (ed.), *Images of Issues: Contemporary Social Problem.* New York: Aldine) (**attention deficit disorders; autism spectrum disorders; behavioural disorders; labelling theory**).

LEEDS DECLARATION The proposal, growing out of a 1993 conference of epidemiologists, held at Leeds University, to reintegrate **epidemiology** with public health, and to move epidemiology away from **risk factor** analysis. The Leeds Declaration argued that the focus of epidemiology should be 'upstream', on the social and political factors that produce disease, rather than on the diseased individual, whose condition is the outcome of social arrangements. The declaration also pointed out that experimental models based on the natural sciences are not adequate to the task of understanding the patterning of disease and that qualitative studies of the individual's experience of their condition, and of their **life chances** are needed (Nuffield Institute for Health (1993) *Directions for Health: New Approaches to Population Health Research and Practice. The Leeds Declaration.* Leeds: University of Leeds) (**health determinants**).

LEGIONNAIRES' DISEASE   Infection with the micro-organism, legionellae. The first outbreak was in 1976 at a meeting of the American Legion in Philadelphia, though retrospective cases going back to 1947 have now been identified. An illustration of **building related illness**, the micro-organism breeds in cooling towers and evaporative condensers, and is inhaled as water mist by the individual. Treatment is now through antibiotics, though at the initial epidemic thirty-four out of 221 infected individuals died (**sick building syndrome**).

LIBERAL FEMINISM   Liberalism developed in the eighteenth century as a political philosophy emphasizing the rights and freedoms of the individual. While at first applied only to men, the argument that it should be extended to women was developed by **Mary Wollstonecraft** and John Stuart Mill in the *The Subjection of Women* (1869). One of the basic tenets of liberalism is that the economic fate of every individual should be determined through their own efforts, and by their own merits, rather than be based on heredity. This argument underpins Equal Opportunity Commissions, which demand equal opportunities for women in the job market and the right to move to the upper reaches of it. Liberal feminists focus on the clear inequalities in women's participation in medicine, and especially in the specialties (that is those areas of medicine requiring postgraduate qualifications). Where women do get into postgraduate medicine, it is often in the spheres of psychiatry and paediatrics – two areas associated with care and nurturing; women medical graduates do not tend to go on to postgraduate work; they typically end up in part-time GP work, with smaller caseloads; and earn lower salaries than their male counterparts. Liberal feminists do not see problems with organized medicine, do not analyse medicine's location within a class structure, and do not see it as part of a patriarchal society (**Marxist feminism**; **radical feminism**; **socialist feminism**).

LIFE   Defining when life begins, and what constitutes life, like **death**, is central to health social studies and medicine, and inherently about ethics and morality. It is also an issue that cannot be resolved by an appeal to the biological facts. Some religious groups consider life to begin with conception and a 'life' from that point on, while other groups consider it to be the ability of the fetus to sustain itself, and that until it can do so, it is a part of the mother's body and under her control. She can therefore choose to have an **abortion**. At the other end of life the diagnoses of being in a **coma**, or in a **persistent vegetative state** raise problems of the ethics of turning off life support systems and the practice of **euthanasia** (**ethics, medical**; **physician assisted suicide**).

LIFE CHANCES   A concept in Weberian sociology, the likelihood an individual has of having access to socially valued economic and cultural goods. In **Weber's** assessment these are not solely determined by class position as defined by the labour market, but are determined by membership of positively or negatively valued status groups, as, for example, by ethnic group. Life chances are unequally distributed, limiting access to, for example, health services and medical care, and thus shape an individual's experience of life (**class; cultural capital; ethnicity; socio-economic status; stress**).

LIFE COURSE ANALYSIS   The longitudinal study of the effects of life events on an individual's health. The contrast is with 'snapshots' of an individual at a given stage of their lifecycle. The interest in life course analysis has been spurred by research into the long-term impact of early childhood experiences on adult health. It is a qualitative research procedure, which integrates the individual's biography into their social context, though it can take a biological determinist form. This is particularly so in the **latency model** which proposes that genetic, intrauterine or perinatal factors have a long-term impact on health. In the pathways model the emphasis is on cumulative life-time health stressors, starting with the impact of the parents' socio-economic position and the role of inherited social disadvantage (Bifulco, A. and Moran, P. (1998) *Wednesday's Child: Research into Women's Experience of Neglect and Adult Depression*. London: Routledge) (**attachment theory; Barker hypothesis; Midtown Manhattan study**).

LIFECYCLE   The passage of an individual through well defined stages of life, such as infancy, childhood, adolescence and adulthood, with social roles appropriate to each stage. In medicine, these are taken to be biologically specifiable periods with their own characteristic diseases, as in, for example, the diseases of childhood. As historians have argued, it must be remembered that these stages are culturally and historically specific, so that, for example, childhood did not exist in the medieval period (Ariès, P. (1973) *Centuries of Childhood*. London: Jonathan Cape). In health social studies these stages are not prescribed by biological markers but are socially ascribed categories that will be experienced differently depending on class, gender and ethnicity. Anthropologists use a lifecycle approach to show that what the West takes to be biological givens (e.g. **menopause**) are differently experienced (if at all) in other cultures (**age; ageing; ageism; life course analysis**).

LIFE EVENTS AND DIFFICULTIES SCHEDULE   The occurrence of major negative life events, such as the death of a loved one, have long been recognized as having an impact on an individual's health, and particularly their mental health (**stress**). Early attempts to measure the impact of life events were based on self-report questionnaires. However qualitative data – the account of the context of the event, questions about its timing and relationship to the onset of subsequent disorder – could only be elicited through semi-structured interviews, methods laid out in the schedule (Brown, G. and Harris, T. (1978) *The Social Origins of Depression*. London: Tavistock) (**social support**).

LIFE EXPECTANCY The age to which a person, born in a given year, can expect to live. In the history of medicine the concept of life expectancy is a highly contested concept. It was favoured in the nineteenth century, as a measurement by Darwinists, who argued that it demonstrated the survival of the fittest. Sanitary reformers argued that life expectancy was not an individual characteristic, but the product of the individual's social environment, and hotly contested its use. Rather than measure life expectancy at the individual level, they argued that it was life expectancy under different social conditions that should be documented. Contemporary research demonstrates that life expectancy is a product of class position, gender and ethnicity, with males in the upper classes living longer than working class men, women outliving men, and whites outliving other ethnic groups (**indigenous peoples**).

LIFE HISTORY A qualitative research method, based on intensive interviewing, in which the researcher seeks an understanding of life events and process as they appear to the individual (Denzin, N. (1989) *Interpretive Biography*. Thousand Oaks, CA: Sage) (**memory work; narrative accounts of illness**).

LIFE SCAPES A term coined by Edelstein to capture the impact of living in toxic environments, contaminated by waste dumps or poisoned water. Trust is eroded – of other individuals, in the environment – and there is a loss of a sense of self-control over health issues. The fact that these dumps are located in poor and low staus areas contributes to the **burden of disease** these communities carry (Edelstein, M. (1988) *Contaminated Communities: Social and Psychological Impacts of Residential Toxic Exposure*. Boulder, CO: Westview) (**popular epidemiology**).

LIFESTYLE Usually considered to be a individual choice, health social studies demonstrates the ways in which our lifestyles are determined by our **class**, **gender** and **ethnicity**, that is, our position in the social structure. While the **new public health** identifies smoking, alcohol consumption and diet, for example, as freely chosen risk behaviours they are socially patterned (**lifestyle choices; risk factor epidemiology**).

LIFESTYLE CHOICES The argument that individuals can freely choose health or illness enhancing behaviour. However lifestyle choices – particularly the reasons that people drink, smoke or make poor dietary choices – has to do with advertising and access to information rather than individual choice. Importantly, when lifestyle choices are controlled for in studies of the social distribution of diseases they account for less than a third of the differences in the rates of disease (**Whitehall Studies**). Extensive studies have shown that it is almost impossible for people to change their lifestyles in the absence of changes to their social environment. In the **Multiple Risk Factor Intervention Trial** conducted in the USA, counsellors and psychologists supported a group of highly motivated men, in the top

10 per cent risk group for coronary heart disease, over a six-year period, to change their eating and smoking behaviour. The trial demonstrated only modest changes to behaviour. Unless the factors that predispose people to adopt unhealthy lifestyles – work stress for example – are addressed individuals are relatively powerless to change their behaviour (Multiple Risk Factor Intervention Trial (1982) 'The multiple risk factor intervention group – risk factor changes and mortality results', *Journal of the American Medical Association*, 248: 1465–76) (**health determinants**).

LIFESTYLE FACTORS   In the media and popular medicine it is asserted that lifestyle factors are the major cause of the experience of sickness and disease, particularly in the lower socio-economic groups. However lifestyle accounts for only one third of the difference in disease rates between those at the top of the social system and those at the bottom. The claim that lifestyle factors play a major role is also contested in the literature. A study of Gerona, Spain, which has very low heart attack rates, found that the 2,024 people in the sample had very high risk factors such as the prevalence of hypertension, the number who smoked, increased high density cholesterol and high lipoprotein and mean cholesterol levels (Masia, R. et al. (1998) 'High prevalence of cardiovascular risk factors in Gerona, Spain', *Journal of Epidemiology and Community Health*, 52: 707–15) (**cardiovascular disease; risk factor epidemiology; Type A behaviour pattern; Whitehall Studies**).

LIFEWORLD   In sociology, a term to describe those areas of human life which escape the dominance of the state and consumer capitalism. Important in the sociology of health as a term used to capture the experience of illness, rather than its construction as a disease, by medicine (**Husserl; pragmatism**).

LIMINALITY   The lesser experience of social life following the diagnosis of a chronic illness such as cancer or AIDS (**stigma**). In the first stage of liminality there is a loss of a sense of control, and uncertainty. In the second stage the person takes steps to construct a story of their illness, a **narrative** that will make sense of their experience and allow them to communicate it to others. Their attempt to give it meaning to others also gives it meaning for them. This liminal state of constructing and communicating meaning in the face of the inexplicable stays with these people for the rest of their lives (Little, M. et al. (1998) 'Liminality – a major category of the experience of cancer illness', *Social Science and Medicine*, 47: 1485–94) (**disease identity, dependency; stigma; theodicy**).

LOCUS OF CONTROL   A social psychological concept referring to the way in which an individual explains what happens to them. Those with a high internal locus of control see their actions as their own responsibility, with a sense of control over their destiny. Those with an external sense of the locus of control see their lives as the product of external factors that they are helpless to deal with. A strong sense of internal locus of control corresponds to access to information, control over time, and resources to deal with the situation. It is therefore a sociological rather than a psychological variable (**accounts of illness**).

LONDON EPIDEMIOLOGICAL SOCIETY Founded in 1850, the society drew together the intense statistical research activities of the mid-nineteenth century around health and illness patterns, and laid the foundation for **epidemiology**. The society flourished, with *The Journal of Public Health*, founded in 1855, publishing its findings. However with the development of **bacteriology** epidemiology waned and the journal ceased publication in 1859 (**Farr; Graunt; Snow; social history of medicine; social medicine**).

LONG TERM CARE (LTC) The provision of ongoing medical, physical and emotional support to the chronically ill, the disabled and the elderly, usually by women in the home. In turn, because they live longer, women are left unsupported in their own needs for long-term care (**ageing; care in the community; hospital at home**).

LOGOCENTRISM The privileging of rational, logical argument as the only source of reliable knowledge. Used in critiques of medical knowledge to highlight the way in which medical knowledge disallows the patient's story of their illness.

M

MCDONALDIZATION/MCDOCTOR A term coined by George Ritzer in 1983 to describe the increasing bureaucratization of all aspects of social life, from the way we order and consume food, through to the structuring of our leisure activities in theme parks. In medicine, with the increasing role of investors in the hospital and general practice markets, and the rise of insurance companies as third party payers, the argument is that we are witnessing a **deprofessionalization** of medicine as it becomes increasingly rule-following and less based on clinical skills. The rise of the 'one stop fits all', 24 hour walk in clinic, has resulted in a loss of professional autonomy as doctors have to meet turnover targets, fulfil set referral levels, and work to the clock in the same way as employees at McDonalds (Ritzer, G. (1988) 'The McDonaldization of society', *Journal of American Culture*, 6: 100–7) (**corporatization; managerialism; medical dominance; proletarianization; substantive rationality**).

MCKEOWN, THOMAS (1911–88) Between 1950 and 1988 Professor of Social Medicine at the University of Birmingham Medical School. A historical epidemiologist, he demonstrated that every major disease of the nineteenth century was brought under control, not through scientific medicine – the **germ theory** of disease – but through sanitary reform of the city, control of the production of foodstuffs, and control of the impact of industrialization on the environment. He concluded that professionalized medicine contributed less than 1 per cent to the decline in mortality from infectious disease (McKeown, T. (1979) *The Role of Medicine*. Princeton: Princeton University Press) (**social medicine; Whig histories of medicine**).

MCMASTER HEALTH INDEX QUESTIONNAIRE A self-administered, generic (that is, not disease specific) measurement instrument which provides non-clinical ratings of health status with quality of life measures based on physical, social and emotional functioning (**health status assessment**).

MADNESS (**antipsychiatry; asylums; Bedlam; mental illness**).

MADNESS AND CIVILIZATION Foucault's account of the treatment of the insane in the West. The book is both a sociological account of the social functions of psychiatry and a historical account of the emergence of insanity as a category in the West. Sociologically *Madness and Civilization* was published in English at the height of the antipsychiatry movement, which quickly adopted it. In particular the argument is that the reform of **Bedlam** under the influence of **Pinel** was not a breakthrough in the humane treatment of the mentally ill that progressive historians presented it as. Rather it was the refinement of the incarceration of the mentally ill, sequestering them in asylums. *Madness and Civilization* was also influential in the **labelling theory** tradition, that mental illnesses were not real diseases, but the product of psychiatric classificatory systems, existing to police the population through **medicalization** of deviant behaviour. For Foucault, the apparently naturally occurring and objective features of social life – sanity in this instance – are cultural and historical products. In *Madness and Civilization* he documents historically the transformations in the way the mad have been conceptualized. In the medieval period madness was not a distinct feature of social life. In the renaissance it starts to become a characteristic of man, and in the classical age (1650–1800) with the great confinement, becomes antithetical to reason (Foucault, M. (1965) *Madness and Civilization*. New York: Random House).

MAGIC BULLET The term used to describe drugs that when administered attack only the diseased part of the body and have no impact on the rest of it. Coined by Paul Ehrlich (1854–1915), the

founder of chemotherapy, the term came into wide popular usage to describe the triumphs of modern medicine associated with the discovery of sulphonamides and penicillin. However, their impact on infectious diseases was far less than the impact of improved living conditions, food and employment (**antibiotics; McKeown; social medicine; technical fix**).

MAINSTREAMING On the one hand a development of the social right of people with **disabilities** to be treated as 'normal' and integrated into the community. On the other a policy to reduce costs to the state of the provision of health and welfare services through reducing specialist services (Mandiberg, J. (1999) 'The sword of reform has two sharp edges', *New Directions for Mental Health Services*, 83: 31–44) (**care in the community; deinstitutionalization; market; neoliberalism**).

MAGNETIC RESONANCE IMAGE (MRI) (**biotechnology; medical technology**).

MALE STOICISM The gendered expectation that men will deny, repress and control their emotions. This aspect of **hegemonic masculinity** means that men's healthcare needs are not expressed and when expressed lead to a later diagnosis of conditions with a reduced likelihood of successful treatment. Male stoicism may either reflect the necessity for men to maintain their dominant position or be a damaging consequence of hegemonic masculinity on them (Courtenay, W. (2000) 'Constructions of masculinity and their influence on men's well-being: a theory of gender and health', *Social Science and Medicine*, 50: 1385–401) (**gender**; **gendered health**; **hegemonic masculinity**; **men's health**; **support groups, online**).

MALNUTRITION   Lack of food of a sufficient quality to maintain a healthy life. A major problem in the third world, and amongst the bottom socio-economic groups in Western society. The cause is poverty with 15 per cent of the world's population affected by the condition. Malnutrition is a consequence of protein deficient diets, Vitamin A, iodine and iron deficiencies. These deficits mean that, when not dying of starvation, people in the third world suffer from stunted development, are more susceptible to infectious diseases, with more fatal outcomes than in the West, and have a badly impaired quality of life (McIntosh, A. (1995) 'World hunger as a social problem', in D. Maurer and J. Sobal (eds), *Eating Agendas: Food and Nutrition as Social Problems*. New York: Aldine de Gruyter) (**diet**; **nutrition**).

MALPRACTICE   The delivery of wrongful or below standard medical care resulting in harm, disability or death to the patient. Malpractice suits – taking the doctor to court – have been rising steadily, partly because patients are better educated, and partly because the courts now allow expert testimony from others than just doctors about the situation. The increase in cases, and the judgments of the court in favour of the patient has meant increasing medical insurance premiums and the rise of the practice of **defensive medicine (iatrogenic/iatrogenesis)**.

MALTHUS, THOMAS (1766–1834)   Author of *An Essay on the Principle of Population* published in 1798 in which he argued that any efforts to ameliorate the living conditions of the working class would only enable them to breed more, thereby returning them to poverty. Equally conservatively he argued that the human species' urge to breed outruns its ability to produce food. The only solution, apart from war, pestilence and famine, was moral restraint – celibacy and delayed sexual gratification – on the part of the working class until they had saved enough to breed. Malthus' law stated that the population would increase geometrically, while the food supply would only increase arithmetically (**masturbatory insanity**; **social Darwinism**).

MAMMOGRAPHY SCREENING PROGRAMME Public health initiative for women to present for examination of their breasts to enhance the early detection of breast cancer. **Liberal feminists** welcome the initiative as developing women focused health services, and empowering women by making them aware of their bodies. **Foucauldian-feminists** point to the very mixed scientific evidence about the usefulness of breast cancer screening and argue that what appears to be a discourse of empowerment leads women into a double bind: they are frail and potentially always sick, yet they are autonomous and active agents, responsible for their own bodies. Yet their activism actually leads them into further subjugation. From this perspective screening programmes have subverted feminism incorporating some of its central points – autonomy, self-responsibility and control of the body – into a medicalized, patriarchal gaze (Kuni, C. (1993) 'Mammography in the 1990s: a plea for objective doctors and informed patients', *American Journal of Preventive Medicine*, 9: 185–9) (**breast cancer; surveillance medicine**).

MANAGED CARE   A form of control over the prescribing and referral activities of doctors. Healthcare insurers limit what can be prescribed, what tests can be ordered and what treatments can be administered to keep down costs. These attempts by third party payers to limit medical autonomy present a significant challenge to **medical dominance** (**Corporatization; preferred provider organization; proletarianization**).

MANAGERIALISM   In the healthcare system the rise of an administrative group, replacing older medical professional groups in hospitals and government health agencies. Managerialism is based on the assumption that services can be streamlined, that doctors and nurses can be made more efficient, and that patients can be discharged more quickly from hospitals, with the criteria of success being profitability (**casemix; clinical pathways; diagnostic related groups; neoliberalism; new public management; pressure groups**).

MANIC DEPRESSION   The diagnosis of a condition, also called bipolar illness, in which the persons swings between elation and despair. As with the diagnosis of major depression and schizophrenia, women are over-represented and hospitalized more than men for mania (Hendrick, V., Altshuler, L. and Gitlin, M. (2000) 'Gender and bipolar illness', *Journal of Clinical Psychiatry*, 61: 393–96) (**mental illness**).

MARITAL STATUS   Marital status is closely linked to health, with married people being healthiest, then the never married and the widowed, and then with the poorest health, the divorced. The supposition is that the married are more socially integrated, have stronger social networks and higher self-esteem. Early research suggested that while marriage was good for men's mental health, it was bad for women's. Current research still points to the 'double shift' of housework and paid work that women experience but suggests also that overall married women experience higher self-esteem and better standards of health (Arber, S. (1991) 'Class, paid employment and family roles: making sense of structural disadvantage, gender and health status', *Social Science and Medicine*, 32: 425–36) (**gender; social networks analysis; social support**).

MARKET   In Western societies the sector of social life in which goods and commodities are exchanged for profit. Certain social goods – health – were protected from the market under the **welfare state**. This is because the health sector has characteristics that mean that it forms an imperfect market. These are: the information asymmetry between the doctor and the patient, where the patient does not know what the best treatment for their condition is. Unlike other markets we are not in a position to shop around, or evaluate what we are buying. The second is price inelasticity, in that we can never pay too much for our health. Unlike other markets, prices do not act as a signal of what people are prepared to pay, but rather what they have to pay. We will pay what is demanded which leads into the third characteristic. The medical market is under provider control – the doctor tells us which of the services provided by the doctor we need and must purchase. The fourth characteristic is the problem of moral hazard, that is individuals can take steps to avoid the consequences of their actions. The classic case is taking out insurance against a known risk, which then reduces the tendency to avoid the risk, knowing that we will have the resources to protect ourselves from the consequences of our actions. With the rise of neoliberalism, conservative governments have moved to implement policies that make health a commodity just like any other on the market. The evidence is that introducing market based delivery systems reduces access, results in poorer services, and makes it even more difficult for the poor to engage with health services (White, K. and Collyer, F. (1998) 'Health care markets in Australia: ownership of the private hospital sector', *International Journal of Health Services*, 28 (3): 487–510) (**citizenship**;

commodification; **corporatization**; **gift relationship**; **medical-industrial complex**; **neoliberalism**; **new public management**; **perverse incentives**).

MARX, KARL (1818–82) Political activist and social theorist, Marx provided an analysis of modern industrial societies as fundamentally class based societies. The bourgeoisie, the owners of the means of production, exploited the proletariat, who having nothing else to sell in market society, sold their labour power. This meant that, having sold that which made them human, that is, their ability to create and modify nature, the experience of life under capitalism was one of **alienation**. Marx argued that because of the contradiction between the form of property relationships (private property) and the productive capacity of industrialized societies capitalism would ultimately break down. Most twentieth-century social theory has been in one way or another a response to Marx's arguments. His impact, as developed in health social studies, has been immense in providing an explanation of how diseases are socially produced and distributed in capitalist societies (**capitalism**; **class analysis**; **commodification**; **Engels**; **health determinants**; **ideology**; **Marxist approaches**; **materialism**; **neo-Marxism**; **social gradient of disease**).

MARXIST APPROACHES In a Marxist approach the function of medicine is the maintenance of the capitalist social system.

The medical profession controls labour through its control of the sick certificate, while the theories of disease it develops and enforces, individualizes the causes of disease and ignores social factors thus performing an ideological function in stabilizing the status quo. Medical knowledge and technology do not have a separate existence from capitalist social relations, rather they are the product of them. The biologism (the belief that social relations can be understood as natural phenomena), the scienticism (the belief that the understanding of social relations should be based on the methods of the natural sciences), the mechanistic image of the body (that the mind is separate from the body, and the body constructed of distinct but interdependent parts) and the positivistic concept of disease (that diseases have singular causes that attack independent parts of the body and are cured by drugs and technology) are not capitalist overlays on medical knowledge, but constitute medical knowledge under the capitalist mode of production (Navarro, V. (1980) 'Work, ideology and medicine', *International Journal of Health Services*, 10: 523–50) (**alienation; capitalism; class analysis; commodification; Engels; health determinants; ideology; Marx; Marxist feminism; materialism; neo-Marxism; social gradient of disease**).

MARXIST FEMINISM   The original formulation (Zaretsky, E. (1976) *Capitalism, The Family and Personal Life*. London: Pluto Press) of Marxist feminism draws on Engels' argument in *The Origins of the Family, Private Property and the State* (Engels, F. 1984 [1884], Moscow: Progress Publishers).

The original division of labour is the family based on biology, and under capitalism takes the form of monogamous marriage in which the husband stands in relation to the wife as the bourgeoisie is to the proletariat. A capitalist society requires this form of private ownership of the wives' fertility, since the owners of capital need to ensure that they are passing their property onto their legitimate offspring. For Marxist feminists capitalism and patriarchy are enmeshed and the freedom of both the workers and of women require the overthrow of capitalism (**feminism; liberal feminism; radical feminism; socialist feminism**).

MASTERS AND JOHNSON   William Masters (1915–2001) and Virginia Johnson (1925–) along with **Kinsey** were among the first to attempt the objective study of human sexual relations. In 1964 they opened the Masters and Johnson Institute and in 1966 published *The Human Sexual Response* (New York: Lippincott Williams and Wilkins). They explored the physiology of sex in a laboratory setting, observing people masturbating and having intercourse. They postulated a four-stage model of sexual response – excitement, plateau, orgasm and resolution. Their narrowly biological account of sexuality leaves out the meanings of sex for the individuals involved (**Hite report**).

MASTURBATORY INSANITY   A disease of men in the eighteenth and nineteenth centuries. Its existence is explained by social historians in terms of the need to control populations, and to produce individuals with internalized self-control. **Thomas Malthus** argued that human beings were driven by the urge to eat and to reproduce, and further, that reproduction would always outrun the production of food. Thus there was a perceived need to control people's desires, and to internalize moral actions such as the delay of gratification and self-denial. It was in this political context that medical thought developed with a focus on reproduction and sexuality. The concern with sexual promiscuity had a parallel in economic theory: one should save one's money and not be a spendthrift. These two social concerns were brought together in the idea that one should save one's sexual abilities in the same way that one should save money. Masturbatory insanity provides a good example of the way in which medical thought is structured and sustained by the social, political and economic concerns of the social groups producing it, and of the social control function of the medical profession (Englehardt, H. (1981) 'The Disease of masturbation: values and the concept of disease', in A. Caplan, H. Englehardt and J. McCartney (eds), *Concepts of Health and Disease*. Reading, MA: Addison-Wesley) (**agoraphobia**; **anorexia nervosa**; **drapetomania**; **hysteria**).

MATERIALISM   In health social studies, explanations of social life which argue that the material organization of society, and especially of the economy, determine not only what people think, but also why they get the diseases they do, and die of the conditions that kill them. In medicine, with the **mind–body dualism**, the theory of the body as a set of inter-related systems, independently of the patient's consciousness, leading to the treatment of disease in a **mechanistic** fashion (**diet**; **employment**; **health determinants**; **housing and health**; **idealism**; **Marxist approaches**; **occupation**).

MATERIALIST ANALYSES   Explanations of disease that emphasize the social, political and economic factors beyond the control of the individuals that adversely affect their health. These factors range from the large-scale physical organization of the urban space, the ways in which the hazards and pollutants of industrial and dockside areas are concentrated, to lead poisoning along industrial highways, to lack of access to transport (**diet**; **housing and health**; **occupation**; **pollution**; **structural explanations**).

MATERNAL MORTALITY   Deaths of women associated with childbearing and birth. It is the number of mothers' deaths due to complications of birth, divided by the number of births. Historically, the decline in maternal mortality in the West, was a product of the introduction of sanitary reform to the hospital, and in particular, was reduced dramatically when surgeons had to wash their hands between operations. In the contemporary world the main cause of maternal death, about 50 per cent, is caused by unsafe abortion (Tonks, A. (1994) 'Pregnancy's toll in the developing world', *British Medical Journal*, 108: 353–54) (**abortion**).

MAUSS, MARCELL (1872–1950) Anthropologist, sociologist and Émile Durkheim's nephew. For sociologists of health his most important work was in a brief essay on the **body** published in 1935. Mauss was concerned to demonstrate that the use of the body can take a wide variety of forms and is not biologically dictated. He argued that our cultural and historical location (he did not deal with class) will determine how we carry out such various tasks as running, marching, swimming and walking, and even how we learn to position our limbs. For Mauss the experience and use of the body are the product of socialization, a process he called the development of 'techniques of the body'. Within any given society these techniques would reflect not only fashion, but more importantly educational levels and would be used to mark out levels of prestige. The body then is not only socially produced, but it mirrors and reproduces the hierarchies of the social structure by which it is produced. Furthermore, control of the body is central to a more generalized **social control** that allows for the stable reproduction of social relationships. The control of the body is central to the maintenance of social order. As Mauss put it: being educated and socialized into specific ways of deportment – Mauss called it habitus – works as a 'retarding mechanism, a mechanism inhibiting disorderly movements' thereby contributing to the stability of social life (Mauss, M. (1973 [1935]) 'Techniques of the body', *Economy and Society*, 2: 71–88) (**Bourdieu; gift relationship**).

MEAD, GEORGE HERBERT (1863–1931) Author of *Mind, Self and Society from the Standpoint of a Social Behaviourist* (1934) proposing a philosophical and sociological theory of the self. Mead argued that the self is the outcome of the human ability to see ourselves as others see us. It is thus a dynamic product of social interaction, with social reality understood as a reflexive, symbolic sphere, rather than as pre-given, fixed and stable. Mead's approach was influential in the development of **symbolic interactionism**, which has been an influential school of **microsociological** studies in the health area (**Chicago School of Sociology; personality; pragmatism**).

MECHANISTIC In the history of medicine, in the eighteenth century, the claim made that for medicine to develop it had to conceptualize the body as an object, with no reference to metaphysical issues, such as its relationship to God. Vitalists, by contrast, emphasized the body as part of the wider purpose of things, arguing that humans were not just part of nature, but imbued with a spirit or force. In contemporary usage mechanistic is used pejoratively to label professional medicine for treating the individual as an object, for conceptualizing disease as distinct from the self, and for defining treatment in terms of biochemicals and surgical procedures (**Cartesian; holism; mind–body dualism; reductionism; vitalism**).

MEDIBANK Australia's national public health system, introduced in 1974 (following vehement opposition from medical practitioners) by a reforming Labor government, it allowed for the private provision of medical services which are publicly funded. It was dismantled by the incoming Conservative government, and following the election of another Labor government, replaced with Medicare in 1983. The intention was that doctors would not charge over a common fee, which meant that patients would still have to pay about 15 per cent of their fees, and that doctors would bulk-bill the government, rather than leaving the patient out of pocket, while waiting for reimbursement from the government. Like the USA's Medicare, the system is provider driven, open to over-servicing, and outright fraud (**Australian Medical Association; fee-for-service; perverse incentives**).

MEDICAID   A US public health insurance programme, a form of pauper relief, though under 35 per cent of those Americans living in poverty have access to it (**health insurance; uninsured**).

MEDICARE   A public health insurance programme, introduced in the United States, in 1965, to protect the elderly from the impact of acute healthcare costs. In 1972 it was extended to cover people with chronic conditions. While it covers 37 million Americans, it is very expensive, being based on a **fee-for-service** model, allowing for provider-driven costs and **perverse incentives** (**health insurance; uninsured**).

MEDICAL ANTHROPOLOGY   The study of the beliefs and practices of medicines in other cultures, held up for examination against the taken for granted scientificity of Western **biomedicine**. It is grounded in **sociobiology** and **social Darwinism**. Like the **sociology in medicine** approach it has increasingly been challenged by theoretical developments in anthropology which no longer privilege Western medical beliefs, but place them on a par with other belief systems (Guypta, D. (1988) 'For a sociology/anthropology of illness: towards a delineation of its disciplinary specificities', *International Sociology*, 3 (4): 403–13) (**anthropology of health; medical anthropology, critical; sociology in medicine; sociology of medicine**).

MEDICAL ANTHROPOLOGY, CRITICAL Developing in the 1980s an approach that emphasizes social inequality of resources and power as determinants of health status. It adds a concern with the political and economic aspects of healthcare experiences to anthropology's usual concern for the impact of culture on peoples' actions and understanding of their situation (Baer, H., Singer, M. and Johnsen, J. (1986) (eds), 'Towards a critical medical anthropology', special issue of *Social Science and Medicine*, 23 (2) (**anthropology of health; sociology in medicine; sociology of medicine**).

MEDICAL DISCOURSE   The power of the medical profession to construct areas of life as under their definition and control. The key characteristics of medical discourse are that it locates the problem of disease in the individual's body (rather than the social factors that produce the body) and explains the cause of disease as either in **nature**, or in the individual's freely chosen **lifestyle**, and in either case, outside of social, political and economic relationships (**disease; feminism; ideology; Foucault; Marxist approaches; medical gaze; medicalization; psy-professions**).

MEDICAL DOMINANCE   Elliot Freidson argued that the medical profession dominated the health sector, not because it was the humanitarian, scientific elite that it portrays itself as, but because it was politically well organized. It has a monopoly of practice guaranteed it by the state, enjoys autonomy over its own work, and defines for the wider society the issues that medicine has control over. Specifically medicine subordinates other health practitioners, limits their area of practice, and excludes those that it cannot otherwise control or incorporate. Freidson's work marked a consolidation of the sociology of knowledge into an examination of medicine, medical knowledge and medical practices as political and social accomplishments. The current status of medical dominance is much debated. (Freidson, E. (1970) *Profession of Medicine: A Study of the Sociology of Applied Knowledge.* New York: Dodd and Mead; Freidson, E. (1970) *Professional Dominance.* Chicago: Aldine) (**Apothecaries Act; corporatization; deprofessionalization; Flexner Report; internet-informed patient; McDonaldization/ McDoctor; professionalization; proletarianization; professional trajectory**).

MEDICAL GAZE   A concept in Foucault's analysis of the transformation of medicine in the eighteenth century, when the symptoms observed by the doctor and reports by the patient which had formed the basis of diagnosis, were replaced by the observed body, the disease and the medical interpretation. Foucault located this transformation, not in the knowledge base of medicine, but in the changing political context of the decline of sovereign power and the diffusion of power throughout society. The decentralization of political power required a new form of **disciplinary power**, in which bodies could be monitored and the population categorized. The new pathological medicine secured for the doctor the right to access the patient's body (**anatomo-politics; bedside medicine; biopower; psy-professions**).

MEDICAL GEOGRAPHY   The study of the impact of the natural and social physical environment on health (**housing and health**). While the impact of the environment has been known since Hippocrates and his studies of malaria, the first modern demonstration was in the work of **John Graunt** who showed that living in cities was unhealthier than living in the country. The role of space played an important part in the debates about the causes of mental illness in the 1930s in studies of schizophrenia in Chicago (Macintyre, S., Ellaway, A. and Cummins, S. (2002) 'Place effects on health: how can we conceptualise, operationalise and measure them?', *Social Science and Medicine*, 55: 125–39) (**mental illness**).

MEDICAL-INDUSTRIAL COMPLEX 'A large and growing network of private corporations engaged in the business of supplying healthcare services to patients for profit – services hitherto provided by non-profit institutions or individual practitioners'. At the base of this complex is the corporate ownership of hospitals, and the interlocking ownership and production of technological and diagnostic machinery. This vertical integration of hospital ownership and horizontal integration of technological goods and services has been facilitated by neoliberal governments who assume, against the evidence, that private market initiatives are more efficient than state supplied services (Relman, A. (1980) 'The new medical-industrial complex,' *New England Journal of Medicine*, 303: 963–70) (**corporatization; neoliberalism; privatization**).

MEDICALIZATION The historical process in which medicine replaced religion and law as the dominant institution of **social control**. It also refers to the spread of medical definitions and processes into areas of life which have only a tangential relationship to the body and disease (**gambling**). When medicine was developing in the eighteenth and early nineteenth centuries it focused on the individual's body and the biology of disease. Disease was understood primarily as an aspect of the sick person's body. As a new science, medicine was attempting to mimic the natural sciences and to produce objective explanations of disease. In the twentieth century, medicine

redefined its area of competence to include the individual's psychological, economic and social circumstances. This development of the '**biopsychosocial**' model of disease reflects the increasing development of individualization in modern societies. With it, both individuals and medicine, become more concerned with workings of the whole person, and the need for individuals to develop internal mechanisms of social control, rather than externally administered ones (Conrad, P. and Schneider, J. *Deviance and Medicalization: From Badness to Sickness*. Philadelphia: Temple University Press) (**attention deficit disorder; autism spectrum disorders; behavioural disorders; drapetomania; hysteria; labelling theory; learning disabilities; post traumatic stress disorder; reproduction**).

MEDICAL OUTCOMES STUDY (MOS) A short health survey, the SF-20, for use with large numbers of patients in practice settings (Stewart, A. and Ware, J. (1992) *Measuring Functioning and Well-Being: The Medical Outcomes Study Approach*. Durham, NC: Duke University Press) (**health status assessment**).

MEDICAL MODEL The taken for granted way of thinking about sickness and disease in Western society is called the medical model. That is, most of us usually believe that being sick or diseased is a straight forwardly physical event. It is the consequence of a germ or a virus or bacteria entering the body and causing it to malfunction. The cure or the solution to the problem lies in taking professional medical advice and usually some form of drug that wipes out the offending organism and restores our body to a stable physical state. So for most of us being sick is a biochemical process that is natural and not anything really to do with our social life. This medical model however, applies to a very limited range of acute medical conditions (**clinical gaze**; **medical discourse**; **nature**; **sociology of medicine**).

MEDICAL POLICE   In the eighteenth and nineteenth centuries a link was drawn between the health of the population and the power and prosperity of the state. In this perspective implementing health policies based on environmental controls and monitoring the behaviour of individuals was the task of the law administered by the police. Initially developing in France and Germany the first chair in Medical Jurisprudence was established at Edinburgh University in 1807 by King George III. The concept was picked up in England in 1809 with J. Roberton's *Treatise on Medical Police* and H. W. Rumsey's (1856) *Essays on State Medicine*. The approach was ultimately overwhelmed by the **germ theory** of disease and the development of **biomedicine** (White, K. (2001) (ed.), *The Early Sociology of Health and Illness*. London: Routledge) (**Chadwick**; **Frank**; **sanitation**; **Snow**; **social medicine**; **Villerme**; **Virchow**; **Whig histories of medicine**).

MEDICAL PROFESSION   The occupation licensed by the state which can diagnose

disease and prescribe drugs for their treatment (**allopathy/allopathic**; **corporatization**; **deprofessionalization**; **McDonaldization/ McDoctor**; **medical dominance**).

MEDICAL PSYCHOLOGY   In contrast to the **sociology of medicine** medical psychology studies the way in which the personality and cognitive processes of individuals influence their susceptibility to disease and illness. Whereas health sociologists argue that individual behaviour – particularly health risk behaviour such as smoking or drinking – are the product of structural factors, medical psychologists identify their source in such characteristics as 'Type A' personalities, or in low self-esteem, or in having an external **locus of control**. This focus on the individual excludes the wider social factors that shape and determine the scope for individual action. Medical psychology is increasingly turning to **genetics** as the explanatory variable in an individual's behaviour and thus is moving further away from health sociology (**IQ controversy**; **lifestyle**; **Type A behaviour pattern**).

MEDICAL SOCIOLOGY   A term first used by **Elizabeth Blackwell** to highlight the intersection between social issues such as sexuality and religion and medicine. Following the work of **Parsons** in the 1950s medical sociology became the academic discipline assisting professional medicine in pursuit of understanding patients and their actions, particularly their compliance or non-compliance with medical orders, and **help-seeking behaviour**. As sociology became more critical of medicine (**antipsychiatry**) the term was replaced by variants of health sociology or sociology of health (**sociology in medicine; sociology of medicine**).

MEDICAL TECHNOLOGY   The US Office of Technology Assessment defines medical technologies as 'the drugs, devices, and medical and surgical procedures used in medical care and the organization and supportive systems within which such care is provided'. The role of the office is to assess the economic value and safety of medical technologies. In the UK the **National Institute of Clinical Evidence** provides the same role. Sociological research on medical technologies takes three forms. First, there are those approaches that see technological developments as a determining force in society. Such approaches emphasize, for example, the impact of new technologies of surveillance, such as genetic testing, as independent forces shaping social relationships. The second approach emphasizes the role of social factors, particularly the political and economic, in determining technological developments and implementation. The third approach is based on the interdisciplinary fusion of science and technology studies and the sociology of medical technology emphasizing the interplay between the social shaping of technologies and the technological shaping of the social (Timmermans, S. and Berg, M. (2003) 'The practice of medical technology', *Sociology of Health and Illness*, 25: 97–114). Social historians of medicine link medical technologies to wider developments

in society. Pickstone, for example has suggested that the inter-relations of the social and the technical have produced four historical periods in medicine: biographical medicine; analytical medicine; experimental medicine; and techno-medicine, the last coming to dominate from the end of the nineteenth century with the rise of universities, research laboratories and capitalist firms investing in drugs and technology (Pickstone, J. (2000) *Ways of Knowing: A New Science, Technology and Medicine.* Manchester: Manchester University Press) (**actor-network theory; bedside medicine; biotechnology; Fleck; health technology assessment; social construction of technology approach; technological fix; Whig histories of medicine**).

MEDICAL UNCERTAINTY   Notwithstanding advances in medical knowledge much Western medicine is practised in the absence of knowledge of the cause of disease and the effect of treatment and thus involves large elements of 'magical' thinking, for example, that doing something is preferable to doing nothing (Parsons, T. (1951) *The Social System.* Glencoe: Free Press). This characteristic of medical knowledge presents as a sociological and psychological problem to medical practitioners who must carry on as if their scientific knowledge was complete. (Fox, R. (1980) 'The evolution of medical uncertainty', *Milbank Memorial Fund Quarterly*, 58: 1–49).

MEMORY WORK   An emancipatory feminist method of analysis, in which women, as part of a group, write their health stories over a period of up to two years. By working collaboratively, the argument is, women can free themselves from patriarchal power structures, as they examine both their resistance to, and victimization by patriarchy (Haug, F. (1987) *Female Sexualisation: A Collective Work of Memory*. Tr. E. Carter London: Verso) (**feminism**).

MENOPAUSE   The cessation of menses (periods) in women associated with physical discomfort and mood swings. While often thought to be a biological universal, anthropological study suggests that the experience is culturally shaped, with Japanese women, for example, not experiencing the hot flushes, irritability and tension associated with the process in other Western countries. Feminist sociologists argue that menopause has been constructed by Western medicine in the process of medicalizing the lifecycle of women, and that its treatment as a 'disease', cured by **hormone replacement therapy**, reflects patriarchal demands on women that they remain sexually active and attractive for men (Lock, M. (1993) *Encounters with Ageing; Mythologies of Menopause in Japan and North America*. Berkeley: University of California Press) (**medicalization; menstrual cycle; premenstrual syndrome**).

MEN'S HEALTH   Understanding men's health as determined by their gender is a recent development given the focus of feminists on the impact of gender roles on women's health. As a consequence of their gender role men under-report physical symptoms, have a machine-like relationship to their body, have a individualistic view of their health, do not participate in support groups, delay seeking medical advice, and make 'bad' patients, refusing to present for check ups and examinations. Chronic illness challenges key attributes of masculinity – their ability to stay in control, act rationally, not complain and 'be a man' (Cameron, E. and Bernardes, J. (1998) 'Gender and disadvantage in health – men's health for a change', *Sociology of Health and Illness*, 20: 673–93) (**gender roles; hegemonic masculinity; male stoicism**).

MENSTRUAL CYCLE   The regular (roughly 28 days) shedding of the lining of the uterus by women. While a significant occurrence in most women's lives, in Western cultures there are no ceremonies to mark it, and very little public discussion or reference to it in popular culture. In other cultures it is marked as the sign of the power and potency – for good or evil – of women (**medicalization; menopause; premenstrual syndrome**).

MENTAL HEALTH   (**mental illness**).

MENTAL HOSPITALS   Specialized institutions in the twentieth century for the custody of those diagnosed by psychiatrists as sick. With the rise of the **antipsychiatry** movement and consumer rights for patients they were gradually closed and care of the mentally ill moved into the community, without proper resources to provide it **asylums**; **Bedlam**; **care in the community**; **deinstitutionalization**; **manic depression**; **mental illness**).

MENTAL ILLNESS   Sociologists have long demonstrated the social distribution and differential diagnosis of mental illness. Faris showed in 1939 that while manic-depressive psychosis appears randomly distributed the diagnosis of schizophrenia was more common in poorer areas. His work was among the first to test and dismiss the '**social drift**' **hypothesis**, showing that poverty preceded illness, rather than that sick people moved down the system (Faris, R. and Hollingshead, A. (1939) *Mental Disorders in an Urban Area*. Chicago: University of Chicago Press). Class position is significantly correlated to the diagnosis of mental illness and the form of treatment. The lower classes are more likely to be diagnosed with psychosis, enter treatment through the legal system, and are more likely to receive biological treatment than psychotherapy (Hollingshead, A. and Redlich, R. (1958) *Social Class and Mental Illness*. New York: Wiley). In Marxian analysis increases or decreases in those diagnosed as mentally ill are shown to be closely linked to the economy. Increases in the number of the mentally ill reflect the increase in surplus unemployed people at times of economic crisis, while in times of high economic demand they diminish. Additionally **asylums** are argued to 'mop up' the casualties of the labour market (Brenner, H. (1973) *Mental Illness and the Economy*. Cambridge, MA: Harvard University Press). Feminist sociologists have explained the consistent over-representation of women in psychiatric populations as a function of women's social roles as wife and mother (Gove, W. (1972) 'The relationship between sex roles, marital status and mental illness', *Social Forces*, 51: 34–44). In Foucault's analysis the category of insanity is a label to sort and segregate the population, administered by state mandated professionals (Foucault, M. (1967) *Madness and Civilization*. London, Tavistock). In his analysis a whole range of 'normal' human problems – from sexual preferences, drug use, body shape, and deportment – (**abnormal**) are put through the prism of the '**psy-professions**' in which normalization is the key, and thus extends beyond the professionally defined mental illness of psychiatry (**antipsychiatry**; **serious and ongoing mental illness**; **technologies of the self**; **therapeutic community**).

MERCY KILLING   The active intervention by another person to bring about the death of an individual judged to have no future quality of life due to injury or terminal disease. In the USA it has been championed by Jack Kevorkian, a medical practitioner, who believes in **physician assisted suicide**. He has faced murder charges, but been found not guilty for assisting patients to die (**ethics, medical**; **do not resuscitate**; **euthanasia**).

META-ANALYSIS   In epidmiology the combining of statistical results from a number of smaller studies (on the same topic) to increase sample size and therefore the validity of the findings (Sackett, D.

and Spitzer, W. (1994) 'Guidelines for improving meta-analysis', *The Lancet*, 343: 910) (**Cochrane Centre; evidence-based medicine**).

METANARRATIVES In current usage, the description of overarching or grand theories of society, for example, Marxism or feminism. As argued by Lyotard, these are now held to be impossible given transformations in social life that have led to the breakdown of a stable, objective social reality, and the development of **postmodernist** forms of social organization. Furthermore history is no longer seen as linear, or having a teleology, that is, a specifiable endpoint. Thus knowledge can be had only of the local and the specific (Lyotard, F. (1984) *The Post Modern Condition: A Report on Knowledge*. Tr. G. Bennington and B. Massumi. Minneapolis: University of Minnesota Press).

MIASMA The miasmatic theory of contagion postulated that infectious disease was caused by specific atmospheric conditions, a proposal originating with **Hippocrates**. The idea was particularly important in the development of public health in the nineteenth century, drawing attention to the state of decomposing animal and vegetable substances in urban spaces. **Edwin Chadwick** in his *Inquiry into the Sanitary Condition of the Labouring Population* (1842) argued that the atmospheric changes caused by putrefying materials caused infectious disease. This led to a wide range of urban reforms, around factories, houses and streets. It must be recognized though that this focus

did not see poverty and industrialization as the cause of disease (**contagion; social medicine**).

MICROSOCIOLOGICAL Approaches in sociology that focus on small-scale interactions, (rather than large social structures) as within a family, or between a doctor and a nurse, or within specific institutions such as asylums or hospitals. These approaches – **ethnomethodology, symbolic interactionism** and **phenomenology** – have been very influential in health studies in the United States. The approach is marked by participant observation in the field and the results offer depth rather than breadth in their findings. The approach is associated with the **Chicago School of Sociology** and the works of **E. Hughes A. Strauss** and **E. Goffman**, in for example, *Asylums: Essays on the Social Situation of Mental Hopsitals and Other Inmates* and *The Presentation of the Self in Everyday Life*. The approach is based on **grounded theory** that is the direct examination of social life, rather than a priori theorizing by the researcher. Macrosociologists have been critical of the lack of attention to factors such as class or gender, that is, power relations, which shape micro level interactions. Nevertheless these approaches have produced outstanding studies in sociological studies of health and illness, as well as of health institutions (**dying trajectories; Mead; Schutz**).

MIDTOWN MANHATTAN STUDY A project to explore the links between inequality experienced in childhood, deprivation in adulthood and the impact on health over the lifecycle. This type of research attempts a dynamic construction of a person's health status over the lifecycle (Langer, T. and Michael, S. (1963) *Life Stress and Mental Health: The Midtown Manhattan Study*. New York: Free Press) (**life course analysis**).

MIDWIVES Traditionally women who assisted in the birthing process. Subordinating midwifery to male medical control was one of the earliest achievements in the development of professionalized medicine. In the process birthing was transformed from the business of women and medicalized into an event requiring male intervention and control. By taking over birthing, male medical practitioners gained access to the family as a market for their services, thus furthering their professionalization. The consequences of the entry of the male practitioner was a sharp rise in maternal mortality through puerperal fever, which was spread by doctors who had not washed their hands (Donnison, J. (1977) *Midwives and Medical Men*. London: Heinmann).

MIND–BODY DUALISM Ascribed in the development of Western thought by social scientists to **Descartes** the distinction made in medicine between the objective, factual and knowable aspects of the body and its disorders, and the fundamentally unknowable states of consciousness of the person with the disease or disorder. The transformation of the person from a subject into a body as an object was fundamental to the development of Western medicine, facilitating the development of **mechanistic** models of the body, and underpinning the treatment of disease using biochemical and technological interventions. The development of the concept, embodiment, is one attempt by sociologists to overcome this dualism (**bedside medicine; behaviourism; body; dualism; embodiment; medical gaze; positivism**).

MIND–BODY RELATIONSHIP Notwithstanding the **mind–body dualism** the recognition by medical practitioners that how the person thinks, feels and interprets their condition affects the course of disease, the treatment outcomes, and even the perception of pain. The attempt to take on board the findings of sociologists and psychologists of health was the development of the **biopsychosocial** model of disease which flourished in the late 1970s and early 1980s. (Engel, G. (1979) 'The need for a new medical model: a challenge for biomedicine', *Science*, 196: 129–36) (**body; embodiment; placebo effect**).

MINERS' NYSTAGMUS Coal miners in Britain, from the nineteenth century onwards (culminating between World War I and World War II as the most expensive compensated illness in the mining industry) were diagnosed with oscillating eyes, weight loss, tremors and depression. The condition was negotiated as a disease at the intersection of the growth of the welfare state, professionalizing medicine and the unions. When this constellation of political and economic factors changed the condition ceased to appear or to be diagnosed. There are clear parallels between this condition and the development of **repetitive strain injury** in the 1980s (Figlio, K. (1982) 'How does illness mediate social relations? Workmen's compensation and medico-legal practices, 1890–1940', in P. Wright and A. Treacher (eds), *The Problem of Medical Knowledge: Examining the Social Construction of Medicine*. Edinburgh: Edinburgh University Press) (**chronic fatigue syndrome**).

MODERNITY The period from about 1700 to the 1970s in the West. The term encapsulates the transformation of Western Europe from a rural, religious, feudal society to an industrialized, urbanized, rationalistic culture. It provides the framework within which scientific medicine develops, and privileges scientific knowledge over other ways of knowing. It was a period characterized by a belief in progress based on science and technology, and that a science of society could be developed allowing for prediction and control of human affairs. From the 1970s on, significant changes occurred at the level of the economy transforming the factory base of production in the West, leading to a decline of the working class (**postmodernity**), and culturally, there was a loss of certainty about the ability of science – social and natural – to produce stable knowledge of nature or society (**metanarratives**; **post-Fordism**).

MORAL CAREER In **Goffman's** sociology, the impact of being labelled mentally ill is the first stage in the person embarking on a transformation in their social role, from person, to mentally ill, in which their identity is stripped and their accountability as rational actors denied (Goffman, E. (1959) 'The moral career of the mental patient', *Psychiatry: Journal of Interpersonal Relations*, 22 (2): 123–42) (**degradation ceremonies**; **depersonalization**; **stigma**).

MORAL ENTREPRENEURS A term coined by Howard Becker to characterize those groups who make it their business to raise public concern around issues, and particularly to transform them into public problems, with an individualistic explanation of why these problems occur (Becker, H. (1963) *Outsiders: Studies in the Sociology of Deviance*. New York: Free Press). A good example is the construction of the 'drink-driver' as 'the' problem in car crashes, and not the brewers or distillers, or the designers of cars, or the engineers who design the roads (Gusfeild, J. (1981) *The Culture of Public Problems: Drink Driving and the Symbolic Order*. Chicago: University of Chicago Press). In health sociology the concept is used to demonstrate the ways in which what used to be bad behaviour (for example inattentiveness in boys) is transformed into diseased behaviour (the boys now have **attention deficit disorder**), a process of **medicalization**, which obscures other explanations of their behaviour, such as the size of classes in schools, or the necessity for both parents to have a job to survive economically, with concomitant impact on family life (Conrad, P. and Schneider, J. (1992) *Deviance and Medicalization: From Badness to Sickness*. Philadelphia: Temple University Press) (**morality and medicine**).

MORAL HAZARD   In the insurance industry, the phenomenon whereby insured individuals do not change their behaviour knowing that any risk they take will be compensated for (**markets**).

MORALITY AND MEDICINE   Definitions of a bodily state as a disease is often as much a product of moral concerns as they are of scientific ones. In fact, medicine can be seen to be a set of moral claims about the good life and the healthy body, delivered in the language of an objective and value free science. This especially the case with the **new public health** which is based on moral judgements about good citizens: those who maintain their body weight within a normal level; conduct their lifestyles in appropriate ways by keeping fit, reducing their drinking and stopping smoking. This targeting of individuals as immoral when they get sick from obesity, alcohol use, or smoking **blames the victim** and provides a dense smokescreen around those social, political and economic facts that produce and distribute disease, and which shape and limit individuals' lifestyle choices. (Brandt, A. and Rozin, P. (1997) *Morality and Health*. London: Routledge) (**Canguihelm**; **citizenship**; **courtesy stigma**; **disease**; **labelling theory**; **moral entrepreneurs**; **normal**; **stigma**; **stigmatized risk group**).

MORBIDITY   The number of diagnoses of a given disease or other condition in a given population at a designated time, usually expressed as a rate per 100,000. Unlike the **medical model**, health sociologists argue that patterns of disease are systematically produced by social relationships and unequally distributed in society, with those at the bottom being sicker and dying sooner than those at the top (**gender**; **health determinants**; **social class**; **social gradient of disease**).

MORTALITY   The number of deaths due to a given disease or other condition in a given population at a designated time, expressed as a rate per 100,000. Patterns of mortality are the product of social relationships and not a random biological event (**class**; **death**; **Engels**; **gender**; **health determinants**).

MOTIVATED DEVIANCE   Talcott Parsons argued that the strains of modern society – its competitiveness, its individualism, and the strains of the nuclear family – could lead individuals to try and avoid their social responsibilities by going sick. Thus sickness can be a form of motivated deviance to resolve the tensions of one's social roles. It is for this reason, Parsons argued, that the medical profession controls and limits entry to the sick role, and only when legally diagnosed as diseased can an individual enter the **sick role**. The importance of Parsons' insight is that being sick is not simply a biological fact, but a social accomplishment. The limitation is that in some circumstances the attempt to have a condition diagnosed as a disease may be the only alternative for individuals caught in intolerable strain, as for example with **repetitive strain injury** following the reorganization of office work in the 1980s (**chronic fatigue syndrome; deviance**).

MULTIPLE RISK FACTOR INTERVENTION TRIAL (MRFIT)   In this study conducted in the USA, a group of highly motivated men, in the top 10 per cent risk group for coronary heart disease, were supported by counsellors and psychologists over a six-year period to change their eating and smoking habits. However, the trial showed that only modest changes to behaviour could be sustained. The trial also demonstrated the limitation of intervening at the individual level. For every one of the men who did modify their behaviour nothing was being done to prevent others from adopting the same lifestyles. That is, the factors that predispose people to adopt unhealthy lifestyles – work stress for example – are ignored in interventions trying to treat people who have already adopted them (Multiple Risk Factor intervention Trial. (1982) 'The multiple risk factor intervention trial – risk factor changes and mortality results', *Journal of the American Medical Association*, 248: 1465–76) (**cardiovascular disease; lifestyle; risk; risk factor epidemiology**).

N

NARRATIVE ACCOUNTS OF ILLNESS In order to make sense of chronic illness, disability and the experience of disease human beings try to tell a story of their condition. Sociologists and anthropologists study the way the stories of illness are told by individuals. These storylines serve the function of explaining the experience and process of illness, and can be shown to be constructed around themes of restitution, chaos and quest (Frank, A.W. (1995) *The Wounded Story Teller. Body, Illness and Ethics.* Chicago: University of Chicago Press). Narrative accounts are particularly important in the context of chronic illness where they: 1 transform illness events and construct a world of illness; 2 reconstruct one's life history in the event of chronic illness; 3 provide an explanation and understanding of illness; 4 provide a form of strategic interaction in order to assert or project one's identity; and 5 transform illness from an individual into a collective phenomenon (Hyden, L. (1997) 'Illness and narrative', *Sociology of Health and Illness,* 19: 48–69). It is important to remember that while the sufferer's account of their experience is different from that provided by the medical practitioner, it does not speak for itself and needs to be analysed in terms of the social factors which shape the account (**biographical disruption**; **chronic illness**; **quest narratives**).

NATURALISTIC PARADIGM In sociology, the study of social interaction in the field as it actually occurs. Such studies involve participant observation, **in-depth interviews** and **ethnographic** presentation of findings. They are based on the assumptions of the qualitative research tradition, that social reality is dynamic and unfolding, rather than pre-given or stable. In this approach the researcher is as much a part of the subject under study as the participants. The approach explicitly rejects the methods of the natural sciences in the study of human interaction. (Lincoln, Y. and Guba, E. (1985) *Naturalistic Inquiry.* Newbury Park, CA: Sage) (**Chicago School of Sociology**; **Kant**; **qualitative research**; **verstehen**; **Weber**).

NATUROPATHY A form of herbal medicine, flourishing in nineteenth-century America in frontier conditions where self-treatment was the only option for healthcare. Recent trends indicating a large rise in herbal self-treatment in the United

States and other Western countries are taken as indicative of dissatisfaction with **allopathic** medicine and the decline of **medical dominance** (Baer, H. (1992) 'The potential rejuvenation of American naturopathy as a consequence of the holistic health movement', *Medical Anthropology*, 13: 369–83) (**complementary/alternative medicine; homeopathy**).

NATIONAL HEALTH SERVICE (NHS) As part of the post-World War II political settlement between capital and labour in Britain, led by Minister of Health Aneurin Bevan, the Attlee Labour government extended the national insurance system to provide free medical treatment to all in 1948. The policy was fiercely rejected by the British Medical Association, which saw it as a form of government control of the profession and an intrusion on its autonomy. Resistance faded as it was soon realized that under the NHS the private doctors did far better and had securer sources of income.

NATIONAL INSTITUTE OF CLINICAL EVIDENCE (NICE) A UK initiative which provides medical practitioners with information about **evidence-based** treatments in an attempt to bring about quality and cost control in medical practice. This initiative is congruent with **neoliberalism** and the decline of medical dominance as the state and insurance companies seek to reduce services and costs (**actor-network theory; health technology assessment; medical technology; social construction of technology approach**).

NATURE In Western society we operate with a routine conceptual distinction between culture and nature. However the health social sciences demonstrate that what is taken to be natural or cultural is historically specific and shaped by social factors. Things that were 'natural' yesterday are medical problems today. Women's 'diseases' provide a good example. Pregnancy, until the development of gynaecology and obstetrics, was regarded as a natural event. Now it is constructed as a hazardous condition requiring constant medical supervision (**childbirth**). Thus classificatory schemas putting some things in 'nature' and others in 'culture' are historically specific and the outcome of social and political interactions. When we appeal to nature to explain events we are, in fact, appealing to human constructions that are the product of culture.

NATURE/NURTURE DEBATE An ongoing debate in Western societies about how much of an individual's characteristics are determined by birth, how much by the way they are brought up, or how much is determined by the social group they are born into? In social studies of health, twin studies are utilized to examine the relative impact of heredity or culture on what genetically identical individuals get sick of or die from. Twin studies consistently point to the impact of environmental factors rather than genetically determined outcomes. For example, twin studies, of the length of life of twins reared independently, found that rather than their shared genetic makeup determining their health status, environmental factors played a greater role in determining their life span. They also died of quite different diseases than a genetic determinist model would suggest (Hayakawa, K. (1992) 'Intrapair differences of physical aging and longevity in identical twins', *Acta Genetica Med. Gemellol*, 41: 177–85) (**cultural determinism; genetics; ethnicity; IQ controversy**).

NEEDS ASSESSMENT, HEALTH   The estimate of health needs in a population or group, undertaken by epidemiologists and public health practitioners with the aim of improving health services (Wright, J., Williams, R. and Wilkinson, J. (1998) 'Development and Importance of Health Needs Assesssment', *Britsh Medical Journal*, 316: 1310–13) (**inverse care law; Jarvis' law**).

NEGOTIATED ORDER   Associated with the work of **Anselm Strauss** in the **symbolic interactionist** tradition, studies of total institutions such as asylums showing how individuals negotiate, that is, work their way around, the bureaucratic structures placed on their lives. The key argument is that to focus on the formal institutional patterns of an organization will miss how individuals make sense of, and shape the institution to their own ends, working to maintain a sense of self (**degradation ceremonies; depersonalization**). The general sociological point is that social order is far less stable than is presupposed in **functionalist** accounts and is maintained in active social interaction (Strauss, A. (1978) *Negotiations, Varieties,*

Contexts, Processes and Social Order. San Francisco: Jossey Bass) (**bureaucracy; Chicago School of Sociology; microsociological; pain**).

NEOLIBERALISM   A term used to describe the resurgence of the political doctrine that individuals are best left to look after themselves and reflecting the dismantling of the **welfare state** and the modification of the idea of **citizenship** by conservative governments, since the mid-1980s. Under the imperative of the World Bank and the International Monetary Fund loan and credit arrangements, both developing and developed countries are dismantling their healthcare services, and the public education sector, as well as privatizing – that is selling off – public utilities such as electricity, water, rail and port services. The consequence has been the redevelopment of the infectious disease thought to have been brought under control by the mid-twentieth century (Longbottom, H. (1997) 'Emerging infectious diseases', *Communicable Diseases Intelligence*, 21: 89–93) (**corporatization; diseases of poverty; healthism; new right; privatization**).

NEO-MARXISM   Social science approaches which accept Marxist analyses as the base of understanding contemporary Western industrialized societies, but also attempt to take into account social changes not foreseen by Marx. These include complex ownership patterns and the development of a managerial class, as well as the failure of capitalist society to polarize into two classes, and the failure of revolutionary class-consciousness to develop in the working class. Neo-Marxists also attempt to explore the relationship between class structure and inequalities based on gender and ethnicity. In general neo-Marxists accept that non-economic forces have to be accounted for in explaining patterns of inequality (**critical theory; Frankfurt School; ideology; Marxist approaches; Marxist feminism**).

NEUROSES   An unreasonable fear and/or high level of anxiety. In Freudian psychoanalysis it is a defence mechanism, though not a particularly useful one, in the attempt to cope with emotions from the past. Women are diagnosed as neurotic at higher rates than men, and prescribed more anti-depressants and anxiolytics than men (**anxiety; Freud; mental illness; psychoanalysis**).

NETWORK ANALYSIS   (**social networks analysis**).

NEW GENETICS   Recent developments in medicine following the invention of recombinant DNA technology in 1973. The strong claim, usually in the mass media, is that this will allow for the testing, identification and intervention in the genetic make-up of humans, and particularly the identification of and prevention of genetically caused diseases. Geneticists themselves are more cautious in their claims about the advances that have been or will be made given the complexity of the interaction between genes and the social environment and the multiple genes implicated in most diseases. The developments have raised serious concerns about the likelihood of increasing oppression based on claims about the genetic basis of individuals' social attributes, particularly in terms of gender and ethnicity (Cunningham-Burly, S. and Boulton, M. (2000) 'The social context of the new genetics', in G. Albrecht et al. (eds), *Handbook of Social Studies in Health and Medicine*. London: Sage) (**cloning; geneism; genetic determinism; geneticization; IQ controversy**).

NEW PUBLIC HEALTH   The 'old' public health refers to initiatives to prevent disease through environmental interventions, whether of sanitation or of workplaces and housing conditions. The 'new' public health focuses on **risks** and what are assumed to be peoples freely chosen **lifestyles**, thus ignoring structural features of society, and inducing us to be our own agents of social control (**epidemiology; governmentality; morality and medicine; risk; technologies of the self**).

NEW PUBLIC MANAGEMENT   Under the impact of **neoliberalism**, reforms in the public sector (that is, the state sector) introducing labour market flexibility, performance management systems and flexible specialization. The outcome is work intensification, longer hours and in the hospital, increased bureaucratic control over nurses and junior doctors (**benchmarking; clinical pathways; corporatization; market; privatization**).

NEW REPRODUCTIVE TECHNOLOGIES (NRTS)
A range of medical processes to either monitor pregnant women or to intervene in the process of conception and pregnancy. Feminist sociologists examine the ways in which these technologies are determined by patriarchal assumptions about the necessity to bear and rear children as the 'normal' social role of women. When linked to the **new genetics** the concern is that women are being transformed into breeding test-tubes (Stacey, M. (1992) (ed.), *Changing Human Reproduction: Social Science Perspectives.* London: Sage) (**assisted reproductive technologies; childbirth; donor insemination; in vitro fertilization; reproduction**).

NEW RIGHT   A political movement arising in the early 1980s, under Prime Minister Margaret Thatcher in England, and President Ronald Regan in the United States which re-asserted (as had occurred in nineteenth century capitalist societies) that the role of the state should be minimal in a market economy. State functions should be **privatized** or **corporatized** on the assumption that actors in the private market would perform them better. In healthcare this led to the **new public management** in which market principles were introduced into hospitals. The results have meant the routinization of medical work and a decline in the care provided to patient's as nurses and doctors attempt to meet 'production' targets (**citizenship; market; neoliberalism; welfare state**).

NEW ZEALAND MAORI   As with other **aboriginals** there are massive inequalities between Maori and pakehaa (whites) in New Zealand. They have lower life expectancy, higher incidence of diseases such as hepatitis B, and significantly higher age-specific death rates from heart attacks. Whereas for whites, health is linked to socio-economic status – job and income – for Maori it is much broader: a healthy person is one who understands his or her culture, family and extended family links. The loss of self-esteem that comes about from not having these links (which colonization and urbanization have undermined) is an important factor in the subsequent adoption of poor lifestyle activities (**lifestyle choices; lifestyle factors**).

NIGHTINGALE, FLORENCE (1820–1910)
The founder of modern nursing, separating nursing out from religion and allowing middle class women a role independent of the home. While radical in her claims that nursing was an occupation, she was also very much the product of Victorian patriarchal values, in seeing it as in a subordinate role to male medical practitioners, and in her opposition to the registration of nurses (Woodham-Smith, C. (1950) *Florence Nightingale.* London: Constable) (**Dix; nursing**).

NOMINAL GROUP PROCESS   A group process to generate ideas, encourage creative thinking and enhance organizational decision making and problem solving. The group process allows for a wide range of ideas to be expressed, and minimizes the influence of dominant individuals. It is useful as a way for health policy developers to expand their traditional agendas (Jones, J. and Hunter, D. (1995) 'Consensus methods for medical health service research', *British Medical Journal*, 311: 376–80) (**Delphi technique**; **focus groups**).

NONPROBABILITY SAMPLING TECHNIQUES
In statistics sampling is usually organized to reflect the structure of the whole population. In qualitative health social studies samples are usually chosen, not because they are representative, but because they pose particular issues of interest to researchers or because groups have approached researchers for help. More generally in social research nonprobability sampling may take the form of convenience sampling (that is using a population because of ease of access, as in first year psychology students); snowball sampling whereby the researcher gains access to group through referral from one member to the next; or in a **case study** approach, where one institution is examined.

NORMAL   Conforming to a preferred pattern of behaviour. In Western medicine disease is a disruption of what is presumed to be the biologically normal. There are at least six distinct senses of the term: 1 commonness, usualness, in a statistical sense of lying within the range of variability of a double value of standard deviation on either side of a normal Gaussian curve; 2 averageness, that is, that which has the highest frequency of occurrence; 3 typicalness, that is, conforming to some standard of typicality; 4 attaining adequate performance;

5 attaining optimal performance; and 6 a naïve conception based on a number of the preceding conceptions. Most medical accounts of normality make use of either number one or two. The problem with statistical accounts of normality as explications of disease is that they are difficult to operationalize. For example, consider whole populations affected by epidemics of the plague or parasitic infections. Using a statistical concept of normality, it is now logically impossible to classify the population as diseased (Vacha, J. (1978) 'Biology and the problem of normality', *Scientia*, 113: 823–46). Similar difficulties are met in utilizing an explanatory framework of normal function, that is, concepts of disease which are based on the functions of parts failing to contribute to the goals of the whole organism. On this account of disease, it is not possible for an organ to be non-diseased, and yet lose its function. However this is quite possible: with increasing technological innovation in artificial reproduction, human sexual organs may completely lose their function in reproduction (Margolis, J. (1976) 'The concept of disease', *The Journal of Medicine and Philosophy*, 1: 238–55) (**abnormal**; **Bachelard**; **Canguihelm**; **disease**; **Fleck**; **new reproductive technologies**).

NORMS   Sets of expectations about how individuals should act in situations. In **Parsons'** sociology norms are the internalized ways of acting specific to social roles, as in for example, the norms of being a doctor or a patient. **Microsociological** approaches reject explanations of social action based on norms, arguing instead that individuals actively construct and maintain their social roles, as they make sense of the world (**deviance**; **ethno-methodology**; **phenomenology**; **symbolic interactionism**).

NUREMBERG CODE   Ethical guidance for the medical profession following the Nuremberg trial of twenty German medical practitioners for crimes against humanity, after World War II. Under the impact of **eugenics** medical practitioners carried out extensive medical experiments in concentration camps on those deigned unfit to live, or not fit enough to labour. The most infamous, Dr Mengele, who attempted to demonstrate, among other atrocities, that different 'races' responded differently to the same disease by injecting them with typhoid and the like, escaped trial. The 1964 **Helsinki Declaration** distinguished therapeutic experiments – research which had a beneficial impact on patient care – from non-therapeutic experiments which had no benefit for the patient. However, it provided no sanctions against the latter (**Belmont Report**; **ethics, medical**; **Hippocrates**; **informed consent**; **IQ controversy**; **racism**; **Tuskegee syphilis experiment**).

NURSE PRACTITIONER   Nurses who with additional training are allowed in some jurisdictions to carry out tasks usually only conducted by doctors, as in the diagnosis of diseases and the prescription of drugs. Depending on your perspective this is either a breakthrough for professionalized nursing, or with the increasing specialization of medical practice, the medical profession off-loading the more routine tasks of patient care to a subordinate occupation (**medical dominance**).

NURSING   The occupation that provides care to the sick and dying. Because of its links with mothering, its apparent reflection of women's natural caring role, and its subordination to medicine, it has been engaged in ongoing struggle from the late nineteenth century to be recognized as a **profession** (**doctor/nurse game**; **emotions**; **Florence Nightingale**; **medical dominance**).

NUTRITION   Food and liquids that sustain life. Nutritional deficits – and their contribution to disease and death – are a product not of any worldwide shortage of food, but of the politics of its distribution. The aggressive marketing of Western food to third world countries – for example, baby formulas – have directly contributed to infant mortality in the third world. In Western societies dietary choices are not **lifestyle choices** but the product of what is marketed to different groups in society. Supermarkets in poor areas are predominantly stocked with 'convenience' foods and have less fresh fruit and vegetables than similar shops in well-off areas (**diet**; **malnutrition**).

OBESITY Medically, being 30 per cent over the ideal body weight for age and height. Depending on the statistics (which are hotly debated) obesity affects 30 per cent of Americans, with 61 per cent being overweight. While not a disease Medicare in the United States listed it as an illness in 2004 opening the way for insurance-covered treatment programmes. While the cause of obesity lies in high sugar and fat processed foods, most medical accounts explore the role of genetics and heredity. Focusing on **lifestyle** or **blaming the victim** will not produce a solution: control over the quality of foodstuffs and activity programmes in schools will (**anorexia nervosa**; **eating disorders**).

OBJECTIFICATION Used in health studies as a shorthand term for the way that medicine transforms individuals and their bodies into objects for it to practise on. The transformation of the person into a patient was critical in the development of Western medicine, and the focus of Foucault's *Birth of the Clinic*. Notwithstanding efforts to transform medicine, as for example, in the development of **biopsychosocial** models of illness, the **mechanistic** and **scientistic** assumptions prevent it from developing a humanistic view of the patient as person (**bedside medicine**; **reductionism**).

OBJECTIVITY In **positivist** social research the attainment and maintenance of a disinterested stance and the use of statistical methods, the data of which are presented as facts, as the hallmark of research. **Behaviourism** in psychology was the most developed form of this research. Sociologists in the Durkheimian tradition similarly argue that sociology can be a science of social facts, which are external to the individual, have an objective existence and can be studied for their law-like patterns, as Durkheim sought to demonstrate in his study *Suicide*. Health social researchers in the qualitative tradition argue that objectivity is not possible in the social sciences since its data are conscious individuals who react back on the researcher. **Microsociological** approaches – **ethnomethodology**, **symbolic interactionism** and **phenomenology** – all emphasize the contingent nature of knowledge and its situational production and argue that objectivity is not possible (**Kant**; **verstehen**; **Weber**).

OCCUPATIONAL CLOSURE The construction of boundaries around an occupation determining who can practise it. In medicine this has been the outcome of the development of medical dominance, whereby only legally qualified persons can practise medicine. Dominant occupations also control and specify the roles of other adjacent occupations, for example, in the case of medicine, nursing (**credentialism; medical dominance; professionalization**).

OCCUPATIONAL DISEASE A range of disorders directly attributable to a person's employment such as **asbestosis, repetitive strain injury, brown lung disease** (pneumoconiosis), brown lung diseases (byssinosis) or tunnel worker's asthma (silicosis). Unlike workplace injuries and deaths which can be shown to be caused by workplace organization, occupational diseases can evolve over a long timespan allowing employers, with the support of medical practitioners, to reject responsibility for their workers' condition and to avoid paying compensation. Employers' use medically justified arguments to argue that it is the characteristics of the individual that caused the disease rather than environmental conditions. (Smith, B. (1981) 'Black lung: the social production of disease', *International Journal of Health Services*, 11 (3): 343–59) (**class analysis; employment; industrial disease; occupation and health; social gradient of disease**).

OCCUPATIONAL HEALTH AND SAFETY ADMINISTRATION The US agency charged with ensuring safe working conditions. Industrial sociologists point out that much of the data agencies such as this work with is provided by employers with a vested interest in presenting their industry as safe, and of any problems in it as due to the workers, shortcomings, such as **accident proneness (blame the victim; employment; industrial disease; occupation and health; occupational disease**).

OCCUPATION AND HEALTH Our occupation exposes us to a wide range of physical and psychosocial risks. These range from high-risk industries in which occupation can be easily shown to be the sole cause of cancer, as in the asbestos industry. Overall it is estimated that 20 per cent of all cancer deaths can be attributed to occupation. The **stress** of work environments that combine low autonomy and high workloads in an unsupportive environment has been claimed to be the cause of up to 35 per cent of cardiovascular mortality (Johnson, J. et al. (1996) 'Longterm psychosocial work environment exposure and cardiovascular mortality among Swedish men', *American Journal of Public Health*, 86: 324–31). In Australia an estimated 500 workers die each year at work, a further 2,200 die of work related cancers, and 650,000 are injured or become sick directly because of their work (Mathers, C. et al. (1999) *The Burden of Disease and Injury in Australia – Summary*. Canberra: Australian Institute of Health and Welfare) (**class analysis; employment; industrial disease; occupational disease; Occupational Health and Safety Administration; social gradient of disease**).

ORAL HISTORIES Qualitative research method in which the person's perspective is given prominence and the role of the researcher is to capture as accurately as possible the subject's experience and perspective. Oral histories can be either about the whole of a person's life, or about specific parts of it (as in after the diagnosis of a terminal illness). Oral histories are used to capture the uniqueness of one individual's experience as a model for others sharing some or all of the individual's characteristics (**case studies**).

ORGAN DONATION Granting permission allowing the medical profession access to a body part for transfer to another person. It may be either following death when a large range of organs can be 'harvested' – from the cornea, to the liver, lungs, heart, or kidneys – for some other person, or in the case of a living donor, an organ which can be survived without, for example, one of the kidneys, donated specifically for a sibling or designated other, such as a spouse. Sociologists have examined the social and psychological dynamics of such a decision, particularly as it relates to the case of a living donor. Flowing from the logic of the **gift relationship** (Fox and Swazey have argued that organ donorship is fraught with difficulties. 1, the donating individual may feel profoundly ambivalent about the offer; 2, the recipients may find themselves feeling that they have a part of another person in their body; and 3, that for the recipient, there is no way to repay the gift. The institutional solution to this last problem is to ensure anonymity of the donor, such that the recipient can feel no obligation to make restitution (Fox, R. and Swazey, J. (1992) *Spare Parts: Organ Replacement in American Society*. New York: Oxford University Press).

ORGAN TRANSPLANTATION The transfer of a body part from one human to another. These procedures have raised complex ethical questions about the status of **death** as 'brain-dead' individuals are kept on respirators to maintain their tissue. Organ transplantation processes also blur the distinction between 'experimental' and 'therapeutic' medicine, which raises tensions in terms of the **Helsinki Declaration** (**xenotransplantation**).

ORTHODOX MEDICINE The practice of medicine as licensed by the state, and whose practitioners exercise dominance over other health practitioners. It is based on a **mechanistic** model of the body, and presents curative interventions based on drugs and interventionist technologies. Social historians argue that its rise to dominance was because its treatment – individualized, technical and drug based – correspond to the political and economic requirements of liberal capitalist societies (**allopathy/allopathic**; **alternative medicine**; **Flexner report**; **ideology**; **medical dominance**; **social medicine**).

OSTEOPATHY Founded by American Andrew Taylor Still in 1892, an alternative medical practice which, like **chiropractic**, seeks to heal the body through the manipulation of the spine and joints. In the USA osteopaths are legally recognized as medical practitioners, though subordinated to **allopathic** practitioners. Patients with chronic back pain use osteopathy and chiropractic as complementary forms of treatment, consulting allopathic practitioners for other health issues. As part of their successful claim to legitimacy osteopaths and chiropractors restrict their practice to spinal problems and have given up claims to be holistic health practitioners (Coulter, I., Hays, R. and Danielson, C. (1996) 'The role of the chiropractor in the changing health-care system', *Research in the Sociology of Healthcare*, 13A: 95–117) (**complementary/ alternative medicine**).

OTTAWA CHARTER The World Health Organization's Ottawa Charter for Health Promotion – Towards a New Public Health (1986) emphasized improving people's health through attention to the social, economic and physical environment as the source of illness and disease (**Healthy Cities Project**).

OUTSOURCING Under **neoliberal** policies putting on the **market** services previously undertaken by the state in the mistaken belief that that this will be more efficient and cost effective (**citizenship; contracting out; new public management; privatization; welfare state**).

P

PAIN Acute or chronic physical discomfort. Pain is studied in health studies to demonstrate the impact of social and cultural factors on its experience and to demonstrate the limitations of the biomedical model of illness. Pain may become the core of a person's identity, being understood as an assault on the self, and a form of protracted suffering. Anthropologists have consistently demonstrated cross-cultural variations in the construction of situations as painful and in the experience of different levels of what is to count as pain. Similar differences have been shown to exist between socio-economic groups and ethnic groups in Western societies (**chronic pain**).

PANOPTICON Jeremy Bentham's design for a prison that maximized the surveillance of the inmates and minimized the number of warders. The circular building had a central column from which the guard could see into each cell without the prisoner knowing whether or not they were being observed. Thus prisoners had to behave at all times, leading them to police themselves. The model provided the central metaphor for **Foucault's** *Discipline and Punish*, in which he argued that in

modern societies, with their requirement to manage large populations, the biomedical and **psy-professions**, through their concept of normalcy induce us all to police ourselves in terms of the presentation of our bodies and make normal our psyches (**carceral society; technologies of the self**).

PARADIGM Associated with **Thomas Kuhn** who in *The Structure of Scientific Revolutions* argued that scientific knowledge was formed and sustained by communities of scientists who shared the same world view and sets of assumptions about the nature of reality and how to investigate it. A paradigm formulates specific sciences' problems and provides the ways in which to attempt to solve them. In the sociology of health the concept was developed as 'thought collectives' by **Ludwig Fleck** some thirty years prior to Kuhn (**epistemological break; thought styles**).

PARSONS, TALCOTT (1902–79) A leading American sociologist of the twentieth century who made important contributions to the sociology of health. Parsons argued that contemporary society, while having a capitalist economy, had non-capitalist social relations at its core; in short his sociology was an engagement with **Marxism**. He argued that the professional role in modern society was a distinctive one, based on altruism and an ethic of care, thus putting a break on the egotism and competitiveness of capitalist market relationships. The medical profession provided a key example for his analysis and he identified their non-profit orientation, their orientation towards the collectivity, their treatment of all individuals with the best possible practice based in scientific knowledge as a break on competitive market-based social systems (1951, *The Social System*. Glencoe: Free Press, especially Chapter 10). Despite this medico-centric account Parsons argued strongly against any understanding of sickness as purely biological. Cultural and social norms will determine what counts as disease and how it is treated. For Parsons, to be sick is to enter the **sick role**, which is controlled by the medical profession. Their task is to prevent individuals from opting out of their social roles, or by responding to the strains of modern society, through the 'motivated deviance' to be sick. ('The definitions of health and illness in the light of American values and social structure', in E. Jaco (ed.), *Patients, Physicians and Illness*. Chicago: Free Press). Parsons' analysis has been subjected to extensive empirical criticism, but this should not obscure the theoretical power of his analysis of medicine as an institution of **social control** and of the way in which social structures, particularly the family, determine an individual's health and illness

(**structural-functionalism**; **voluntaristic theory of action**).

PARTICIPANT OBSERVATION   A form of qualitative research in which the researcher enters into the world of those under study, attempting to understand the world as they experience it. It may be covert, with the group, club, ward or institution, for example, unaware that it is under study, or it may be overt, with the group knowing that one of its members is conducting a study. As a technique it can produce powerful analyses of the experience of institutions as in **Goffman's** analysis of asylums, or the study of medical socialization in *Boys in White: Student Culture in a Medical School* (Becker, H., Geer, B., Hughes, E., and Strauss, A. (1961) Chicago: Chicago University Press). The technique was developed both in anthropology and in the **Chicago School of Sociology**. Critics point out that the observer may be selective in what they perceive (especially if participating covertly) and may not be given access to all the relevant matters if overt researchers.

PATIENT ROLE   An individual's identity on entry to the sick role. In **Parsons'** analysis the patient must comply with the doctor's orders and want to get well. With the changing status of medicine – the growth of a more educated public, for example – the 'role' has been re-defined as a much more active engagement between the doctor and the patient. It has been argued that with the growth of chronic illness – such as diabetes – many patients actually know more about their condition and its management than their doctors, thus reversing, or equalizing the power imbalance that exists between a doctor and a patient (**doctor–patient relationship**; **sick role**).

PATIENT SELF DETERMINATION ACT Enacted in 1991 by the US Congress, all US healthcare facilities receiving Medicare or Medicaid monies must inform patients of their right to determine end-of-life decisions (**advanced care directives**; **do not resuscitate**).

PATRIARCHAL MEDICINE The embedded assumptions in medical knowledge that women are inferior to men. Feminist sociologists have identified the ways in which medical knowledge reinforces stereotypes of women: it is sexist in the sense of discriminating against women by distinguishing them from the more positively valued image of men. This may be overt, as in studies asserting that women have smaller brains. More commonly it is through ignoring women entirely (**clinical drug trials**). Patriarchal medicine constructs men as rational, logical, clear and unemotional; women are the opposite – intuitive, emotional and unreliable (**dualism**). Medical knowledge is also phallocentric in that women are referred to in general terms that refer only to male characteristics (Grosz, E. (1988) 'The in(ter)vention of feminist knowledge', in B. Caine, E. Grosz and M. de Lepervanche (eds), *Crossing Boundaries: Feminism and the Critique of Knowledge*. Sydney: Allen and Unwin) (**feminism**; **patriarchy**; **sexism**).

PATRIARCHY The dominance of men over women, in which medicine plays a large role in Western societies. Women's bodies are defined in contrast to the good, healthy, male body and found wanting. Hence women are, by definition, inferior, sicker and more at risk of biological disorder than men. In performing this analysis medicine moves from the social category of mother, of houseworker, to biological category, of menstruating, pregnant and menopausal, and combines by sleight of hand the two, obscuring the social basis of 'women's problems'.

PERSISTENT VEGETATIVE STATE (PVS) Following the withdrawal of life support systems, the self-sustaining continuation of heartbeat and breathing, raising complex issues of the classification of someone as dead (**coma**; **death**; **do not resuscitate**).

PERSONALITY Usually taken to be the stable set of characteristics that individuals bring to social interactions. Beyond this there are widely differing accounts of what it is, from Eysenck's **behaviourist** account that it is based in the brain and therefore very stable, to **G. H. Mead's** theory of the interactive self which is constantly being adjusted and developed depending on the nature of interactions with others. Different 'types' of personalities have been linked with specific diseases, as in **Type A behaviour pattern** though these approaches are largely discredited and are a form of victim blaming. Health social studies favours dynamic models of an interactive self, creating meaning and making sense of situations rather than passively responding in fixed ways to them (**blame the victim**; **identity**; **role**; **social interaction**).

PERVERSE INCENTIVES   In health systems based on a fee-for-service payment system, the motivation for the doctor to act in his/her financial interest, rather than in the interest of his/her patient's health and to order inappropriate tests, over-prescribe drugs, and to perform unnecessary surgery (Rodwin, M. (1993) *Medicine, Money and Morals: Physicians' Conflicts of Interest*. (New York: Oxford University Press) (**fee-for-service**; **market**; **supplier induced demand**).

PETTY, WILLIAM (1623–87)   A colleague of **John Graunt** Petty founded 'political arithmetic', the accumulation and synthesis of political, economic and social survey data related to health. Petty's motivation was the creation of a strong state, which he argued had to be based on a healthy workforce (Banta, J. (1987) 'Sir William Petty: Modern Epidemiologist (1623–1687)', *Journal of Commonwealth Health*, 12: 185–98) (**social medicine**).

PHARMACY   A specialized shop for the dispensing of drugs, and the only legal source of drugs prescribed by a medical practitioner. Pharmacy, as an occupation, continues to try and define itself as a specialized para-medical profession, though now pharmacists rarely make up their own preparations, dispensing prepackaged drugs supplied by multinational companies.

PHARMACEUTICAL COMPANIES   Companies that produce and market prescription and over the counter drugs, among the largest and most profitable multinational companies. Drug companies aggressively market their products both to doctors, and in the United States, direct to consumers through TV advertising of prescription drugs. In 1993 the US Congress estimated that drug companies made an excess profit of US$2 billion (**adverse drug reactions**).

PHARMACOGENETICS   The attempt to predict an individual's reaction to drugs, based on knowledge of the individual's genetic structure. While the promise is for individualized drugs, the cost is extensive genetic testing, and the outcome, much more likely, the re-development of drugs for niche marketing at phenomenal profit for companies (Hedgecoe, A. and Martin, P. (2003) 'The drugs don't work: expectations and the shaping of pharmacogenetics', *Social Studies of Science*, 33: 327–64).

PHENOMENOLOGY   In the philosophy of **Edmund Husserl** the attempt to apprehend through deep introspection the forms of consciousness and of experiences. Thus the focus is on the inner lifeworld of individuals. In qualitative health research the attempt to elicit the individuals' understanding of the situation. The approach emphasizes the analyses of the lifeworld, and the subjective, intentional component of human action. As with **Weber** and qualitative approaches, the methods of the natural sciences are rejected as inadequate to the task of examining human interaction (case studies; Gadamer; Heidegger; Husserl; microsociological; oral histories; verstehen).

PHENOMENOLOGICAL SOCIOLOGY Developed in America by **Alfred Schutz**, adapting Husserl's philosophical position, to argue that sociology should capture the meaning of events to the individual, and not the meaning of the individual's meaning to the sociologist. His approach has been broadly influential in health studies as a riposte to reductionist accounts of illness and disease (**Gadamer; Heidegger; Husserl; microsociological**).

PHYSICIAN ASSISTED SUICIDE The accelerated death of a terminally ill patient, using resources at the doctor's disposal, that is, drugs, and with the patient's agreement, to ensure a pain-free death. It is probably not uncommon, but because it is illegal no evidence (other than anecdotal) is available (**euthanasia; mercy killing**).

PIAGET, JEAN (1896–1980) A highly influential Swiss psychologist in the mid-twentieth century. Piaget postulated a set of logical stages that infants and children proceed through as they mature (sensory-motor stage; pre-operational stage; concrete operations and formal operations). His theory of child development was criticized for ignoring the social and emotional aspects of the child's development.

PINEL, PHILIPPE (1745–1826) French physician, who though not a psychiatrist, led the transformation in the treatment of the mentally ill in the nineteenth century. He argued that insanity, where it was not organic, was the outcome of psychological processes and would respond to moral, humane treatment rather than the then accepted methods of incarceration, shock treatment and deprivation. His work, *Medico-philosophical Treatment on Mental Alienation* (1801) influenced **William Tuke**, the English Quaker who led the reform of **Bedlam (American Psychiatric Association; asylums; insulin coma therapy**).

PLACEBO EFFECT The successful treatment of a condition due to the administration of an inert substance such as a salt or sugar pill. Health social scientists argue that it demonstrates the impact of cultural beliefs on treatment practices – you will get well if you believe you are being treated, and shows that the mind is not separate from the body as proposed by Western medicine. Before any new drug is licensed it must be tested with a placebo arm, that is, administered to a group of patients, while another group receives a placebo, with neither doctor nor patient knowing who is receiving which, and clear benefit from the active drug demonstrated (**Cartesian; clinical drug trials; Hawthorne effect; mind–body dualism; Thomas theorem**).

PLURALIST APPROACHES A political theory that argues that power is distributed between social groups in society and that the state is an arbiter of the competition for social goods. In health studies the approach was developed by Robert Alford, who identified three major interest groups: the professional monopolists, such as doctors, who control their work conditions; the corporate rationalizers, who pursuing profitability and accountability, seek to challenge the professional monopolists (**medical dominance**); and the third group are the lay community, who because of their diffuseness have least power in health services and policies. Pluralist approaches are in contrast to Marxist and feminist approaches which argue that power is monopolized either by the ruling class and/or men, and that the state is a participant in maintaining this inequality (Alford, R. (1975) *Health Care Politics.* Chicago: University of Chicago Press) (**managerialism; medical dominance; power; social control**).

POLITICAL ECONOMY Approaches in health studies that emphasize the determining role of economic interests in both producing disease and in shaping the way it is dealt with. Marxists argue that medicine plays a number of crucial roles in capitalist society: it blames the victims of diseases, which are produced by the capitalists' pursuit of profit, for their own conditions. The medical profession acts as an agent of social control of the working class, individualizing and depoliticizing disease, and controlling access to the sick certificate. Furthermore, the very way in which disease is treated, with drug based, high cost **technical fixes**, which do not cure people, but are enormously profitable, are pursued. Medicine in capitalist

societies reflects the characteristics of capitalism: it is profit oriented, blames the victim, and reproduces the class structure in terms of positions of dominance in the medical occupations, with white males at the top, and in terms of who can afford access to healthcare (**Marxist approaches**).

POLLUTION Atmospheric pollution has a major impact on the health of individuals, especially as its effect is often confined to specific areas, such as proximity to nuclear energy plants. It may also be experienced as a consequence of the structure of the city, with heavily used industrial roads running through areas of poor quality housing and low income areas. For example, 27 per cent of African American children living in inner city slums have elevated blood lead levels, compared with 2 per cent in the suburbs (Freid, M. (2000) 'Poor children subject to environmental injustice', *Journal of the American Medical Association*, 283: 3055).

POPPER, KARL (1902–94) An influential philosopher of science who argued that to be scientific a theory had to be falsifiable, and that science should be a search for refutations of theories rather than search for defences of them. He was critical of positivism, since the accumulation of facts could never prove a theory, but also of Marxism and Freudianism, which he argued were unfalsifiable ideologies (Susser, M. (1986) 'The logic of Sir Karl Popper and the practice of epidemiology', *American Journal of Epidemiology*, 133: 635–48) (**case control studies; causal**

inference; Fleck; induction; Kuhn; paradigm; positivism).

POPULAR EPIDEMIOLOGY   Epidemiology focuses on individuals and their **lifestyle** accumulating lists of risk factors, and blaming individuals for their diseases. On the other hand community based environmental action groups identify the risk to individuals' health, not in their behaviour, but in the actions of industrial corporations dumping toxic chemicals, polluting the atmosphere and waterways. Because these companies regularly operate in poor areas they exacerbate the social gradient of disease, adding to the insult of poor socioeconomic standing, a profoundly hazardous environment in which to live. (Brown, P. (1995) 'Popular epidemiology, toxic waste and social movements', in J. Gabe (ed.), *Medicine, Health and Risk*. Oxford: Blackwell) (**blame the victim**; **risk factor epidemiology**).

POPULATION GROWTH   In the mid-1990s the world population was around 5.7 billion, with the United Nations estimating its growth to 12.5 billion by 2050. While overall world population growth has declined since the late 1960s it has continued to increase in the poorest countries, where it is intertwined with poverty and environmental destruction and constitutes a major public health problem. Any solution must combine addressing the question of poverty and fertility rates. However, international policy on the issue confronts secular liberals with religious conservatives and polarization is the outcome

(McMichael, A. (1995) 'Confronting a one child world', *British Medical Journal*, 311: 1651–2) (**demographic entrapment**).

POSITIVISM   At its most general level an **epistemological** position which claims that knowledge should be based on observation and the collection of facts. It assumes the existence of a stable, objective world external to the individual and amenable to sensory verification. It has six key components. 1 A belief that the methods and procedures of the natural sciences are appropriate to the social sciences. 2 Only phenomena which are observable count as valid knowledge (**behaviourism**). 3 Scientific knowledge involves the explanation of how phenomena are linked to other phenomena. 4 Science involves the discovery of universal laws (patterns or regularities) which allows for predictions to be made about human actions and events. 5 Science is deductive since hypotheses are derived from theories and then empirically tested. 6 The social scientist is objective and values do not enter the research process. In health social sciences each of these propositions is largely rejected (**bias**; **case control studies**; **causal influence**; **Chicago School of Sociology**; **Kant**; **qualitative research**; **Weber**; **verstehen**).

POST-FORDISM   The break with large-scale factory production systems (which was called Fordism, after Henry Ford's car plants in the USA) to more flexible forms of production aimed at niche markets. Some sociologists argue that this change in production marks a definite shift out of capitalism (**postmodernity**). It has been used to explain the rise of **consumerism** in contemporary healthcare, with the shift from universal to targeted healthcare (Nettleton, S. and Harding, G. (1994) 'Protesting patients: a study of complaints submitted to a family health service authority', *Sociology of Health and Illness*, 16: 38–61).

POSTMODERNISM A movement in art, architecture, and literature which in contrast to the rigid rules of composition in modernism, sought through pastiche, contradiction, and in delving into the irrational aspects of human creativity to explode the restrictions around artistic production. In literature, James Joyce's *Ulysses*, in painting Picasso's *Guernica*, and in architecture the *Georges Pompidou Centre* in France.

POSTMODERNITY A term used in sociology to describe the changes in modern society. Broadly these are the decline of the industrial sector; the associated decline of the working class; the decline in unionization and the decline in occupation as a source of identity; and the weakening of the rigid distinction between public and private sectors, with their associated gender division of labour. Some sociologists argue that these transformations have freed individuals from the old constraints of occupation and class, and that we are moving out of capitalism while others point to the growth in part-time, service sector jobs as new forms of capitalist exploitation (**citizenship**; **post-Fordism**; **social wage**; **welfare state**).

POST STRUCTURALISM Originating in literary analysis, the attempt to deconstruct texts to show the underlying binary oppositions that they are built on. The focus on the ways in which binary oppositions sustain the vision of the world have provided an important way for health research scholars to unpack **dualisms** such as doctor/patient; doctor/nurse; cure/care; male/female and so on, emphasizing that these are **social constructions** of reality and do not reflect an underlying natural order of things (Derrida, J. (1977) *Of Grammatology*. Tr. G. Spivak. Baltimore: John Hopkins University Press).

POST TRAUMATIC STRESS DISORDER (PTSD) Following World War I and the documentation of the experience of shell shock Kardiner posited the existence of a traumatic neuroses, laying the basis for PTSD (Kardiner, A. (1941) *The Traumatic Neuroses of War*. New York: Paul B. Hoebener). PTSD was first listed in the American Psychiatric Association's *Diagnostic and Statistical Manual* in 1980. Early attempts to formulate a diagnosis appeared in DSM-I (1952) as gross stress reaction. According to DSM-IV the memory of a past traumatic incident relives itself in the present. Individuals diagnosed with PTSD persistently re-experience the trauma; make persistent efforts to avoid stimuli associated with the trauma; and have persistent increased arousal and high levels of anxiety. The condition is of considerable interest to sociologists of psychiatry since its inclusion as a disease was highly contentious, representing the rejection of prevailing Freudian and psychodynamic based explanations of **anxiety**, and their replacement with the medical model and was intricately linked to reactions to the Vietnam War. (Young, A. (1995) *The Harmony of Illusions: Inventing Post-traumatic Stress Disorder.* New Jersey: Princeton University Press) (**antipsychiatry**; **compensation neuroses**; **medicalization**; **social constructionism**).

POVERTY   At one end of the spectrum a lack of 'minimum necessities of merely physical efficiency' (Rowntree, S. (1901) *Poverty: A Study of Town Life.* London: Macmillan). Absolute poverty destroys health through poor nutrition, housing, impaired growth and early death (**diseases of poverty**). However it is well demonstrated that as levels of absolute poverty are ameliorated 'relative' poverty stills plays a significant role in undermining individuals' health. Economists such as A. Sen have argued that this is because there is a cultural aspect to poverty and inequality particularly around issues of self-esteem which make individuals vulnerable to sickness and disease (Sen, A. *Inequality Re-examined.* Oxford: Clarendon Press) (**class**; **diseases of affluence**; **inequality**; **social gradient of disease**).

POWER   In **Marxism** power is the ability of the ruling class to control the working class. In this the medical profession plays the role of controlling access to the sick certificate, obscures the social and economic basis of disease, and through the prescription of drugs and the use of technology provides a profitable arena for capitalists to invest in. In **feminism** power is the ability of men to dominate women. Medicine facilitates this by constructing them as weaker and more sickly than men, constructs their reproductive roles as the natural basis for the gender division of labour, and treats their complaints as psychological. In **Foucault's** work, power is implicit in all social relations, and since the nineteenth century is an aspect of the processes by which we make and represent ourselves, especially through our bodies. He calls this **disciplinary power** (**pluralist approaches**; **social control**).

POWER/KNOWLEDGE   Foucault's neologism for the modern medical and social sciences. The new academic disciplines of the nineteenth century – psychology, psychiatry, and medicine, and the social sciences – were not only disciplines in the sense of codified bodies of knowledge, but disciplines in the sense of prescribing how people should act and behave, the lifestyles they should adopt, and in establishing norms of behaviour they could enforce. Thus they are exercises in power/knowledge. Knowledge is not disinterested – it is linked to forms of **social control** (**conventionalism**; **de Saussure**).

PRAGMATISM   A theory of knowledge that essentially argues that since all knowledge is provisional, the best that can be hoped for is that what works should count as true. It provides the underpinnings of **microsociological** traditions in the USA and was developed out of the work G. H. Mead (1863–1931), John Dewey (1859–1952) and C. H. Peirce (1839–1914) (**Thomas theorem**). Its importance for social accounts of health and disease is that it emphasizes the social shaping of technology, that expert knowledge is itself socially located (**social construction**), partial and incomplete, and that the perspective of the person who is 'dis-eased' is a valid voice in the definition of the situation (**epistemology**; **lifeworld**).

PREFERRED PROVIDER ORGANIZATIONS (PPOS)   Doctors, hospitals and health service providers that insurance groups enter into contract with to provide services to the groups they have insured, at a discounted rate. This also allows the insurer to specify the tests and referrals that they will cover, thus controlling outlays, limiting **medical dominance** and restricting access to services by the insured (**health maintenance organizations**; **managed care**).

PREGNANCY   The carrying of a fetus by a woman from conception to birth or abortion. In Western societies the experience is medicalized, and in **feminist** analyses, this is the outcome of **patriarchal medicine's** domination of women (**childbirth**; **infant mortality rate**; **medicalization**; **reproduction**).

PREMENSTRUAL SYNDROME (PMS)   The alleged impact on women's emotional stability caused by hormonal changes at the time of menstruating. The condition was

first identified in 1931, though whether it exists, what causes it and how to treat it are widely contested, both by feminists and medical practitioners. The diagnosis of PMS has been shown to be closely linked to workforce requirements: when women workers are needed diagnosis of the condition fades, and when women are being excluded from the workforce it increases. Other explanations for its existence link PMS to the increasing number of obstetricians and gynecologists who need to find a market for their work, while other researchers show the active participation in its construction by multinational drug companies. For feminists the issue is in striking a balance between the **medicalization** of women, by allowing that PMS is a disease, thus placing women under the control of patriarchal medicine, and reinforcing the position that women are determined by their biology, while at the same time providing women with access to a legitimate account of the discomfort which may accompany menstruation (Gurevich, M. (1995) 'Rethinking the label: who benefits from the PMS construct?', *Women and Health*, 23 (2): 67–98) (**diagnostic limbo**; **menstrual cycle**).

PRESCRIPTION   The written order of the doctor to the pharmacist to dispense a drug to a patient. All studies of doctors' prescribing behaviour show that therapeutic need, based on a clinical diagnosis, is only one part of the picture. There are marked variations in doctors' prescribing habits, across size of practices and with regional variations (Davis, P. (1997) *Managing Medicines: Public Policy and*

Therapeutic Drugs. Buckingham: Open University Press).

PRESSURE GROUPS　(**managerialism**; **pluralist approaches**).

PREVALENCE　The number of instances of a given disease or other condition in a given population at a designated time, expressed as a rate per 100,000 (**incidence**).

PREVENTIVE MEDICINE　Health policy initiatives designed to produce an environment conducive to health. In Western societies this takes the form of state controls over the production of food, of sanitation and legislation to control environmental pollution. Under **neoliberalism** many of these functions are under threat, and capital lobbies the state to weaken legislation so as to improve profitability (**public health infrastructure**).

PRIMARY CARE　The provision of health services by doctors to ambulatory patients, usually in solo or group general practices, in the suburbs.

PRIVATE MEDICINE　The organization of the delivery of medical services based on an individual contract between the patient and the doctor. Organized medicine has always resisted attempts to bring it under state control as socialized medicine. The most privatized health care system, the US, is also the most expensive (**fee-for service**; **market**; **perverse incentives**).

PRIVATIZATION　Under the impact of **neoliberal** policies, the attempt by governments to shift their public responsibilities for the provision of health, education and welfare onto the private sector. The underlying assumption, with little or no evidence to support it, is that the state is inefficient as the provider of these services. Privatization can take a number of forms in the health sector. First, it may involve contracting out specific hospital services, for example, cleaning and catering, but also clinical and diagnostic activities, pathology and obstetrics. A second form is to allow investors to build private hospital facilities in the grounds of large public hospitals. A third is to allow private operators to construct or lease a public hospital and to run it as a private institution in a for-profit contract arrangement. There is no evidence that these processes reduce costs, improve services, or maintain equity in access to medical services (Collyer, F. and White, K. (1997) 'Enter the market: competition, regulation and hospital funding in Australia', *Australian and New Zealand Journal of Sociology*, 33 (3): 344–63) (**corporatization**; **epidemiological polarization**; **medical-industrial complex**; **new public management**).

PROFESSION　A form of occupational closure in which a group is allowed by the state to administer its own members. In the history of medicine the medical profession has gone through three stages. Under a patronage system in the eighteenth century the patient had power over the doctor; with the rise of the hospital in the nineteenth and twentieth centuries the profession exercised collegial control over its members; with the rise of laboratory medicine the profession's power is mediated by the state (Johnson, T. (1972) *Professions and Power*. London: Macmillan) (**bedside medicine**).

PROFESSIONALISM　　The characteristics of an occupation held to distinguish it from other occupations in the division of labour that are oriented to the profit motive. As identified by **Talcott Parsons** in his analysis of medical practitioners these are universalism, neutrality about the condition under treatment, an orientation towards the collective good and the delivery of the best technical and scientific service available, independent of the patients' social characteristics (**medical dominance**). (Parsons, T. (1951) *The Social System*. Glencoe: The Free Press) (**sick role**).

PROFESSIONALIZATION　　The process whereby an occupation monopolizes knowledge, expands to take over other occupations' roles, expels competitors, and through political activities, protects itself from incursions into its field of practice (Gieryn, T. (1983) 'Boundary work and the demarcation of science from non-science: strains and interests in professional ideologies of scientists', *American Sociological Review*, 48: 781–95). A variation is the analysis of the process by which an occupation limits, excludes, and subordinates competitors (**medical dominance**) (Willis, E. (1989) *Medical Dominance*. Sydney:

Allen and Unwin) (**Apothecaries Act**; **credentialism**; **encroachment**; **occupational closure**).

PROFESSIONAL TRAJECTORY　　The identification of the stages by which an occupation becomes a profession through emergence, consolidation and institutionalization, processes shaped not by scientific facts, but social, political, and economic factors (Bucher, R. and Strauss, A. (1961) 'Professions in process', *American Journal of Sociology*, 66: 325–34) (**medical dominance**) .

PROLETARIANIZATION　　A term used in Marxist theories of the medical profession to describe the rise of corporate medicine in which doctors become employees working under similar conditions to workers in other parts of the economy (McKinlay, J. and Arches, J. (1985) 'Towards the proletarianization of physicians', *International Journal of Health Services*, 15: 161–95) (**deprofessionalization**; **medical dominance**).

PSYCHIATRY　　The branch of medicine that deals with disorders of the mind. Because psychiatric classifications of disease (for example, until the mid-1970s homosexuality) often closely reflect political, social and cultural values, it arouses considerable controversy and scepticism about its claims to be scientific (**American Psychiatric Association**; **asylums**; **antipsychiatry**; **Bedlam**; **mental illness**; **morality and medicine**; **post traumatic stress disorder**).

PSYCHOANALYSIS A wide range of therapies, developing from the work of Freud, which emphasize the role of the unconscious in determining the ways we act, and in particular unresolved sexual desires originating in childhood. While still practised, especially in the United States, because it is unprovable, it is largely discredited (**anxiety**; **Freud**; **Popper**; **talking therapies**).

PSYCHONEUROIMMUNOLOGY/PSYCHONEU-ROENDOCRINOLOGY (PNI/PNE) Branches of medical research which study the impact of social stress on the body. Five physiological markers of stress have been identified: the level of glycoslated proteins; the impaired working of the immune system; a homeostatic mechanism out of balance; the actions of peripheral benzodiazepine receptors; and the relationship of hip to waist size (Kelly, S., Hertzman, C. and Daniels, M. (1997) 'Searching for the biological pathways between stress and illness', *Annual Review of Public Health*, 18: 437–62) (**learned helplessness**).

PSYCHOSOCIAL FACTORS Those factors that link an individual's experience of health and illness and their social position. As with the social gradient of disease these are differentially distributed. The higher the individual is placed in society – in terms of income, education and so on, the better their health, and the more psychosocial factors facilitate their health: autonomy at work, access to services, knowledge of health practices, and an internal **locus of control**. Those down the social system who experience chronic stress at work, cumulatively stressful life events (poverty, unemployment, insecure housing) with little or no autonomy over their work conditions, have poorer social support, smaller social networks, less access to services and an external locus of control, resulting in them being more passive and fatalistic about their health. It is important to keep in mind that psychosocial factors are not psychological factors, but the product of an unequal society (Rutter, M., 'Psychosocial influences: critiques, findings and research needs', *Development and Psychopathology*, 12: 375–405) (**health determinants**; **social drift hypothesis**; **social support**; **stress**).

PSYCHOSOCIAL RISKS The long-term experience of stressful life events correlated with physiological changes in the body. Tracking the link between the biological and the psychological is the aim of the new areas of **psychoneuroimmunology/ psychoneuroendocrinology**. Physiological markers of increased stress that have been identified are glycosylated proteins, the immune system, homeostasis, peripheral benzodiazepine receptors and the waist–hip ratio. While psychosocial risks are manifest in the individual body sociologists seek to explain their origin in specific social structures, especially of **class**, **gender** and **ethnicity**. (Kelly, S. et al. (1997) 'Searching for the biological pathways between stress and health', *Annual Review of Public Health*, 18: 437–62) (**job strain**; **stress**).

PSYCHOSOMATIC ILLNESS In Western medicine, with its distinction between mind–body, those conditions for which there is no apparent physical basis, and therefore are based in the mind (**biopsychosocial**; **placebo effect**; **somatization**; **Thomas theorem**).

PSYCHOSURGERY The therapeutic techniques of psychiatry – surgical interventions such as frontal lobotomies, electro-convulsion therapy and mind altering drugs. Critics of psychiatry have argued that these technologies are connected to professional interests in experimentation and the bureaucratic requirements of a smoothly functioning institution, whether the hospital or the asylum (**antipsychiatry**). The continuing discrepancies in gender differences in the application of these techniques – women are more likely to be treated in these ways than men – provide ongoing concern for feminists (Busfield, J. (1986) *Managing Madness: Changing Ideas and Practices*. London: Hutchinson) (**insulin coma therapy**).

PSYCHOTHERAPEUTICS The use of drugs in psychiatry to treat mental illness. The treatment of conditions such as depression with drugs overlooks the role of social factors in producing and distributing the condition in society. Women are significantly more likely to be prescribed antidepressants and anti-anxiety drugs than men (**antipsychiatry**; **insulin coma therapy**; **mental illness**).

PSY-PROFESSIONS A neologism to capture the group of modern helping occupations (psychiatry, psychology, medicine, social work) who shape and impose our subjective understandings of ourselves. In Foucault's analysis these occupational groups developed through the nineteenth century as new forms of **power/knowledge** to police the population by telling them how to behave (knowledge) and enforcing correct forms of behaviour by controlling access to institutions such as the hospital, asylum and prison (power) (**discourse**; **Foucault**; **technologies of the self**).

PUBLIC HEALTH Developing from the mid-nineteenth century in Britain the recognition of the impact of the social environment on people's health, though in its broadest sense going back to **Hippocrates**. Public health in a capitalist society is directed towards screening populations for treatment by private practitioners; blaming the victims of social circumstances for their condition; individualizing explanations of disease through pointing to **lifestyle factors** and with the development of risk factor **epidemiology** keeping the population in a heightened state of alarm about their health. Developed countries spend less than 1 per cent of their health budgets on public health, since it is generally a non-profitable enterprise (**Chadwick**; **new public health**; **sanitation**; **social medicine**).

PUBLIC HEALTH INFRASTRUCTURE The provision of clean water, the control over sanitation, foodstuffs, and housing conditions by the state. Under the impact of **neoliberalism** these social initiatives have been wound back, and consequently there is now a resurgence of infectious diseases in developed societies (Longbottom, H. (1997) 'Emerging infectious diseases', *Communicable Diseases Intelligence*, 21: 89–93).

PURCHASER-PROVIDER SPLIT An initiative to make health services more accountable for their expenditures by separating the functions of supplying and paying for services, so that for example a hospital has internal markets when different sections deal with each other (**new public management**).

QUACKERY   One way in which orthodox medicine maintains its boundaries and excludes competitors, is label them as frauds or quacks. More generically, claims to medical scientific competence without appropriate state mandated qualifications, and using methods of diagnosis or treatment not recognized by the orthodox medical profession (**allopathy/allopathic**; **complementary/alternative medicine**; **Flexner report**; **professionalization**).

QUALITATIVE RESEARCH   Following **Max Weber** qualitative researchers study human social life as the outcome of social interaction and distinguish action from behaviour (**behaviourism**). By distinguishing these Weber sought to demarcate the methods of sociological research as distinct from those methods used in the natural sciences (**positivism**). Working within a German tradition that emphasized the uniqueness of the social sciences, Weber argued that sociology must develop unique methods to explain social life. Of particular importance is Weber's **verstehen** methodology. For Weber sociological research had to account not only for the regularities and observable patterns of social life but also the meanings and intentions of social actors (Outhwaite, W. (1975) *Understanding Social Life: The Method Called Verstehen*. London: Allen and Unwin). Applied to the sociology of health, the focus is not on the 'objective' characteristics of disease but on the way in which people make sense of their situation when sick. For example the experience of deafness, epilepsy, diabetes or multiple sclerosis go beyond the medical description of these conditions. Sociologically speaking these are stigmatizing conditions, experienced as moral as much as physical conditions. (Schneider, J. (1988) 'Disability as moral experience: epilepsy and self in routine relationships', *Journal of Social Issues*, 44 (1): 63–78) (**grounded theory; Kant; interactionist sociology; narrative accounts of illness; stigma; symbolic interactionism**).

QUALITY ADJUSTED LIFE YEARS (QALYS) A statistical measure of the benefit of a medical intervention on the patient's subsequent enjoyment of life. QALYS were devised by health economists as a way of assessing the value of different interventions, with an eye to making resource distribution more objective in competing claims for healthcare (Carr-Hill, R. (1989) 'Assumptions of the QALY procedure',

Social Science and Medicine, 29: 469–77) (**burden of disease**; **health related quality of life**).

QUALITY OF LIFE   The development of the idea, in the 1970s, that medical measures to save life and/or cure disease should also take into account the impact on the quality of life, that is whether they diminished or enhanced personal well being and happiness (Bowling, A. (1997) *Measuring Health: A Review of Quality of Life Measurement Scales*. Buckingham: Open University Press) (**health related quality of life**; **quality adjusted life years**; **sickness impact profile**).

QUANTITATIVE RESEARCH   Research methods emphasizing the use of statistical analysis and the presentation of a study's findings using statistical methods. While not necessarily antithetical to qualitative research, there is generally a divide between the two. The use of statistical methods in the social sciences is an aspect of **positivism** and generally rejected by those in the qualitative tradition. In **clinical epidemiology** statistical methods are used to generate **risk factors** but pay little attention to the causal factors underlying the correlations generated (**qualitative research**; **reductionism**).

QUARANTINE   The isolation of infected individuals or regions in the case of the outbreak of infectious or epidemic disease. In the nineteenth century, debate focused not on the scientific merit of quarantine, but on its impact on trade, and was opposed by the merchant class (**contagionism**; **germ theory of disease**; **miasma**).

QUESTIONNAIRES   A form of survey research, the administration of a set of questions to the research population. In closed-ended types, a form of structured interview in which exactly the same questions are put to respondents in the same order, and usually designed to allow the responses to be coded for computer analysis. This form is much favoured by those in the positivist tradition, designed to enhance **objectivity** and establish factual data. It presumes in advance what it is that is to be studied and prevents the respondent from injecting their own meanings into the study. In the open-ended form there is more scope for the respondent to state their views.

QUEST NARRATIVES   One of the most predominant themes in Western culture, the stories of their illness told by patients as they pursue a cure for their condition, or seek to transcend it and to find meaning in it. It is the dominant motif of movies of the young, stricken down by terminal illness and their journey to a new self-understanding as they come to terms with their condition (**biographical disruption**; **narrative accounts of illness**).

RACE The sorting of the population into biologically unique groups, or races, on a claimed biological basis, has been a prominent feature of twentieth-century medicine and some of the social sciences, such as biologically reductionist forms of anthropology, psychology and sociobiology. However, it has been well demonstrated that there are no basis for the division of human species into races, and there are more genetic differences within a group than across human groups. The designation of a group as a 'race' is a socially accomplished labelling and not the reflection of a biological reality. Politically and ideologically race functions to 'scientifically' explain the subordinate position of a group and to make their place in the social structure look natural, inevitable and unchangeable. It does this by asserting that their (negatively valued) cultural characteristics are physically inherited (Rose, S., Lewontin, R. and Kamin, L. (1984) *Not in Our Genes: Biology, Ideology and Human Nature.* Harmondsworth: Penguin) (**ethnicity; eugenics; heredity; IQ controversy; reductionism**).

RACISM The systematic treatment of a group in society as of a different category of persons on the grounds that they have a different biological constitution, claimed to be marked by skin colour. The claim is based on an appeal to supposedly scientific fact, usually constructed to support the argument that an underprivileged group is 'naturally' deficient in characteristics that would otherwise allow them to be successful. By extension, the argument is that inequalities built on skin colour are natural, inevitable and unchangeable. Racism may be expressed by individuals in the form of stereotypes and prejudices about people of different colour or **ethnicity**, or it may be institutional, a set of assumptions historically produced and supported by entrenched policies, which do not rely on individual intent for their operation, but are part of the way the system functions (**African Americans; indigenous people; IQ controversy; race; reductionism; Tuskegee syphilis experiment**).

RADICAL FEMINISM A form of feminist analysis that asserts the fundamental biological differences between men and women. Woman's body is privileged over man's, and it is in women's interest to wrest control of their fertility and reproductive abilities from men. For radical feminists the family is the basis of the hierarchical sexual division of labour, and must be overthrown. Woman are in a class of their own and the sexual division of labour is the most basic form of oppression. It is women's role in childbearing which is the cause of their oppression, and only when technology relieves them of this role will freedom be possible (Firestone, S. (1974) *The Dialectic of Sex: The Case for the Feminist Revolution*. New York: Morrow) (**birth control**).

RANDOMIZED CONTROL TRIALS (RCTS) A process for investigating the impact of a new medical practice, but most commonly a new drug. The patients are divided into two groups, one receiving the new treatment, while the other is treated with the existing best practice. The aim is to minimize the role of social or psychological reactions of the patient to the treatment process. In the randomized double-blind controlled trail the doctors administering the new treatment do not know which treatment they are working with, thereby minimizing any impact they may have on the process. Because RCTs are limited to experimental conditions they are of limited value when it comes to assessing psychological or sociological aspect of treatment and the delivery of health services to patients (**clinical trial; Cochrane Centre; evidence-based medicine; placebo effect**).

RATIONALIZATION In the sociology of Max Weber, the greater and greater intrusion of science and calculability into everyday life, making it more predictable, but without giving an answer to the ultimate questions of the meaning of existence. Health sociologists demonstrate the ways in which the doctor–patient encounter is more and more rationalized to fit specified outcome targets of the number of patients seen, the number of prescriptions written, and the number of referrals for tests written, but with no attention to the role of suffering or physical deterioration as a part of human existence. As a key concept in Weber's work it parallels that of **alienation** in Marx and **anomie** in Durkheim (**McDonaldization/McDoctor**; **rational legal authority**).

RATIONAL LEGAL AUTHORITY In modern societies individuals comply with orders, based on rules and regulations, which are formally enacted and enshrined in law. The contrasts are with charismatic authority, where individuals comply because of the perceived outstanding qualities of an individual, or traditional authority, in which compliance is based on adherence to age-old practices of doing things. In medicine nurses comply with the directions of doctors, based not on any personal characteristic of the doctor, but because the doctor has the legal authority to diagnose and treat disease and to direct para-professional groups in subordinate occupations (**bureaucracy; doctor/nurse game; occupational closure; profession; Weber**).

REDUCTIONISM The logically fallacious argument that the workings of a complex whole can be reduced to the workings of its parts (the whole is always greater than the sum of its parts), thus in medicine, of the body to its organs, then to its cells, then to its genes, then to its DNA. Reductionism is also an epistemological position that asserts that all knowledge can be reduced to one scientific methodology, that of the natural sciences, and particularly to physics. This was the dream of positivist sociology, especially as laid out by its founder Auguste Comte (1798–1857) (**holism**; **mechanistic**; **positivism**; **vitalism**).

REFLEXIVITY   In the sociology of knowledge the question is not whether an approach is true, but how a claim to knowledge comes to be substantiated. This means the construction by the sociologist is as open to dispute as the claim to knowledge by those under examination. Reflexivity is the process by which the sociologist inquires into their own basis for knowing the situation, such that they ask the same questions of themselves as investigators, as they do of those whose knowledge is under investigation. At the core is the problem of relativism, that all accounts of a situation are value laden, and that independent knowledge of the situation is not possible (**social instruction/constructionism**; **sociology of scientific knowledge**).

REIFICATION   A concept developed by Hungarian Marxist Georg Lukacs (1885–1971) to describe the process in capitalist societies whereby social relationships come to be seen as relationships between things. Thus in work, workers see themselves as selling their labour power, a

thing, to employers, which prevents them from seeing that they are in a social relationship of exploitation (**alienation**). In medicine, reification occurs when disease is seen as existing independently of the patient, and the encounter between the doctor and the patient ceases to be about the social processes that produced or distributed the disease in the first place, and a successful intervention is one that addresses the technical problem at hand. In this medicine performs the **ideological** function of obscuring social relationships as the basis of disease and focuses on the individual patient's body (Waitzkin, H. 'A critical theory of medical discourse: ideology, social control and the processing of social context in medical encounters', *Journal of Health and Social Behaviour,* 30: 220–39).

RELATIVISM   An **epistemological** position which holds that all knowledge is culturally dependent, and that there is no way of objectively choosing between different belief systems. In **social constructionism** the argument is extended to the contents of medical science: medical knowledge reflects its historical, political, gendered and economic shaping by the wider society (which it in turn shapes), rather than being a objective account of nature (**Fleck**; **reflexivity**; **scientific method**).

RELIABILITY   The confidence with which a researcher can claim that their findings represent reality. In the quantitative tradition reliability is measured by the replicability of the study by other researchers who reach the same conclusions. In the qualitative tradition reliability is more likely to be measured by the extent to which the study's findings are supported by the group under study (**research methods**).

REPETITIVE STRAIN INJURY (RSI) The debate over RSI provides a case study of the social production of disease as different parties fight to construct its meaning. To some commentators – generally employers – it is the outcome of a general lack of tone, poor posture and unfitness. Others – generally representatives of the unions involved – focus on equipment and work processes, suggesting that the conditions of employment in modern offices, with the lack of control experienced by the worker and the drudgery of the work, inevitably give rise to the complaint. Yet for others – the psychiatrists – it is a form of **compensation neurosis** and/or a form of hysterical conversion syndrome, or the product of the medico-legal system. Thus, whether or not RSI is a disease, or will become a disease, is a political issue, and the outcome not of biological factors but social relationships. Furthermore sociologists who enter the debate, particularly those who utilize a constructionist perspective will themselves become actors in the definitional process as their work is appropriated by representatives of different positions to suit their own interests. (Hopkins, A. (1989) 'The social construction of repetitive strain injury', *Australia and New Zealand Journal of Sociology*, 25: 239–59) (**chronic fatigue syndrome; deviance; miners' nystagmus; occupation and health; post traumatic stress disorder**).

REPRODUCTION In biology the process of conceiving, carrying and delivering members of the next generation. From a sociological perspective how this process is accomplished is a social, cultural and political act. Historical and anthropological research demonstrates the wide cultural variability in the construction of pregnancy and birth, while feminist approaches examine the role of patriarchal medicine in Western society in determining women's social roles on apparently scientific grounds (Macintyre, S. (1977) 'The management of childbirth: a review of sociological research issues', *Social Science and Medicine*, 11: 447–84) (**childbirth; gender roles; medicalization; new reproductive technologies; pregnancy**).

RESEARCH METHODS The range of techniques used in the natural and social sciences to investigate their subject matter. In the social sciences they divide into quantitative and qualitative methods, based on different assumptions about the nature of the social that they investigate. For those in the quantitative tradition, based on **positivism**, social life is to be examined in the same way as, for example, geologists study the earth: society is a fixed, independent reality, which the social scientist studies as a value-free scientist using statistical and mathematical models for reporting their findings. The aim of research is to provide valid and generalizable findings without bias. Those in the qualitative tradition emphasize the negotiated, fluid nature of social life, and use methods emphasizing interpretation, in-depth discussions with their respondents and **participant observation**

of social life as it actually occurs. The impetus for this approach is in the writings of **Weber** and the **Chicago School of Sociology**. The aim of research is explanation and understanding, often in ways that are not generalizable, by researchers who stand on equal footing with their respondents. While the two traditions can be blended the different assumptions about the nature of social reality and of the purpose of social research means that researchers are predominantly in one tradition or the other (**Kant**; **reductionism**; **triangulation**; **verstehen**).

RETIREMENT   The withdrawal of an individual from the workforce, normally at a legally prescribed age. In disengagement theory this marks the gradual withdrawal from active social life as the individual prepares for death. Activity theorists emphasize the continuities in social engagement and the opening up of new opportunities for personal growth (**age**; **ageing**; **ageism**).

REVOLVING DOOR SYNDROME   Originally used to describe the impact of the **deinstitutionalization** of the mentally ill, the repeated re-admission to hospital for crisis management of their condition. It refers more broadly to the continuing crisis management of at-risk groups whose condition is ameliorated by constantly accessing health and welfare services, but who are never effectively dealt with (Woogh, C. (1986) 'A cohort through the revolving door', *Canadian Journal of Psychiatry*, 31 (3): 214–21).

RISK   With the development of statistics in the nineteenth century it became possible to calculate mathematically the probability of an event, and in the health area, of disease or death (**Graunt**; **Petty**). In this tradition risks are objective features of life. In a Foucauldian analysis it is argued that risks are socially constructed, particularly in the **new public health**, to direct attention to individual lifestyle choices and to detract attention from structural causes of disease (Lupton, D. (1999) *Risk*. London: Routledge) (**Multiple Risk Factor Intervention Trial**; **surveillance medicine**).

RISK FACTOR EPIDEMIOLOGY   The focus on individual behaviour as the cause of disease, replacing the focus of nineteenth-century **epidemiology** on the social causes of disease. In focusing on the proximate causes of disease – diet, cholesterol or hypertension for example – risk factor epidemiology individualizes the cause of disease and excludes the distal social causes. Risk factors need to be placed in their social context so as to see how individuals are exposed to them and have limited resources to respond to them. It is the lack of resources to respond to risks that is the fundamental cause of disease patterns. There is limited evidence for the role of risk factors in the cause of disease with socio-economic position intervening to protect those at the top of society, independently of their lifestyle (Link, B. and Phelan, J. (1995) 'Social conditions as fundamental causes of disease', *Journal of Health and Social Behaviour*, Extra Issue: 80–94) (**healthism**; **lifestyle factors**;

Multiple Risk Factor Intervention Trial; popular epidemiology; Whitehall Studies).

RISK SOCIETY The development of global threats of pollution and nuclear hazards, which threaten rich and poor countries alike, have given rise to the concept of risk society. Thus not only are the poor at risk, but the rich as well. At the core of the concept is the paradox that many risks can only be identified by experts, at the same time as expert knowledge is more and more questioned (Beck, U. (1992) *Risk Society*. London: Sage) (**healthism**).

RITES OF PASSAGE The ceremonial marking of the transition of the individual from one social status to another, as for example, in the marriage ceremony, the transition from being single to being a couple. While usually used in relation to positive role transitions, marking enhanced status in the group, rites of passage may also relate to the transition to a degraded social status, as in the **degradation ceremonies** which mark an individual's transition into the categories of mentally ill or criminal (**courtesy stigma**; **Goffman**; **stigma**).

ROLE The set of characteristics associated with a social position independently of the personal characteristics of the individual who holds the role. Thus in Parsonian sociology (**Parsons**) doctors fulfil their role by their use of the best scientific treatments, delivered to patients independently of the patient's social characteristics, for the good of the community rather than the pursuit of self-interest. In Parsons' model, roles are positions which individuals are socialized into and over which they have little control. As developed in **structural functionalism**, the assumption is that society is a stable set of expectations of how others will act, which can be objectively studied. In the **symbolic interactionist** tradition, roles are negotiated between individuals as they test out others' perceptions of their performances. In this usage society is fluid, negotiated and interactive (**Chicago School of Sociology**; **Mead**).

RSI (**repetitive strain injury**).

RYLE, JOHN (1889–1950) Along with the **Webbs** an ardent campaigner for social medicine in Britain following World War I. Ryle linked poor health to social inequality and injustice, arguing that medicine was about reform at all levels of society, from schools to factories. He was the first professor of social medicine at Oxford.

S

SAMPLE SIZE The number of subjects in a study. This may range from whole populations, as in morbidity and **mortality rates** to single individuals, as in life history research (**case studies**).

SAMPLING In quantitative research, seeking to generalize to the whole population a representative group is devised and analysed, a technique known as probability sampling. Sampling allows quantitative researchers to make claims based on statistical inference about the whole population (**causal inference; nonprobability sampling techniques**).

SANITATION The maintenance of the environment – particularly housing, water and food supplies – to protect people's health. The publication of **Chadwick's** report on sanitary conditions of the working class drove the nineteenth century public health movement, resulting in an amelioration of the impact of capitalist industrialization. While advocating public health reforms the sanitary movement identified the cause of disease with the **miasma** arising from rotting garbage and not from the poverty produced by the underlying economic system (Rosen, G.

(1974) *From Medical Police to Social Medicine: Essays on the History of Health-care.* New York: Science History Publications) (**Engels; McKeown; social medicine**).

SCHIZOPHRENIA A diagnosis in psychiatry based on symptoms reported by the patient, including hearing voices, hallucinations and the sense of being under the control of some outside agent. The condition, because of different rates of diagnosis in different countries, has given rise to considerable controversy. In particular it has been shown to have been used in Russia through the mid-twentieth century to label political dissidents, and rates of diagnosis are still high in the United States by international comparison. The **antipsychiatry** movement argued that it was, then, a medicalized form of political control of individuals who resisted patterns of normal behaviour. There is considerable debate in the anthropological literature about whether schizophrenia is culturally specific to European and North American societies (Barrett, R. (1988) 'Interpretations of schizophrenia', *Culture, Medicine and Psychiatry*, 12: 357–88) (**antipsychiatry; mental illness**).

SCHUTZ, ALFRED (1899–1959) An
Austrian social philosopher who fled from
Nazism to the United States in 1939,
Schutz brought the phenomenology of
Husserl into sociology with his *The
Phenomenology of the Social World*
(orig. 1932, 1972, London: Heinemann).
Schutz's major focus was on how social
actors understand situations from a subjective perspective and what meanings they
attach to their actions. He argued that
unless sociologists really grasped the
meaning of the situation for the person, all
that they did was lay their own interpretation of reality over the subjects, a process
he called second-order typification. His
work has been used to underpin the
qualitative research tradition, but like
ethnomethodology and **symbolic interactionism** it has been criticized for its lack
of attention to issues of power and for
the limited generalizability of studies
conducted in this theoretical tradition
(**Heidegger; Husserl; phenomenology;
microsociological**).

SCIENTIFIC METHOD Developing from
the seventeenth century, and epitomized
in the work of Isaac Newton (1642–1727),
the claim that through the observation of
empirical data, theories can be developed
to explain events, and the laws of nature
discovered. Thus it replaced the theological account of the middle ages that knowledge was a product of faith and revelation.
While the image of the scientific method still
holds considerable sway – especially in the
popular press, economics and psychology –
the development of Einsteinian quantum

physics challenged the claim that the
world can be known independently from
the perspective of the observer or that
there are stable laws of nature. It is this
relativistic view of the existence of things
which underlies much interpretive health
studies (**empiricism; Fleck; Kant; Kuhn;
paradigm; relativism; Whig histories of
medicine**).

SCIENTISM The claim that the only
valid knowledge is that based on the
scientific method of the natural sciences
and that social problems are amenable to
technical solutions. Western medicine is
scientistic, rigidly distinguishing the mind
from the body, objectifying the patient,
adopting a **mechanistic** model of the
body, and conceptualizing disease as
independent from social relationships. In
psychology it led to the development of
behaviourism, the attempt to exclude
consciousness from the study of the person
(**embodiment; empiricism; positivism;
reductionism; scientific method; technical
fix**).

SCREENING In public health the targeting of either specific risks that should be
monitored – high blood pressure or cholesterol levels for example – or the identification of parts of the population at risk of
specific disease such as women and breast
cancer, who require regular monitoring.
Critics of the new public health argue that
focusing on individuals and **risk factors**
diverts attention from the social
factors that distribute risks and disease
(**Foucauldian-feminism; mammography

screening programme; new public health; risk; surveillance medicine).

women are socialized have a poorer sense of self than men.

SECONDARY CARE   The assistance given by other members of the family to the primary care-giver (usually the wife/mother) or the person under care, usually indirectly and intermittently (**care in the community**).

SELF-CARE   The maintenance of self-control over our emotions and life, and in terms of health, of our bodies. Under **neoliberalism** self-care of the body is assumed to represent self-discipline. Public health campaigns target **lifestyles** held to be under our control and on which we have to impose our will in the quest for body maintenance. Failure to do so is to fail in our requirement as active citizens to participate in society. The sick body, the disabled body, offends because of its lack of conformity to the ideals of autonomy and control (Schilling, C. (1993) *The Body and Social Theory.* London: Sage) (**bodyism; citizenship; fitness; morality and medicine; psy-professions; somatic norms; technologies of the self**).

SELF-ESTEEM   Viewing oneself positively. People with high self-esteem cope better with illness, possibly because they have a strong sense of control over situations (**locus of control**). Self-esteem is less a psychological variable than a sociological one, associated with economic well being and the ability to access information. Feminists argue that in Western societies

SELF-HELP GROUPS   The voluntary coming together of individuals in similar conditions to share knowledge and support one another. It is the reciprocal nature of relationships in these groups that distinguishes them from the encounter with the professional physician or healthcare system. Groups vary widely in their political stance, with some having overt political agendas to influence policies or treatments (as in HIV/AIDS groups) through to those that see themselves as operating within a pre-defined situation, which may enhance **medicalization**. They have been found to be particularly valuable at the psychosocial level for those suffering from chronic illness, but they may also lead to **desease identity dependency** (Katz, A. (1992) *Self Help: Concepts and Applications.* Philadelphia: The Charles Press) (**lay referral system; support groups, online**).

SELF-SELECTED SAMPLE   Research in which respondents are volunteers and in which no attempt is made to control for the fact that these respondents will be highly motivated and have strong opinions on the topic. For example the work of Shere Hite is based on voluntary responses to a 127 item questionnaire (and within it the respondents could choose which questions to answer or omit). Out of 100,000 questionnaires distributed through women's groups, church groups, magazines and so on she had a response rate of only 4.5 per cent. From this she extrapolated her findings on women's sexuality to the whole population, leading many researchers to reject her work (**Hite Report**).

SEMIOTICS　The study of language, understood not to refer to real objects by their real names (the Adamic theory of language), but as an inter-related system of signs. Based on the work of **Ferdinand de Saussure** who distinguished signifiers – an object, from the object so identified – the signified. He argued that the link between the two was purely conventional (**conventionalism**). The implication of this argument, called the linguistic turn in the social sciences, has been developed in health studies to argue that there is no necessary link between a condition (the signifier), for example, a physical condition, and what we call it (the signified) for example, a disease, than the fact that it has been successfully so labelled (**Bachelard; Canguihelm; labelling theory; medicalization; social constructionism**).

SEPARATION ANXIETY　A concept in **psychoanalysis**, the fear that the child has of being separated from his or her mother. John Bowlby (**attachment theory**) extended the concept to the more general one of maternal deprivation, which occurs, he argues, when the mother does not provide the child with an adequate sense of security (**anxiety; psychoanalysis**).

SEPARATIONS, HOSPITAL　The number of people who leave a hospital either

through a completed procedure, discharge or death. It is often used to determine the trends in morbidity from a disease (**benchmarking; clinical pathways; new public management**).

SERIOUS AND ONGOING MENTAL ILLNESS (SOMI)　The terminology used to describe individuals with mental illness is a product of political and economic factors. In the past these have included idiot, inmate, mental patient, mentally retarded, and insane. In the 1990s under the impact of economic rationalism they were reconceptualized as a client or **consumer** and health policymakers referred to them as service users. Health consumer advocates refer to them as survivors and consumers. SOMI is increasingly used to highlight the special needs of this population and their uniqueness as users of the health services (Pilgrim, D. and Rogers, A. (1999) *A Sociology of Mental Health and Illness.* Buckingham: Open University Press) (**mental illness**).

SEXUAL HARASSMENT　Unwanted sexual approaches ranging from innuendo, inappropriate touching, through to physical assault, and rape, that is, forced sexual intercourse. A United Nations study found that between 8 and 15 per cent of college-aged women had been raped, and between 20 and 27 per cent had been the target of attempted rape. The experience of sexual harassment may be experienced as very stressful, with women often trapped in situations with, for example, no alternative source of employment (Griffith, J. and

Griffith, M. (1994) *The Body Speaks.* New York: Basic Books) (**domestic violence; gender linked health risks**).

SEXISM   The set of institutionally maintained assumptions that women have a lesser role, and are incapable of a greater role to play in society, economically, politically and culturally. Many of these assumptions are claimed to be based on scientifically grounded biological knowledge and are sustained by patriarchal medical knowledge which systematically constructs women's bodies as lesser than men's and as more diseased and in need of medical control. Significant differences in the treatment of men and women presenting to the doctor with the same complaint have been demonstrated. Women are prescribed more antibiotics, hormones, and drugs affecting the central nervous, cardiovascular and urogenital systems. Women are four times more likely to have their activities restricted than men with the same symptoms. These studies support the argument that doctors operate with stereotypical, and sexist, assumptions about their women patients (Sayer, G. and Britt, H. (1997) 'Sex differences in prescribed medications – another case of discrimination in general practice', *Social Science and Medicine*, 15: 711–22) (**clinical drug trials; feminism; medicalization; patriarchal medicine**).

SEX ROLE SOCIALIZATION   The argument that men and women are different not because of biological givens but because they are socialized in different ways. Thus feminine social roles emphasize fragility, dependency and emotional expressiveness. It is argued that this leads women to a greater tendency to experience and report their symptoms to the doctor. Men on the other hand are socialized to repress their emotions, deny their physical symptoms, and are less likely to present to the doctor (Verbrugge, L. (1985) 'Gender and health: an update on hypotheses and evidence', *Journal of Health and Social Behaviour*, 26: 156–82) (**gender; gender linked health risks; gendered health; gender roles; male stoicism; sexism**).

SEXUALITY   (**gender**).

SEXUALLY TRANSMITTED DISEASE (STDS) Diseases spread through sexual intercourse. The oldest is gonorrhea, a non-fatal infection of the urethra. Syphilis was apparently brought back from the Americas by Columbus and rapidly, and fatally, swept over Europe. This probably owed as much to the social conditions of the time – international warfare, increasing population density, urbanization, and the move from the countryside to the city as capitalism developed – which escalated its spread. Sexually transmitted diseases were thought to be under control until the outbreak of HIV/AIDS which was first diagnosed in 1981. Again social factors have played a significant role in its spread, starting with its identification with the homosexual community and a lack of will of conservative governments to act. In the third world its spread is facilitated with the growing movement to the city, and with the lack of work, young men and women turning to the sex industry. Religious resistance to birth control in many countries has led to strong resistance to condom use, and facilitated the spread of the disease. Its impact in third world countries and among the poor in the West is devastating, halving life expectancies, and resulting in over 8 million deaths (**stigmatized risk groups**).

SHAMANISM　The prevention and/or cure of illness in non-Western cultures through the conduct of rituals or practices putting the healer into a trance to intercede with the spirit world. Shamanism may be blended with Western medical services (**biomedical cultures; folk healing; indigenous healing; spiritual healing**).

SICK BUILDING SYNDROME (SBS)　First reported in the early 1980s, the claim by workers (backed up by the World Health Organization that up to 30 per cent of new and remodelled buildings would be a source of complaint) in air-conditioned buildings to suffer a range of respiratory complaints, headaches, sore throats, stuffy noses and itchy eyes. These conditions appear to be linked to time spent in the building but no underlying cause can be identified. One postulated cause is the reduction in building ventilation standards following the oil crisis of 1973. In an effort to reduce energy consumption the amount of outdoor air provided for ventilation was reduced from 15 cubic feet per minute to 5 cubic feet per minute per occupant. Because of this the American Society of

Heating, Refrigerating and Air-Conditioning Engineers has revised its ventilation standard back to 15 cubic feet per minute per occupant. From a Marxist perspective, this attempt to cut costs interacts with work practices and a lack of autonomy on the job and would be 'cured' by transforming work relations (Indoor Environmental Quality, National Institute for Occupational Safety and Health, June 1997, http://www.cdc.gov/niosh/ieqfs.html) (**alienation; building related illness; occupation and health; repetitive strain injury**).

SICK ROLE　The medically sanctioned right to withdraw from normal social obligations on the grounds of ill-health. **Talcott Parsons** argued that given the strains of modern society individuals would be tempted to 'go sick', which he termed '**motivated deviance**'. To prevent this the sick role is a carefully guarded social role with two rights and two duties. The patient's rights are first, withdrawal from their usual social roles, and second, that they are exempt from blame for their condition, since they cannot get well on their own but need help and support. The patient's duties are that they must want to get well – they cannot malinger – and they must seek technically competent help, that is, go to the doctor. Parsons thus saw the medical professional as an agent of **social control**, preventing individuals from opting out of their social roles. At the same time he recognized that 'going sick' may be the only option for an individual facing intolerable social strain, but did not allow it as a valid political response to social strain (**compliance; consultation; deviance; doctor–patient relationship; professionalism**).

SICKNESS IMPACT PROFILE (SIP) A range of research instruments for measuring health related **quality of life**. They combine objective measures of clinical status with subjective evaluations of well being, based on extensive open-ended questioning of patients, professionals and care givers (**health status assessment; Karnofsky's performance status scale**).

SIDE EFFECTS (**adverse drug reactions**).

SIGERIST, HENRY (1891–1957) Historian of medicine and campaigner for public health in America between the wars (Sigerist, H. (1937) *Socialised Medicine in the Soviet Union*. London: Victor Gollancz) (**Webb**).

SIMON, JOHN (1816–1904) Appointed Britain's first chief medical administrator in 1854 and responsible for the development and implementation of a large number of public health provisions, for example, the Local Government Act (1858) and the Sanitary Act (1866) (**Snow; social medicine**).

SMOKING Causally associated with lung cancer, the inhalation of commercially produced and treated tobacco. There are a number of features about smoking: the decline in Western countries was led by the professional, white collar occupations, with men giving up as women increased their smoking; there is a wide social class gradient in smoking with those towards the bottom smoking more; as Western markets shrink, tobacco companies are deliberately targeting under-developed countries as markets. Tobacco consumption and poverty are interlinked, and to reduce the first requires action on the second. Focusing on individuals and castigating them for smoking will blame the victim, and miss the point of why low status groups smoke (**case control studies; causal inference; lifestyle; lifestyle choices**).

SNOW, JOHN (1813–58) A surgeon and one of the first anaesthetists. He is famous for identifying contaminated water as the source of a cholera outbreak in nineteenth-century London. He demonstrated this by removing the handle from the Broad Street water pump, preventing access to contaminated water and showed that consequently the area had less cholera than surrounding areas. Equally though, in his *On the Modes of Communication of Cholera* (1849), he emphasized the role of poverty and overcrowding as a cause of sickness and disease, and that it was these factors that increased the fatalities from cholera (**social medicine**).

SNOWBALLING (**nonprobability sampling**).

SOCIAL CAPITAL Best understood as a development of Durkheim's concept of organic solidarity. Durkheim argued in his book *The Division of Labour in Society* (1933) that social harmony would come about in industrial society through the formation of communities based on shared occupational interests and producing a new moral individual whose actions would be guided by a concern for the common good. Contemporary social capital theorists argue that the increased density of social relationships, with improved communication leads to a revitalized common good and to the alleviation of social conflict. In communities where there is strong social capital – neighbourhood organizations, social clubs and so on – there are also better health rates (Lomas, J. (1998) 'Social capital and health – implications for public health and epidemiology', *Social Science and Medicine*, 47: 1181–8). However there are problems with the social capital approach. The explanation of poor health in the poorer sections of society as the consequence of their lack of certain attributes – that they do not generate social capital – continues a conservative sociological explanation of inequality, suggesting that dysfunctional communities are responsible for their own shortcomings and should solve them on their own. Emphasizing 'social capital' in the absence of addressing inequalities of economic capital makes this approach appealing to right-wing, post-welfare state governments who see it as a cost neutral way of putting responsibility for services that used to be provided by the state back on to the local level **(health determinants; social wage; welfare state)**.

SOCIAL CAUSATION   In general the claim in health studies that sickness and disease are produced by social processes rather than purely biological ones. There are three identifiable models. In **labelling theory** the argument was that social reactions to odd behaviour, based on specific understandings of normal behaviour, could lead to the labelling of the individual as diseased, especially in terms of the context of the social control function of psychiatry (**antipsychiatry**). In the social heritage approach researchers document how the social and economic conditions of the mother during pregnancy lay down a life long pattern of health and disease. In the third tradition the argument is that individuals and groups are differentially exposed to the conditions which cause disease (**materialist**) and that the resources to deal with these conditions is differentially distributed through society (**stress**) (Siegrist, J. (2000) 'The social causation of health and illness', in G. Albrecht et al. (eds), *Handbook of Social Studies in Health and Medicine*. London, Sage) (**disease, social model; social pathology**).

SOCIAL CLASS   (Black Report; class; class analysis; diseases of poverty; social gradient of disease; social inequality; socio-economic inequalities; socio-economic status; Whitehall Studies).

SOCIAL CLOSURE   In the sociology of professions the successful demarcation of an occupation's area of practice achieved through subordinating, limiting or excluding closely allied occupations. Thus medicine subordinates nursing, limits the activities of para-professions such as pharmacy or physiotherapy, and excludes, for example, homeopathy (**social usurpation**). In the sociology of science the resolution of a dispute is by professional fiat rather than (as is usually thought) the workings of the scientific method or an appeal to the 'facts' (**conventionalism**) (**medical dominance**; **professionalization**).

SOCIAL CONSTRUCTION/CONSTRUCTIONISM

As developed in the sociology of health, the argument that concepts of disease and the body are the product of specific socio-historical periods rather than reflections of an independently existing nature or reality. The social constructionist theory of medical knowledge has three major aims: 1 to demonstrate that medical knowledge is socially shaped in the same way that other knowledge claims are, and therefore should not have a privileged position in the diagnosis and treatment of disease; 2 to demonstrate the contextual elements that influence the development of medical thought and by emphasizing the relativistic implications of both historical and anthropological research into medicine, highlight its contextual qualities; and 3 to examine medicine as a social practice, exploring the more general question of how medical knowledge comes to be accepted as a seemingly scientifically neutral body of knowledge. The constructionist approach problematizes reality, particularly the claim that it is understood through an objective natural science; it demonstrates how 'objective' scientific knowledge both shapes and is shaped by social relationships; and it shows

how the technical realm of medical practice is not neutral with respect to social processes (Wright, P. and Treacher, A. (eds) (1982) *The Problem of Medical Knowledge: Examining the Social Construction of Medicine.* Edinburgh: Edinburgh University Press) (**Bachelard**; **body**; **Canguihelm**; **constructionism**; **disease**; **Kant**).

SOCIAL CONSTRUCTION OF TECHNOLOGY APPROACH (SCOT)

Examines the interplay between the social shaping of technology and the technological shaping of society. The central argument is that technological artifacts are open to a wide range of competing interpretations by different social groups and that there is nothing implicit in their existence that makes them technological (Pinch, T. and Bijker, W. (1984) 'The social construction of facts and artefacts, or how the sociology of science and the sociology of technology might benefit each other', *Social Studies of Science*, 14: 399–441) (**actor-network theory**; **biotechnology**; **health technology assessment**; **medical technology**; **National Institute of Clinical Evidence**; **technical fix**).

SOCIAL CONTROL

In the sociology of health generically speaking, the function of the medical profession is to control and police deviant behaviour, legitimated by the apparent scientificity (in contrast to legal and religious definitions of deviance) of the profession's decisions about what constitutes normal behaviour (Zola, I. (1972) 'Medicine as an institution of social control: the medicalization of society', *Sociological Review*, 20: 487–504). In the

Marxist tradition the function of the medical profession is to discipline the working class through control of the sick certificate. In the labelling theory tradition (**antipsychiatry**) behaviour is designated as abnormal or diseased when it does not fit wider norms of acceptable behaviour (**gambling**). In feminist critiques of medicine it is the identification of thinly veiled patriarchal assumptions about women's roles, in particular the construction of her body as diseased, of her lifecycle in terms of reproduction and the construction of her 'natural' roles as wife and mother. In Parsons' sociology the function of the medical profession is to prevent motivated **deviance** by individuals, that is their opting out of their social roles because they find them stressful (**morality and medicine; power; sick role**).

SOCIAL DARWINISM　　The application of Charles Darwin's theory of evolution and the survival of the fittest to human populations with the aim of justifying the existing social order by claiming that it is natural. As Karl Marx pointed out 'it is remarkable how Darwin recognizes among the beasts and plants his English society with its division of labour, competition, opening up of new markets, "inventions" and the Malthussian struggle for existence' (Marx, K. and Engels, F. (1965) *Selected Correspondence.* Tr. I. Lasker. Moscow: Progress Publishers: 128) (**eugenics; Malthus; social drift hypothesis; sociobiology**).

SOCIAL DEATH　　The exclusion of an individual from the group for failure to conform

to social norms. In the Middle Ages lepers were ritually excluded from society following a funeral mass in which a candle was broken. They were then driven out of the town. Contemporary studies of the dying trajectory demonstrate that prior to the announcement of biological death individuals who do not conform to the expected behaviour, especially those having a lingering death, are treated as though they are already dead (Sudnow, D. (1967) *Passing On: The Social Organization of Dying.* Englewood Cliffs, NJ: Prentice-Hall) (**dying trajectories; voodoo death**).

SOCIAL DEGRADATION　　The experience of social, political and economic circumstances which foster ill-health, disease and premature, preventable death. In the history of modern medicine the debate was between the sanitationists (**social medicine**) and those who either saw the improved health rates of the urban poor as a consequence of medical advances, or those, **Social Darwinists** who argued that it was only right that the sick be weeded out and that their condition reflected freely chosen actions on their part (**social drift hypothesis**). The division between the first two is as old as Western society (**hygiene**). As demonstrated by historical epidemiology almost all the health improvements of the nineteenth and twentieth centuries were due to social, political and economic reform (**alienation; health determinants; McKeown; materialist; poverty; social deprivation; social exclusion; social gradient of disease; social inequality**).

SOCIAL DEPRIVATION   The experience of poverty, homelessness and unemployment, that is, social exclusion from the basic minimums regarded as the norm in a developed society, have a major impact on health. Lack of access to valued social, political and economic goods are structured along class, gender and ethnic lines. Women, the poor and the coloured are systematically at risk of more illness and diseases, and in the case of negatively evaluated ethnic groups and lower class men of early, preventable death. In all advanced societies the social gradient of disease has been demonstrated. The experience of relative deprivation, that is of inequality, in and of itself, leads to poorer health, more preventable disease, and early death (**Black report; class; class analysis; diseases of poverty; ethnicity; feminism; social exclusion; social gradient of disease; social inequality; socio-economic inequalities; socio-economic status; stress; Whitehall Studies**).

SOCIAL DRIFT HYPOTHESIS   A variation of **social Darwinism**, the argument that the sick, depressed and stressed, through natural selection, move down the social system and accumulate at the bottom. Once there they experience poverty, and it is because they are sick that they are poor. The contrary argument, for which there is overwhelming evidence, is that because they are poor, they are sick (Blane, D., Bartley, M. and Davey-Smith, G. (1997) 'Social selection: what does it contribute to social class differences in health?', *Sociology of Health and Illness*, 15: 1–15)

(**Black Report; class; diseases of affluence; diseases of poverty; health determinants; mental illness; poverty; social degradation; social deprivation; social inequality; Whitehall Studies**).

SOCIAL DISTANCE   The difference in status between two groups or individuals. The distance between them, one (e.g. a doctor) having more power and authority than the other (e.g. a patient), may mean that they find it impossible to understand the other's perspective (**conversational analysis**).

SOCIAL EXCLUSION   The World Health Organization has identified social exclusion – the experience of poverty, homelessness and unemployment – and a lack of social support and exposure to stress as key causes of disease and early death. These characteristics of individuals' social lives are, in turn, reflections of and shape their participation in the labour market. Issues of socio-economic status, social integration and health and disease are deeply intertwined (Wilkinson, R. and Marmot, M. (1998) (eds), *Social Determinants of Health – The Solid Facts*. Geneva: World Health Organization) (**health determinants; social degradation; social deprivation**).

SOCIAL GRADIENT OF DISEASE   The marked differences in health levels between occupational classes, for men and women, and for all ages. Those at the bottom of the social system have a much higher mortality from almost all causes of disease. Those in the lower classes suffer from more chronic illness, their children weigh less at birth, and they are shorter. The social gradient of disease goes with marked inequalities in access to healthcare, and particularly to preventive services. The key aspect of the social gradient of disease is that it is not accounted for by **lifestyle factors** or **lifestyle choices**. The social gradient of disease has also been demonstrated within the British civil service, that is, within a specific class, demonstrating the impact of relative deprivation, and the crucial role of autonomy and a sense of control over one's work processes (**Black Report**; **class**; **class analysis**; **diseases of poverty**; **ethnicity**; **feminism**; **occupation and health**; **social exclusion**; **social inequality**; **socio-economic inequality**; **socio-economic status**; **stress**; **Whitehall Studies**).

SOCIAL HISTORY OF MEDICINE   Accounts of the development of medicine that are critical of the claims of great men, having great ideas, and developing great institutions for the care of the sick (**Whig histories of medicine**). Feminist historians document the ways in which male medical practitioners actively excluded women, especially midwives, from their traditional role of attending women in childbirth. They also demonstrate that with the take over by male medical professionals, maternal mortality escalated. Historical accounts informed by Marxism show the close parallels between the development of modern medicine and the requirements of the capitalist class: that sickness be defined in

terms of the inability to labour; and that the definition of cure, based on the consumption of drugs and high cost technology, led to profitable outcomes for capitalists (**Flexner report**). Historical epidemiologists have shown that the impact of nineteenth- and twentieth-century medicine on the reduction in infectious disease, and the increased longevity of the population, was minimal, with reforms to the urban environment, working conditions, and access to adequately prepared food, milk, and clean water far more important. Historians of science argue that what passes for medical knowledge reflects the political, social and economic requirements of the medical profession more than it does the health needs of the population (**Bachelard**; **bedside medicine**; **Canguihelm**; **Foucault**; **germ theory**; **infectious disease**; **McKeown**; **medical technology**; **social medicine**; **Stern**).

SOCIAL INEQUALITY   Hierarchies of difference systematically produced and distributed in society such that different groups have more or less access to education, income, health and prestige (**social gradient of disease**). Marxist sociologists argue that all facets of inequality are a function of the economic organization of society and consequent class structure of capitalist societies. Those utilizing Weber's theory of **social status** argue that aspects of inequality may be differentially distributed (for example, the police may be scaled low on income, moderate on education and high on power; the clergy may be well educated, low on income and high on social standing). However, no matter how inequality is measured the following findings have been consistently established: social class differences in mortality are widening; better measures of socio-economic position show greater inequalities in mortality; health inequalities have been shown in all countries that collect data; social selection and measurement artifacts do not account for mortality differentials; social class differences exist for health during life as well as for the length of life; and trends in the distribution of income suggest that further widening of differentials may be expected (**Black Report; class; diseases of poverty; health determinants; poverty; social degradation; social deprivation; social inequality; socio-economic inequality; socio-economic status**).

SOCIAL INTERACTION   Interpersonal associations essential to the maintenance of our self-esteem and sense of self. **Social exclusion** and lack of **social support** lead to sickness and disease. In sociology the nature of this interaction is hotly debated. For those in the **microsociological** tradition social interactions are fluid, and involve constant work by individuals to maintain them. For those in the structuralist tradition, there is less scope for individuality, as **social institutions** prescribe our actions (**structure–agency debate; role; social support**).

SOCIAL INSTITUTIONS   Those stable patterns of **social interaction** that compose the structure of society, such as the family, the legal system or the education system. In the sociology of **Talcott Parsons** these institutions provide individuals with **roles**, which organize their actions in predictable and stable ways (**structure–agency debate; structuralism**).

SOCIAL MEDICINE   A term to describe nineteenth-century sanitary reform and coined by the Frenchman Jules Guerin in the context of reform following the revolution of 1848. In this approach diseases are seen as the product of the social conditions that allow them to develop (**miasma**). **Engels** and **Virchow** argued that it was the social environment of developing capitalism that caused the great diseases of the eighteenth and nineteenth centuries – cholera and typhoid, tuberculosis and diphtheria. In their analyses the overcrowding of the new industrial cities, the development of slums and the new factory organization of labour caused these diseases. Rather than examine the individual's body and search for bacteriological explanations of disease, this model identified the social environment as the source of sickness and ill-health, and suggested cleaning up the slums, keeping the water fresh and enforcing the hygienic production of foodstuffs. Historical epidemiology supports the argument that social reform rather than scientific medicine brought about the transformation in people's standards of health (McKeown, T. (1979) *The Role of Medicine*. Princeton: Princeton University Press) (**alienation; Frank; McKeown; Snow; social history of medicine; Virchow; Whig histories of medicine; Zinsser**).

SOCIAL MODEL OF HEALTH Approaches which explain health and disease, not as the consequence of the working of nature or biology, but of the social organization of society, and in particular the impact of **social inequality** on individuals' health. (**disease, social model; health determinants**).

SOCIAL NETWORKS ANALYSIS An approach that seeks to understand the actions of individuals through the pattern of their social relationships and the impact of social relationships on their health. It aims to demonstrate how such large scale and abstract categories as 'society', 'community' or 'institution' are actually patterned in people's interactions. Often used to track the spread of infectious conditions such as tuberculosis or AIDS, it can also be used to demonstrate the working of **lay referral systems** and the health seeking activities of individuals as they consult with others in their network. For example, it has shown that individuals with strong social networks are at reduced risk of a wide range of diseases (Pescosolido, B. and Levy, J. (2002) 'The role of social networks in health, illness disease and healing,' *Social Networks and Health*, 8: 3–25) (**Framingham study; kinship; social support**).

SOCIAL ORDER How society holds together is a major debate in social theory. One explanation is that we all share the same values and that there is consensus about how society is organized, a view put by **Émile Durkheim** and **Talcott Parsons**. A variation of this perspective has been proposed by **Foucault** who argues that we internalize the norms of, in the case of health, health professionals who work on behalf of the state, to generate concepts of normal behaviour (**abnormal**). Marxists and feminists on the other hand see society being held together since those in positions of power (either the ruling class or men, or a combination of both) ultimately can rely on force to ensure compliance. Those in the **microsociological** tradition reject overarching explanations of either **structural functionalists** or critical sociologists, emphasizing the ways in which individuals actively construct social reality in an ongoing and dynamic way (**critical theory; ideology; Marxist feminism; social institutions; social interaction**).

SOCIAL PATHOLOGY In the nineteenth century the argument that the social organization of society produced disorder in individuals. Put most strongly by **Émile Durkheim** in his study *Suicide* in which he argued that social dislocation caused by urbanization, the decline of religion, the growth of geographical mobility and the increased density of social interactions would lead to increases in suicide. In contemporary social theory, **social capital** theorists continue this tradition, arguing that socially disorganized communities lack forms of social organization – trust and social participation – in an approach which while sociological in not blaming the individual, is politically conservative in blaming the community. Dysfunctional communities are responsible for their own shortcomings and should solve them on their own, without any attention being paid to structural sources of inequality (**anomie**; **social causation**; **suicide**).

SOCIAL SERVICES   The range of services provide by organizations, private and public, to enhance life, ranging from education and public health to the delivery of meals to the elderly and disabled. In the past the state played a large role in the delivery of these services, but under the influence of neoliberal policies' attempts to shed them either on to the community or into the private-for-profit sector (**care in the community**; **citizenship**; **corporatization**; **welfare services**; **welfare state**).

SOCIAL STATUS   A person's or groups' positively or negatively evaluated position in a hierarchical society. **Status groups** share lifestyles, consumption patterns, and leisure activities. Low social status is significantly linked to much poorer health (**class**; **ethnicity**; **socio-economic status**; **status groups**; **Whitehall Studies**).

SOCIAL STRUCTURE   (**agency**; **social institutions**; **structural functionalism**; **voluntaristic theory of action**).

SOCIAL SUPPORT   The focus on **stress** has led to the postulation of the existence of buffers to stress – of coping resources, of coping strategies and social support networks. The major findings

from the social support literature are: 1 social integration is positively linked to mental and physical health and lower mortality rates; 2 perceived emotional support leads to better physical and mental health and helps individuals buffer the impact of major life events; and the most powerful form of support is an intimate and confiding relationship (Thoits, P. (1995) 'Stress, coping and social support processes: where are we? What next?', *Journal of Health and Social Behaviour*, Extra issue: 53–79). In turn each of these three points are mediated by social structural factors. Those with high social status have an enhanced sense of support, and involvement in social networks is positively correlated with high social status (**social inequality**). Social support mechanisms can be analysed as enhancing health status in four ways: 1 through the provision of instrumental, practical help; 2 in the provision of information (**lay networks**); 3 appraisal support in the sense of providing feedback to an individual about their health; 4 and providing emotional support (Berkman, L. et al. (2000) 'From social integration to health: Durkheim in the new millenium', *Social Science and Medicine*, 51: 843–57) (**isolation**; **psychosocial factors**; **psychosocial risks**).

SOCIAL USURPATION   The attempt by a subordinate occupation (e.g. nurses or psychologists) to take over areas of practice from a dominant occupation (e.g. doctors) (**encroachment**; **medical dominance**; **professionalization**; **social closure**).

SOCIAL WAGE　The amount of spending on public health, welfare, education, housing and urban infrastructure by the **welfare state**. In current right-wing Western countries, with the dismantling of the welfare state, policy makers have turned to the community as the site that should produce and deliver these services. While critiques of the welfare state demonstrated that it benefited the middle class, the real material expenditure of the welfare state cannot be replaced by idealist appeals to 'community' or 'social capital' (**care in the community**).

SOCIALIZATION　Usually used to refer to the process whereby children are taught to conform to the norms of society, learning appropriate social skills, which as they mature allow them to take on adult social roles. Within Foucauldian sociology socialization is an ongoing process of managing the self to conform to the edicts of normal behaviour (**psy-professions; technologies of the self**).

SOCIALIST FEMINISM　While taking on board Marxist analyses of the role of class in exploiting both men and women, socialist feminism argues that Marxists do not account for the ways in which women are exploited separately from workers, and why the subordination of women precedes the formation of capitalist societies. Class struggle and overthrowing patriarchy are related but distinct political issues (**cyborgs; feminism; Marxist feminism**).

SOCIOBIOLOGY　The use of principles of evolutionary biology to explain the form of human societies and the conduct of human beings, popularized by E. O. Wilson in *Sociobiology: The New Synthesis* (1975). Because of its key assumptions – that heredity dominates culture; that hierarchy and inequality are inevitable; and that actions, from **altruism** to aggression are behaviours over which individuals have little control and are part of the 'natural' order, it is rejected by most health social sciences. Additionally it is sexist, seeing women's caring and nurturing roles as given by nature, and gentically determinist, ignoring the role of culture (**biological anthropology; genetic determinism; social Darwinism**).

SOCIO-ECONOMIC INDICATORS　Measures of an individual or a group's social position based on variables such as whether they own or rent their home (owners are healthier), whether it is rented in the public or private sector (those in the private sector are healthier), whether they are employed or unemployed (the employed are healthier), their level of education (the higher the healthier the individual) or marital status (the married are healthier than the never married or divorced). (Feinstein, J. (1993) 'The relationship between socio-economic status and health: a review of the literature', *The Milbank Quarterly*, 71: 279–322) (**Black Report; class; diseases of poverty; marital status; social degradation; social deprivation; social gradient of disease; social inequality; socio-economic status; Whitehall Studies**).

SOCIO-ECONOMIC INEQUALITIES The difference in income and wealth between those at the bottom of society and those at the top. Patterns of inequality are widening in England, Australia and the USA. For example the USA is now more unequal than at any period since the 1920s. Over the twenty years from 1974 to 1994 the top 5 per cent of US households increased their share of the nation's aggregate household income from 16 per cent to 21 per cent, while the share of the top 20 per cent rose from 44 to 49 per cent. With the widening of income inequality goes a widening in health inequality. Those groups at the bottom of the social system have higher mortality rates in the majority of diseases, suffer more chronic illness, their children weigh less at birth, and they experience marked inequalities in access to health services (Hahn, R. et al. (1996) 'Poverty and death in the United States – 1973–1991', *International Journal of Health Services*, 26: 673–90) (**Black Report; class; diseases of poverty; social degradation; social deprivation; social gradient of disease; social inequality; socio-economic status; Whitehall Studies**).

SOCIO-ECONOMIC STATUS (SES) A concept in Weberian sociology, referring to an individual's position on the socially valued hierarchy of occupations and income and its impact on their **life chances**. Low socio-economic status means exposure to a range of material threats: slum dwellings, poor ventilation, garbage and overcrowding. It also means exposure to the unregulated labour market, to sweatshops, home-work and piece rates. The poor also become poorer, paying higher cash costs, having less access to informal sources of financial assistance, and are more dependent on insecure cash incomes. In other words, the poorer you are, the more it costs you to live. These features of low socio-economic status translate into lower life expectancy, higher overall mortality rates, and higher infant and perinatal death rates (de la Barra, X. (1998) 'Poverty: the main cause of ill health in urban children', *Health, Education and Behaviour*, 25: 45–59) (**Black Report; class analysis; diseases of poverty; social gradient of disease; social inequality**).

SOCIOLOGY A term developed by Auguste Comte in 1839. His aim was to unify abstract theorizing about social life with empirical observation of social life so as to produce a 'science of society'. As developed by **Émile Durkheim**, sociology became the science of society, studying objectively existing social facts that constrained and controlled individuals. In his study *Suicide* Durkheim attempted to demonstrate that even the most personal and private act was determined by the state of society (**anomie**). In contrast, interpretive sociologists in the micro tradition (**microsociological**) show how individuals as active, conscious, meaning makers shape social reality (**Chicago School of Sociology; ethnomethodology; phenomenology; symbolic interactionism**).

SOCIOLOGY IN MEDICINE Throughout the 1950s sociology applied to the field of medicine was used to assist the dissemination of medical knowledge and to encourage patient compliance with medical directives. In this relationship medicine was the senior partner, and the interaction occurred within a broader cultural context that viewed medicine as the paragon of science and of the rational application of scientific principles and technology to human beings. Within sociology this was the period of dominance of the **structural functionalist** perspective under the impact of **Talcott Parsons** (Twaddle, A. (1982) 'From medical sociology to the sociology of health', in T. Bottomore, M. Sokolowska and S. Nowak (eds), *Sociology: The State of the Art*. London: Sage) (**sociology of medicine**).

SOCIOLOGY OF MEDICINE   The development of a critical attitude towards the claims of professional medicine in the 1960s and 1970s. The argument was that some of the problems in the healthcare system – of access, equity and efficiency – could best be explained by the ways in which medicine was organized, both at the institutional level such as the hospital, and professionally in terms of the activities of the medical profession. The publication of Eliot Freidson's *Profession of Medicine: A Study of the Sociology of Applied Knowledge* (New York: Dobb and Mead) and *Professional Dominance* (New York: Aldine Publishing Company), both in 1970, were turning points in the field. Freidson argued that the medical profession dominated the health sector, not because it was the humanitarian scientific elite that it portrayed itself as, but because it was politically

well organized (**antipsychiatry; medical dominance**).

SOCIOLOGY OF SCIENTIFIC KNOWLEDGE (SSK)   Developing in the 1970s out of the disciplines of history, sociology, anthropology, cognitive psychology and linguistics this approach to the claims of scientific knowledge, relativized the contents of Western science and approached the practices of working scientists in the same way as an anthropologist would approach the workings of those in other cultures. Traditional social analyses of science had sought to demonstrate how social factors affected science from the outside, notably in the works of Robert Merton (*The Sociology of Science: Theoretical and Empirical Investigations*. Chicago: University of Chicago Press) but left unexamined the actual contents of science, which was presumed to be a reflection of reality discovered by the scientific method. Following the work of Thomas Kuhn (*The Structure of Scientific Revolutions* (1962) Chicago: University of Chicago Press) social scientists started to examine the contents of scientific theories as also socially produced. Kuhn argued that the contents of scientific theories were historically, culturally and socially produced (**thought styles**) and changed not because of new knowledge but because of dissatisfaction with old **paradigms** (**Bachelard; Canguihelm; Fleck; Stern**).

SOCIOMEDICAL RESEARCH   Research which examines the interplay between the biology of disease and social, cultural and political factors which shape who gets it, how it is experienced and treated.

SOMATIC NORMS   The construction of norms of the ideal body in contemporary society, where fitness and slimness have become markers of responsible citizenship. Maintaining our bodies, a class based and distributed ability, marks us as decent members of society with internalized self-control and techniques of self-management (**bodyism**; **body politics**; **fitness**; **habitus**; **Mauss**; **morality and medicine**; **self-care**; **technologies of the self**).

SOMATIC SOCIETY   Bryan Turner has argued we now live in what can be called a 'somatic society' where 'major political and personal problems are both problematized within the body and expressed through it' (Turner, B. S. (1996: 1) *The Body and Society*. London: TCS/Sage Edition). HIV/AIDS activists and disability action groups are two good examples of this development (**bodyism**; **body politics**; **habitus**; **somatic norms**).

SOMATIZATION   The experience of abusive social and interpersonal issues expressed as painful bodily symptoms. It has been demonstrated to be a viable response by women to their gender roles, and perhaps the only response available to individuals living under regimes of political terror (Kleinman, A. (1995) *Writing at the Margin: Discourse between Anthropology and Medicine*. Berkeley: University of California Press) (**domestic violence**).

SPECIALIZATION   The division of labour among different occupational groups. This is usually hierarchal, with white males, for example, medical specialists, at the top and women's occupations, usually linked to culturally valued norms of women's roles, such as caring, as in nursing, subordinated to them (**medical dominance**).

SPIRITUAL HEALING   Health practices which are based on a belief in God, gods or spirits as active agents in human affairs, and whose existence can explain sickness and disease, and whose intervention can bring about cure. Belief in spiritual healing is still a large part of Western belief systems, such as in Christian Science and Pentecostal movements (**folk healing**; **indigenous healing**; **shamanism**; **theodicy**).

SPOILT IDENTITY   A term coined by **Erving Goffman** to describe the impossibility of regaining full social membership in a community following diagnosis and labelling as insane, chronically sick, disabled or terminally ill. As Goffman puts it, the person has lost their 'wholeness' (Goffman, E. (1963) *Stigma: Notes on the Management of Spoiled Identity*. New York: Simon and Schuster) (**labelling theory**; **stigma**).

STANDARD POPULATION   A population distribution that is used to create rates that have the same age structure, so that different rates can be properly compared (**age-standardized rate**).

STANDPOINT EPISTEMOLOGY   A position in feminist theories of knowledge that argues the social position of the knower is embedded in what is known. For example, medical knowledge held by men in a patriarchal society will be patriarchal medical knowledge. Against this it is argued that the only adequate knowledge of women's health and women's bodies has to be produced from the perspective, that is, the standpoint, of women (**dualism**; **ecofeminism**; **essentialism**; **feminism**).

STATUS GROUPS   In Marxism class is an objective feature of capitalist society which shapes individuals' lives whether they are aware of it or not. **Max Weber** argued against what he saw as a form of economic determinism, suggesting instead that people formed ideas about themselves and others, independently of class processes, which he called status groups. A status group has a shared lifestyle and may be negatively or positively privileged.

STERILIZATION   Surgical or chemical interventions to prevent conception. In the past the state has authorized the forcible sterilization of groups thought not fit to breed, as for example, occurred in the Australian aboriginal population in the 1960s (**eugenics**; **racism**).

STERN, BERNHARD (1894–1956)   US Marxist sociologist of health and author of *Social Factors in Medical Progress* (1927, New York: AMS Press) an important account of the history of medicine. In it

Stern documents the failure of each of the major medical discoveries of modern medicine to be accepted at the time of their discovery. In an examination of discoveries ranging from Harvey's circulation of the blood, Jenner's vaccination and Semmelweis on asepsis, as well as technical innovations such as Auenbrugger's theory of percussion Stern makes three points: that the practice of medicine is not built on the basis of natural science but is the outcome of political struggle around who has the right to practise it; that technical knowledge is redefined to suit the profession's interest and not defined by an objective biological reality; and that medical belief systems are specific to the cultural, political and economic systems that form their background. These points are essential to the argument that medical practice is about social relationships and not about nature and science as is suggested in orthodox histories of medicine (**Fleck**; **Whig histories of medicine**).

STIGMA   A negatively evaluated social status ascribed to an individual as a consequence of their body (for example deformity), their character (for example, being labeled mentally ill or criminal) or their ethnic group (**racism**). The concept is used in the sociology of mental and chronic illness to explore the consequences of being labelled with a disease and of the individual's attempts to pass as normal in the face of diagnoses as diseased, as for example, someone who suffers from epilepsy being labelled 'epileptic', but wanting to retain a normal life (Goffman, E. (1963) *Stigma: Notes on the Management of Spoiled Identity*.

New York: Doubleday Anchor) (**courtesy stigma; epilepsy; Goffman; labelling theory; liminality; moral career; morality and medicine; spoilt identity**).

STIGMATIZATION   The act of labelling a person as of lesser social standing, transforming their character and social standing in negative ways (**stigma**).

STIGMATIZED RISK GROUP   Groups in the community who because they are stigmatized – such as intravenous drug users – are put a higher risk of sickness and disease, since their stigmatized condition means that they get treated indifferently, since it is held that they are responsible for their condition (**blame the victim; courtesy stigma; morality and medicine**).

STRATIFICATION   A model of society which postulates the hierarchical existence of social groups ranging in status, power and authority. The experience of living in a stratified society has a major impact on people's health and well being (**class; social inequality; socio-economic status**).

STRAUSS, ANSELM (1916–96)   American sociologist of health in the **Chicago School** tradition of **microsociology**. For Strauss organizations, such as psychiatric hospitals, were not as stable as they appeared from outside the organization, and inmates and the workers there had to constantly negotiate order. Similarly in work with B. Glaser, observing the dying process, they demonstrated how death had to be socially

organized. He also did work on the experience of chronic illness, all of the studies reflecting the **grounded theory** approach that he and Glaser developed (**affect management; dying trajectory; negotiated order**).

STRESS   Stressful life events have been linked to heart disease, diabetes, cancers, stroke, fetal death, major depression and low birth weight. While current research on stress emphasizes its subjective experience there is also the important point that stressors impact differently on members of different social groups. For example, women are more vulnerable to changes in their social networks, while men are more vulnerable to changes in their work status (Conger, R. et al. (1993) 'Husband and wife differences in response to undesirable life events', *Journal of Health and Social Behaviour*, 34: 71–88). The development of the idea that stress causes disease has also occurred in the political context of the decline of **class** explanations, particularly in the psychiatry literature, where class has long been recognized as the source of disease (Angermeyer, M. and Klusman, D. (1987) 'From social class to social stress: new developments in psychiatric epidemiology', in M. Angermeyer (ed.), *From Social Class to Social Stress: New Developments in Psychiatric Epidemiology*. New York: Springer-Verlag) (**isolation; psychosocial factors, psychosocial risks; social support; stressful life experiences**).

STRESSFUL LIFE EXPERIENCES   The social stress approach originally conceptualized any socio-environmental change as challenging to the individual. Births as well as deaths, marriages as well as divorce, the good experiences and the bad, were analytically placed together. However it has become clear that there is a **social gradient** linking poor health and negative stressors. Those who are unemployed and homeless, those most at risk of losing their jobs, who are living in poverty, face more ongoing, seriously negative stressful events and experience more sickness (**social degradation; social deprivation; stress**).

STRONG PROGRAMME IN THE SOCIOLOGY OF SCIENTIFIC KNOWLEDGE (SSSK) A research paradigm that through close empirical analysis of the development of scientific 'facts' argues that they are shaped by social interests, independently of whether they are true or false (**social construction/constructionism; sociology of scientific knowledge**).

STRUCTURAL EXPLANATIONS Accounts of the sources of disease that focus on persistent social factors such as employment conditions, gender relationships or the role of the medical profession in categorizing some forms of actions as outside the **normal**. Structuralist explanations may emphasize social stability and harmony, as in **Durkheim** and **Parsons** or social change and conflict, as in the Marxist tradition (**health determinants; materialist analyses; structural functionalism; structuralism**).

STRUCTURAL FUNCTIONALISM One of the original metaphors for society, the organistic metaphor: that society could be conceptualized as an organic whole, with each of its parts contributing to its overall functioning. It is particularly important in the sociology of **Talcott Parsons**. Parsons conceptualized society as a social system of inter-related social structures each of which plays a specific function in bringing about stability and integration of individuals and their social roles. Society is the outcome of various actors performing their social roles, for example, mother, teacher or doctor, in specific social institutions, the family, the classroom and the hospital. The institutions perform the specific functions necessary for the continuation of social life. The family socializes the next generation, the teacher prepares the next generation for work, and the doctor repairs and rehabilitates, allowing individuals to return to, and to continue perform their social roles (**sick role; role; voluntaristic theory of action**).

STRUCTURALISM In the social sciences the position that argues that social life is determined by underlying social forces, for example, the economy in Marxism, or patriarchy in feminist analysis. The position emphasizes the limited, if any, autonomy that individuals have in society. In the work of **Durkheim**, for example, individuals are almost entirely determined by pre-existing social facts which may drive them to **suicide** (**agency; Chicago School of Sociology; interactionist**

sociology; voluntaristic theory of action; Weber).

STRUCTURE–AGENCY DEBATE   In sociology the debate over how much autonomy individuals have in the choices they make and how much their choices are constrained by **social institutions**. **Microsociologists** emphasize the sense-making, meaning constructing actions of individuals, while structural functionalists emphasize the ways in which our social **roles** constrain our actions. In the sociology of health, it is clear that individuals attempt to make sense of what it is that has happened to them, but that by and large what happens to them is determined by their position in society over which they have little control (**biographical disruption; health determinants**).

SUBJECTIFICATION   In health social studies this refers to the requirement of the **new public health** that we internalize the **risks** that it alerts us to, and take steps to protect ourselves from them through changing our **lifestyle**. In Foucault's analysis this development is an aspect of disciplinary power, in which we internalize norms of behaviour, defined by the **psy-professions** (Bury, M. (1998) 'Postmodernity and health', in G. Scambler and P. Higgs (eds), *Modernity, Medicine and Health*. London: Routledge) (**bodyism; bio-power; fitness; governmentality; power/ knowledge; surveillance; technologies of the self**).

SUBSTANTIVE RATIONALITY   Action that is driven by a set of social beliefs and values held to be important in and of themselves. The contrast is with **formal rationality** where action is driven by rule following actions independently of the outcome, as for example, in a bureaucracy. The claim to act in a substantively rational way is one of the key claims of the medical profession (and many of its social analysts – **Parsons**): that it acts, for example, altruistically in the interest of the community or the patient and not for personal gain (**profession; Weber**). With the increasing **commodification** of the medical profession it is argued that substantive rationality is declining, leading to **deprofessionalization** and or **proletarianization** (**rationalization**).

SUDDEN INFANT DEATH SYNDROME (SIDS)   Previously cot-death, the sudden death of an infant for no known medical reason. What we do know is that SIDS is correlated with low socio-economic status, and the youthfulness of the mother and that rather than target at risk individuals, improvements in access to care, living conditions, and support for the mother would make for far better intervention and reduction in rates of SIDS.

SUICIDE   The taking of one's own life. Suicide appears to be a pre-eminently individual and psychological act. In his book *Suicide* (1951, New York: Free Press) **Émile Durkheim** set out to demonstrate that this was not the case and to show that it represented the workings of society on the individual, of what he called social facts. He showed through statistical analysis of suicide patterns in Europe that Protestant, urban, educated and single people were most at risk of committing suicide. These individuals were at risk of anomic suicide because their social bonds were weak, or because they over-valued themselves (egotistic suicide). He argued that members of close knit Catholic rural communities were less likely to commit suicide, because of their strong integration into the group and that when they did it would either be altruistic, sacrificing themselves on behalf of the community, or fatalistic, sacrificing themselves when they had outlived their usefulness. Durkheim's positivist approach has been criticized by interpretive sociologists who argue that 'suicide' is not a 'fact' but a label accomplished in coroner's courts through the interaction of the police, the medical profession and relatives. They suggest that one of the reasons for the apparently low suicide rates in Catholic countries is because of the taboo associated with it and its subsequent under-reporting (Douglas, J. (1967) *The Social Meanings of Suicide.* Princeton: Princeton University Press) (**anomie; Kant; social pathology**).

SUPPLIER INDUCED DEMAND   The medical market is under medical control in that doctors tell us what we need to buy of their services, thus determining the number of procedures they undertake. The impact on the number of surgical procedures and follow-up consultations are well established

in areas where there are high concentrations of practitioners operating on a fee-for-service basis. Tonsillectomy rates, for example, have been shown to vary from 13 per 100,000 persons to 151 per 100,000 in the same geographical area (Wennberg, J. and Gittelsohn, A. (1973) 'Small area variations in health care delivery', *Science*, 182: 1102–8) (**fee-for-service; Jarvis' law; market; perverse incentives**).

SUPPORT GROUPS   Usually patient initiated organizations for the provision of information about their condition and support for each other (**self-help group; support groups, online**).

SUPPORT GROUPS, ONLINE   Internet chat rooms for people to discuss and seek information about their condition. They allow for the sharing of information without embarrassment or shame and are a resource for those whose condition limits their activities. There is some suggestion that men access them more as one way of negotiating **male stoicism** (Braithwaite, D., Waldron, V. and Finn, J. (1999) 'Communication of social support in computer mediated groups for persons with disabilities', *Health Communication*, 11: 123–51) (**internet-informed patient; self-help groups**).

SURGEONS   In the history of medicine the lowest of the medical specialists (hence they were always 'mister' and not 'doctor'), travelling with the army, working essentially as human butchers, amputating limbs and setting bones, and acting as barbers at other times. As anatomy and dissection developed though, the surgeons became key players in the development of modern medicine, since with knowledge of the body in death they could now make effective interventions in life.

SURGERY   Developing as the epitome of scientific medicine, pragmatic and empirical, and thus above the disputes of physicians about the nature of disease, surgeons benefited not only with the development of dissection, but with the development of anaesthetics, an unconscious patient and with asepsis, clean operating theatres, both of which increased the survival rate of their patients. Surgery rates are of considerable sociological interest since they are directly linked to the number of surgeons in an area, and not to any underlying 'real' incidence of a disorder (**Jarvis' Law; perverse incentive; supplier induced demand**).

SURVEILLANCE   In epidemiology the collection of data, as well as the review, analysis and dissemination of findings on incidence (new cases), prevalence, morbidity, survival and mortality. Surveillance also serves to collect information on the knowledge, attitudes and behaviours of the public with respect to practices that are held to prevent **lifestyle** based illnesses. In Foucault's analysis of modern societies, there are two closely related phenomena: 1 the collection and organization of information that can be stored by state agencies and used to monitor the activities of an administered population; 2 direct supervision or control of subordinates by superiors in

particular organizations – schools, factories, prisons, universities, hospitals and bureaucracies. Corresponding to these micro and macro levels of surveillance are **anatomo-politics** – the politics of the body – and **biopolitics** – the politics of population (**Foucault; new public health**).

SURVEILLANCE MEDICINE   The targeting of the 'abnormal' few with 'invisible' diseases in mass surveillance programmes such as screening for breast cancer and cervical cancer that justifies the observation of the 'normal' majority (Armstrong, D. (1995) 'The rise of surveillance medicine', *Sociology of Health and Illness*, 17: 393–404). **Foucauldian-feminist** sociologists link these public health programmes to patriarchy and the medicalization of women's bodies, especially since similar programmes do not exist for male diseases such as prostate or testicular cancer (**mammography screening programme; risk**).

SYDENHAM,   THOMAS   (1624–89) English medical practitioner, one of the first to emphasize **empiricism** as the basis for medicine, he also argued that diseases were specific entities, with their own natural histories and existed independently of the patient. At the same time he rejected anatomy, and thought that the microscope was the tool of the devil since it let us see what God had hidden.

SYMBOLIC INTERACTIONISM   An approach in sociology which emphasizes understanding and explaining the social world from the point of view of the subjective actor. In this perspective social life is about creating, changing and negotiating social roles and status. In health sociology it has been a particularly powerful critique of **Parsons' structural functionalism**. It is associated with the **Chicago School of Sociology** and based on the interactive theory of the self, developed by **G. H. Mead**. Symbolic interactionism provides the basis for the **labelling theorists**, and for **Goffman** to develop his work on **stigma**. It was used to great effect in studies of the dying, showing the ways in which an apparently straightforward biological event was socially negotiated and structured. Along with phenomenology and ethnomethodology it is vulnerable to the criticism of sociologists that it overlooks relations between groups, which are based on inequalities of power, and exploitation (**Chicago School of Sociology; dying trajectories; microsociological; Schutz; verstehen**).

SYMPTOM ICEBERG　　Community studies show that up to one-third of people experiencing symptoms of disease do not consult a doctor about them (**clinical iceberg; illness behaviour; lay referral system; sick role**).

SYNDEMIC　　A term coined by Merrill Singer, an anthropologist, to capture the impact on a population of two epidemics operating together, thereby greatly increasing the burden of disease. The aim was to break with **biomedicine's** simplistic treatment of separate diseases as separate issues, and highlights the role of social conditions, especially poverty and ethnicity, in the spread and experience of epidemics. The US Center for Disease Control has adopted the concept in its work (Singer, M. (1994) 'AIDS and the health crisis of the urban poor: the perspective of critical medical anthropology', *Social Science and Medicine*, 39: 931–48) (**critical theory; medical anthropology, critical**).

T

TABOO (TABU) Social restrictions around sacred places, around sacred groups, as for example, priests, or around access to parts of the body. At its most general level based on an argument developed by **Émile Durkheim** that societies can be analysed as dividing reality into sacred and profane sectors, with the two being kept apart. In the health social studies, of interest, since one of the rights of doctors identified by **Talcott Parsons** is to have access to body parts which otherwise are protected by strong social sanctions from being touched or looked at by others, as in, for example, the sexual organs.

TALKING THERAPIES A term for the range of psychoanalytic and counselling therapies that developed from the end of the nineteenth century. With the rise of industrial capitalism and the breakdown of traditional social networks, a professional group evolved for people to talk to, meeting the needs generated by urban isolation (Gellner, E. (1993) *The Psychoanalytic Movement: The Cunning of Unreason.* London: Fontana) (**counselling; Freud; psychoanalysis**).

TARGETED HEALTH SERVICES The move from the universal provision of health and welfare services as a right of **citizenship** to services based on individual need. A policy of conservative governments in developed countries, the aim is to reduce the costs of the health and welfare systems and to make individuals more self-reliant, or for their families to take more responsibility for them (**informal care; market; neoliberalism**).

TECHNICAL FIX The belief that complex social and political problems can be solved with the discovery of a technical solution. Such approaches ignore the reasons for people's actions and by focusing on the technical ignore the underlying social issues. For example, the argument that infectious disease can be brought under control through vaccination, ignores the role that poverty plays in the spread of these diseases (**medical technology; social construction of technology approach; vaccination; vaccines**).

TECHNOLOGICAL IMPERATIVE If the technology to do something exists, it should be used rather than do nothing. In part this is a response to **medical uncertainty**; in part driven by economic factors, on the one side, that when a hospital has invested in expensive technology it has to use it to pay for it, and on the other side insurance companies will cover the costs (**biotechnology; medical technology; technical fix**).

TECHNOLOGIES OF THE SELF   The practices whereby individuals in modern society constitute themselves as subjects, internalizing the **discourses** of the **psy-professions**, through self-appraisal, monitoring their feelings and emotions and constructing their bodies (Rose, N. (1990) *Governing the Soul: The Shaping of the Private Self*. London: Routledge). The technologies of the self are complemented and reinforced through the discourses of the modern helping professions – psychiatry, psychology, social work, and medicine – the psy-professions. In their dividing practices they sort the population into groups and categories (the sane/insane; the sick/the healthy; the normal/the deviant) based on a claimed scientific understanding of individuals and their actions (Foucault, M. (1988) *Technologies of the Self*. Amherst: University of Massachusetts Press) (**healthism**).

TECHNOLOGY   (**biotechnology; cyborgs; medical technology; social construction of technology approach; technoscience**).

TECHNOSCIENCE   A neologism popularized by Bruno Latour, a French sociologist of science, to indicate the interplay between scientific activities, technical processes and the social accomplishment and presentation of a state of affairs as a scientific fact (Latour, B. (1987) *Science in Action*.

Cambridge, MA: Harvard University Press) (**actor-network theory; social construction of technology approach; sociology of scientific knowledge**).

TELEMEDICINE   The interaction between patient and medical practitioner via a television/video linkup. Proponents argue that it will reduce waiting lists, bring services to rural and isolated areas and allow people with limited mobility to be 'seen' by a doctor. However, the use of the technology itself may disturb the clinical encounter, and the doctor is certainly limited in his/her use of touch as a diagnostic tool (May, C. and Ellis, N. (2001) 'When protocols fail: technical evaluation, biomedical knowledge and the social production of "facts" about a telemedicine clinic', *Social Science and Medicine*, 53: 989–1901) (**deprofessionalization; visual imaging**).

THERAPEUTIC COMMUNITY   Part of the reform of mental hospitals in the 1940s and 1950s in Britain, the establishment of groups of patients within the large asylums, to break down hierarchy and to foster the patients and doctors working together for a cure. At the height of the **antipsychiatry** movement **R. D. Laing** established an antipsychiatry hospital, Kingsley Hall, in London, where the psychiatrists and patients lived together (**deinstitutionalization; mental illness**).

THERAPEUTIC REGIMES   The different ways in which care is delivered in the hospital, with different roles for the patient, the nurse and the doctor in each phase or stage of the patient's condition. The care regime provides support to the dying patient, who is perceived to be on a trajectory towards death (**dying trajectories**), and receives intermittent attention from both the nurse and the doctor; in the acute regime, the patient is the recipient of the heroic interventions of the nursing and medical staff as they seek to stabilize the condition (e.g. of road accident trauma or heart attack). This involves rescuing the patient, followed by intensive care; the rehabilitative regime is the attempt to restore lost functioning of a body part or organ; and the therapeutic regime is the attempt to modify the environment to facilitate cure, as in emphasizing caring relationships or the preparation of children's wards as nice places to be.

THEODICY   The problem of the existence of pain and suffering in the world: how could God let this happen or why has he let it happen to me? While medicine has replaced religion as the source of authority in our society (**medicalization**) its focus on disease as a purely physical occurrence has meant that it has been unable to address what concerns individuals most: the meaning of their disease. (Comaroff, J. and Maguire, P. (1981) 'Ambiguity and the search for meaning: childhood leukaemia in the modern clinical context', *Social Science and Medicine*, 20: 29–37) (**biographical disruption; narrative accounts of illness; spiritual healing**).

THOMAS THEOREM   'If men define situations as real, they will be real in their consequences'. Formulated by W. I. Thomas of the **Chicago School of Sociology**, and the basis for a critique in health sociology of **biomedicine** and **Cartesian** views of the body. For example, in Western medicine drugs are biochemically active substances that should have an impact on the body in a straightforward way. However, how individuals define the situation will be important for what happens. In a study of ulcer treatment drugs it was found that up to 90 per cent of those in the **placebo** group got better, in the same way as if they had been treated by the active drug. How the individual defined the situation – that they were being treated – led their body to respond as if it had been treated. (Moerman, D. (1981) 'General medical effectiveness and human biology: placebo effects in the treatment of ulcer disease,' *Medical Anthropology Quarterly*, 14: 14–16) (**placebo effect**).

THOUGHT STYLES   A concept in the sociology of medical knowledge developed by **Ludwig Fleck**. In it Fleck brings together a philosophical analysis of science – that the discovery of scientific facts depends not upon the discovery of a pre-existing nature – and a sociological analysis of science, demonstrating that the discovery of scientific facts depends on non-scientific factors, such as religious, political or economic considerations. Fleck argued that knowledge is only possible in a scientific community on the basis of a tradition of shared assumptions, and that theories act to produce the questions that can be asked, and predispose the answers that can be given. They are a 'world view' producing the possible realities open to us, and limiting them (**Kuhn**; **paradigm**)

TITMUSS, RICHARD (1907–73) Professor of Social Administration at the London School of Economics, Titmuss established the study of social policy and social administration, shaped the establishment of the **welfare state**, and was influential in the British Labour Party. He wrote widely on inequality and its impact on health and disease. His first book *Poverty and Population* (1936) examined the relationship between preventable death and poor diet and the regional differences in health between the rich south and the poor north of England (Titmuss, R. (1976) *Essays on the Welfare State*. London: Allen and Unwin) (**gift relationship**; **Mauss**).

TOTAL INSTITUTION A social institution (e.g. asylum, hospital, or prison) in which one's whole behaviour is circumscribed and monitored; in which one's individuality is reduced to the homogeneity of the group (as diseased, insane, or criminal); and in which one goes through a degradation ceremony (e.g. head shaved, street clothes removed, and or the assignment of a number rather than a name) to destroy individuality (**asylums; degradation ceremonies; depersonalization; Goffman; institutionalization; negotiated order**).

TOXIC CHEMICALS (**acid rain; life scapes; popular epidemiology**).

TRAIT APPROACH Accounts of professionalization which emphasize the meeting of specific criteria by occupational groups, which can provide an account of why they are called professions, namely that they are allowed to self-regulate and monitor the actions of their members. Trait approaches emphasize the length of training, the altruistic orientation of the group, the basis of their practice in a scientific body of knowledge, and their ability to regulate themselves because of their non-profit orientation. One of the reasons that the approach fell into disrepute is that the list of traits can be extended endlessly. The other reason is that the approach effectively takes the dominant professions, such as medicine, which claims to be a profession at face value, and then proceeds to use these criteria as the criteria for judging what constitutes a profession. The approach was discredited by alternative approaches coming from Weberians and Marxists, who emphasized that the successful claim to be a profession was a product of the power of certain occupations to define themselves as professions and to reap benefits for their members such as state-based mandates to control entry to the occupation and to exclude other occupations from practice (Johnson, T. (1972) *Professions and Power*. London: Macmillan) (**credentialism; medical dominance; professional trajectory; professionalism**).

TRANQUILLIZERS Mood altering, prescription only drugs, such as diazepam (valium). In Western society they are overwhelmingly prescribed to women.

Feminists argue that rather than address the issues of the social roles of women that induce stress and depression – those of wives, mothers, and house workers – the doctors act as an agent of **social control** individualizing the problems of, in this case women, and treating the symptoms but not the causes of their distress (Ashton, H. (1991) 'Psychotropic drug prescribing for women', *British Journal of Psychiatry*, 158 (S10): 30–5) (**gender**; **labelling theory**; **mental illness**).

TRANSACTIVE ACCOUNT   The postulation of a solution to the problem of linking the subjective, individual experience of a condition (**verstehen**) and the objective existence of a condition. A transactive account of a situation would provide an account both from the inside, of the individual's experience, and from the outside, of the conditions the individual is objectively responding to (Eisner, E. (1991) *The Enlightened Eye: Qualitative Inquiry and the Enhancement of Educational Practice*. New York: Macmillan) (**research methods**).

TRANSSEXUAL   An individual whose **gender** identity does not correspond to their biological anatomy, that is a female who is certain that she is a man or, as is more common, a male who is certain that he is a woman. Some may have sex reassignment, using hormones to transform aspects of their appearance and voice (either male to female or female to male) culminating in sex reassignment surgery (Lewins, F. (1995) *Transsexuals in Society: A Sociology of Male to Female*

Transsexuals. Melbourne: Macmillan) (**vaginoplasty**).

TRIAGE   The classification of patients in terms of the urgency of treatment. The Australasian College of Emergency Medicine distinguishes five categories. Category 1 patients require resuscitation and must be treated immediately; category 2 are emergency patients and should be treated within ten minutes; category 3 are urgent and need to be treated within 30 minutes; category 4 are semi-urgent and treated within an hour; and category 5, within 2 hours. Sociologists have demonstrated that attempts to revive patients is based as much on their perceived social status as their medical condition.

TRIANGULATION   The use of multiple methods of investigation to provide confirmation of the validity of research findings. For example, interview data can be cross-matched with public documents and ethnographic participation by the researcher in the community to which the individual belongs. Triangulation is often posited as one way to cross the quantitative–qualitative divide in health social research (Denzin, N. (1978) *The Research Act: A Theoretical Introduction to Sociological Methods.* (2nd edn) New York: McGraw-Hill) (**convergent validity**; **research methods**).

TRICKLE-DOWN THEORY   The claim that if the dominant economic group is allowed unfettered freedom in its activities – that is, to make as much profit as possible – the proceeds will eventually find their way down the system to the poorer members of society. Given the well-demonstrated negative impact of work conditions on people's health, even if it did, it would be needed to care for them and to treat them (**occupation and health**).

TRIPLE JEOPARDY　A concept in **gerontology** that identifies the combined impact of the loss of income, social status and spouse on the health of the elderly. Feminist sociologists are critical of the concept since it neglects the fact that it is women who live longer and that what should be at issue is the intertwining of a lifetime of lower income, lower status work, and less superannuation cumulating in a stigmatized and impoverished old age (**ageing**).

TUKE, WILLIAM (1732–1822) AND SAMUEL (1784–1857)　Quaker grandfather and grandson who led the reform of the treatment of the insane at **Bedlam** and founded a retreat at York for the humane treatment of the mentally ill (Samuel published his *Description of the Retreat* in 1813). Following **Pinel** they argued that if the insane were treated like animals, they would respond as animals, but if treated with respect and care they could recover (**American Psychiatric Association; Foucault**).

TUSKEGEE SYPHILIS EXPERIMENT　Between 1932 and 1972 the US Department of Public Health conducted a natural history experiment by leaving 400 Black sharecroppers identified as having latent syphilis untreated. The justification was that with the successful treatment of syphilis, knowledge of its development to its end stage that is, tertiary syphilis, had been lost. The men were given weekly medical examinations involving blood tests and spinal fluid taps, and were told that these were positive treatments that they needed to keep them healthy. In exchange for participating the men were driven to the clinics, were offered a hot meal and promised that they would not receive a pauper's funeral. A medical experiment such as this could only be planned and carried out against the background of racist assumptions about the value of Black lives. It also reflected racially informed perceptions of black sexuality: that Black men had bigger penises than white men, that this was linked to greater libidos and that they were therefore less moral in their sexual behaviour, and thus, if not explicitly deserving of contracting syphilis, at least implicitly so (Haller, J. (1971) *Outcasts From Evolution: Scientific Attitudes of Racial Inferiority*. Urbana: University of Illinois Press). The study was well known throughout American medical circles, had been reviewed by state ethics committees and passed. It was not discontinued due to any pressure from the medical profession, but as a consequence of journalistic exposé (Jones, J. (1981) *Bad Blood: The Tuskegee Syphilis Experiment*. New York: The Free Press) (**Belmont Report; Helsinki Declaration; Hippocrates; Nuremberg Code; race; racism**).

TYPE A BEHAVIOUR PATTERN (TABP)
Proposed in 1959 as a causative factor in heart disease, competitive, overachieving individuals who are constantly chasing deadlines, inducing stress, heart attack and early death. Type Bs by contrast are unambitious, lack competitiveness and are patient. The concept is now largely discredited given the difficulty of finding lifestyle factors causally associated with coronary heart disease (Helman, C. (1992) 'Heart disease and the cultural construction of time', in R. Frankenberg (ed.), *Time, Health and Medicine*. London: Sage) (**lifestyle factors**).

U

UNCERTAINTY, IN DIAGNOSIS (medical uncertainty)

UNEMPLOYMENT   Unemployment is now recognized to be seriously detrimental to physical and psychological health. Unemployed men and woman are more likely to report fair to poor health than their employed counterparts, and to suffer more chronic illness. The impact of unemployment flows through to the health of the next generation, with the children of the unemployed being significantly sicker than the children of the employed and a vicious inter-generational cycle of chronic disease and early death is set up (**occupation and health; social gradient of disease**).

UNINSURED   In market driven economic systems, with the decline of the **welfare state**, the only way for individuals to protect themselves from accident or the financial impact of the diagnoses of disease is to take out private health insurance. In the USA in 1995 about 43.4 million Americans had neither private insurance, nor could they access **Medicare** or **Medicaid**, that is, they had no financial coverage in the event of disease or accident. With the rise of **post-Fordist** production techniques more and more Americans no longer have health insurance plans provided by an employer and the levels of the uninsured and underinsured are rising. (Rubin, B. (1996) *Shifts in the Social Contract: Understanding Change in American Society*. Thousands Oaks, CA: Pine Forge Press). While the claim by neoliberals is that markets are 'natural' they take enormous amounts of government money to be made viable (that is, profitable to private investors): The Howard (conservative) government in Australia spends over AUS$2 billion a year in subsidies to private health insurers and has introduced penalty clauses into private health legislation, making it more expensive for individuals the longer they delay in entering the 'market' and exiting the government universal health scheme, Medicare (**citizenship; market; welfare state**).

UNION OF PHYSICALLY IMPAIRED AGAINST SEGREGATION (UPIAS) ((dis)ablism; disability)

URBANIZATION   In part, an economic transition where industrially produced goods replace agricultural goods as the source of a nation's wealth, a process, that is, of the growth of cities. In the nineteenth century death rates escalated as agricultural labourers moved from the countryside to the cities in the transition from agrarian economies to capitalist factory work (**Engels**; **social medicine**). Subsequently residence in a city provided access to medical services and treatment. Now, with the explosion of third world cities into populations of over ten million, high urban concentrations equal high environmental pollution, contaminated water supplies and environmental pollution. Whether in the developed or developing world the urban poor are those at highest risk of early death and infectious disease (Horton, R. (1996) 'The infected metropolis', *The Lancet*, 347: 134–5) (**risk society**).

V

VACCINATION The act of inducing a mild experience of a disease by introducing it into to the body to prevent a later more serious or fatal attack The process was initially described to an English audience by Lady Mary Wortley Montagu, who observed Turkish women inserting the fluid from a smallpox pustule into the arm of a healthy person. The 'discovery' (it was a well known folk practice) that cowpox, contracted from cattle, prevented the development of smallpox led to inoculation, culminating in the publication of Edward Jenner's (1749–1823) *An Inquiry into the Causes and Effects of the Vatiolae Vaccinae* in 1798. Since it was a simple matter, costing nothing, it met a good deal of medical resistance as the medical profession fought to take over control of the practice (Hennock, P. (1998) 'Vaccination against smallpox, 1835–1914: a comparison of England with Prussia and imperial Germany', *Social History of Medicine*, 11 (1): 49–71) (**vaccines**).

VACCINES Either a weakened or dead viral or bacteriological substance introduced into the body to induce the immune system to react against it, making the person resistant to future attacks from the same agents. In the medical model vaccines are a magic bullet, preventing and eliminating disease. However historical epidemiologists such as **McKeown** argue that they have had very little impact on death rates. Other commentators such as Dubos have shown that in third world countries, whooping cough, measles and scarlet fever have all been reduced without any specific medical interventions, as economic conditions improved (Dubos, R. (1959) *Mirage of Health: Utopias, Progress and Biological Change*. New York: Harper).

VAGINOPLASTY Male to female sex reassignment surgery, in which the penis is inverted so as to construct a vagina (**transsexual**).

VALIDITY In research the confidence with which it can be asserted that the data measures what it purports to. In **positivist** research the issue is usually of how statistically robust the data is and related to how the sample was selected. In **qualitative research** questions of validity relate more to whether or not the subjects would accept the portrayal of their situation (**causal inference; objectivity**).

VERSTEHEN Interpretive understanding, a concept in German philosophy developed in sociology by Max Weber, who argued that sociology must develop unique methods to explain social life. Central to this was 'verstehen' by which Weber meant that sociological research had to account not only for the regularities and observable patterns of social life but also the meanings and intentions of social actors. Applied to the sociology of health, the focus is not on the 'objective' characteristics of disease but on the ways in which people make sense of their situation when sick (**Chicago School of Sociology**; **microsociological**; **qualitative research**; **Weber**).

VICTIM BLAMING (accident proneness; blame the victim; stigmatized risk group).

VILLERME, RENÉ LOUIS (1782–1863) French doctor and public health activist who used statistics to demonstrate the impact of economic inequality on disease rates and whose work played a large role in the development of **social medicine** (**Chadwick**; **Simon**).

VIRCHOW, RUDOLF (1821–1902) Famous as the theorist of cellular pathology and a political radical, Virchow argued in his study of typhoid in Upper Silesia that epidemics were the product of social structures – of ethnicity, religious intolerance and economic deprivation – and not germs. His cures referred not to medical interventions but to changes in the structures of social relationships. These included educational and religious reforms as well as political reforms that would give independence to national minorities. Hence his famous slogan: medicine is a social science and politics is nothing but medicine on a large scale. He rejected bacteriology and retained a multi-causal model of disease. The distribution of and experience of disease and ill-health were always a product of socio-economic factors, and their treatment and prevention had to be at the social and political level. Along with **Frederick Engels** one of the founders of **social medicine** (Taylor, R. and Reiger, A. (1984) 'Rudolf Virchow on the typhus epidemic in Upper Silesia', *Sociology of Health and Illness*, 6: 321–42) (**Frank**; **medical police**).

VISUAL IMAGING A range of technologies in medicine – from X-rays, ultrasound (using the reflections of high frequency sound waves to construct an image of a body organ), positron emission tomography (computerized radiographic technique to examine tissue) and magnetic resonance imaging (nuclear magnetic resonance of protons to produce proton density images). On the one hand these developments feed into the technical, **reductionist** biomedical model, producing the body as a series of discrete images, completely independently of the subjectivity of the patient. On the other, they expose medical practitioners to surveillance in their use of these diagnostic tools, undermining their clinical skills and their autonomy (**bedside medicine**; **biotechnology**; **cyborgs**; **deprofessionalization**; **reification**; **telemedicine**).

VITALISM   The claim that life cannot be reduced to purely material elements. In the history of medicine, vitalism was overtaken by **mechanistic** explanations of life (Blackwell).

VOCABULARIES OF COMPLAINT   An adaptation of C. Wright Mills' (1949) vocabularies of motive in which Mills argued that the way in which social groups verbalize their understanding of a situation is socially determined. For example, nursing talk around conflict with doctors is a regular feature of hospital life, but it can only be carried out in the absence of doctors. (Turner, B. (1986) 'Nursing, professionalism and job context: the vocabulary of complaints', *The Australian and New Zealand Journal of Sociology*, 22: 368–86).

VOLUNTARISTIC THEORY OF ACTION   A key component of **Talcott Parsons'** sociology of health, though in considerable tension with his **structural functionalism**, the argument that individuals can make choices about how they respond to social life (**structure–agency debate**). Parsons, following the German social theorist **Max Weber**, argued that individuals make sense of their world, they interpret it, give it meaning, and make choices about their participation in it. Fundamentally, while animals behave, humans act. In developing this argument and applying it to health and disease Parsons develops one of the core arguments in the sociology of health. If the medical view of disease is correct, then disease is purely the behavioural response of the human organism to environmental factors over which we, as conscious individuals, can have little effect. However, for Parsons, since sociology deals with action rather than behaviour, the following question can be asked. Are sickness and disease conditions imposed upon us, or do they involve motivational factors on the part of the individual, or is there an interplay between choice, disease and the social role we are in? Parsons' answer was that people can make choices about illness – we can enter into disease so to speak. It was on the basis of this argument that he conceptualized illness, not as a biological condition, but as a social role (**sick role**).

VOODOO DEATH   The belief that death is inevitable following a curse. Sometimes referred to as psychogenic, or mind-induced death. However, the curse is usually accompanied by the withdrawal of material resources, such as water, by others in the group, as well as social exclusion. Death is a combination of a loss of will to live, ostracism and of biological essentials such as food and water (Canon, W. 'Voodoo Death,' *American Anthropologist*, 44: 169–81) (**social death**).

W

WATSON, JOHN BROADUS (1878–1956)
Professor of Psychology at Johns Hopkins University and founder of **behaviourism**. Watson argued that human behaviour could be studied as objectively as animal behaviour, and that in particular, as Pavlov had shown with dogs, that human beings could be conditioned to respond to stimuli (**behaviour modification**). Watson was forced out of academic life following a scandal with a student, and eventually applied his theories in advertising, arguing that it was not the intrinsic property of a good that made us want it but rather the image of our self that was conveyed by our act of consuming it.

WEBB, BEATRICE (1858–1943) AND SYDNEY (1859–1947) Influential health policy activists and social reformers in Britain after World War I. Progressive and left-wing, they helped to produce a health-care system based on **social medicine**, that is, not just focused on sanitary reform, but also political and economic reform. This development was central to the **welfare state (Ryle)**.

WEBER, MAX (1864–1920) German social theorist and one of the founders of sociology. His importance to health social studies lies in his arguments about the necessity for the social sciences to develop their own research methods, distinct from those of the natural sciences (**positivism**). Because human beings actively make sense of their environment they cannot be studied from the outside as inert objects (**behaviourism**). Rather, while society certainly was made up of structured patterns of action which sociologists could study, sociology simultaneously had to provide an account of the subjective meaning to individuals of these patterns. Following the German philosopher Georg Dilthey, Weber used the word 'verstehen' – the attempt to arrive at an interpretative understanding of the individual's perspective – to capture the unique methods of the social sciences. He also argued that regular patterns of action could be extrapolated to **ideal types**, the central features of the situation, as in a bureaucracy, which has been influential in the study of the **hospital (formal rationality; Kant; qualitative research; verstehen)**.

WELFARE SERVICES The provision of public health, education and housing by the **welfare state** to ameliorate the impact of the capitalist economy on the working class. Also known as the **social wage**, which while also benefiting the middle class, did result in a downward redistribution of resources and is the reason for the increase in longevity in Britain after World War II. Under **neoliberalism** these services have been replaced by **market** driven private health, education and housing, and the health gains of the mid-twentieth century are being reversed (Charlton, D. and Murphy, M. (eds) (1997) *Adult Health: Historical Aspects.* London: HMSO) (**citizenship**).

WELFARE STATE   In welfare state capitalism (1950–80), the state managed the economy, guaranteed minimum living standards and administered the population, who by birth right were members of the nation and enjoyed citizenship. Central to the welfare state was the commitment to full employment, citizenship mediated by universalistic welfare policies, and the participation of labour in mass consumption. Since the early 1980s the structural basis of welfare state capitalism has been undermined with the decline of the industrial sector in Western economies and the globalization of capitalist investment strategies. This has also meant a change in the standing of the medical profession, with state policies now directed towards control over the costs and quantity of medical services, that is, intervening in the clinical decision making of the medical profession and thus weakening its dominance (**medical dominance**). The state under neoliberalism has sought to shed its

health and welfare functions contracting them out, **outsourcing** them, or privatizing them with a negative impact on access and equity, as well as reducing the quality, of health services (White, K (2000) 'The state, the market and general practice: the Australian case', *International Journal of Health Services,* 30 (2): 285–308) (**citizenship; corporatization; market; neoliberalism; new public management; welfare services**).

WHIG HISTORIES OF MEDICINE   The triumphal history of medicine emphasizing great men, Florey discovering penicillin; great ideas, the germ theory of disease; and great institutions, hospitals like Guys and St Bartholomew's. In this portrayal modern medicine is presented as a natural science, based in the hospital and the laboratory and responsible for the decrease in mortality and morbidity since the nineteenth century. This view is rejected by researchers in the social history of medicine who argue that the infectious diseases of the nineteenth and early twentieth century were brought under control by the sanitary reform movement. (see as an example, Youngson, A. (1979) *The Scientific Revolution in Victorian Medicine.* London: Croom Helm) (**bedside medicine; Foucault; germ theory; infectious disease; McKeown; medical technology; social medicine**).

WHITEHALL STUDIES   An ongoing longitudinal study of British civil servants. It has shown a three-fold increase in mortality rates between the bottom and the top of the civil service, that is, within the same socio-economic class. In exploring this difference these studies established the limited impact of **lifestyle factors** on health variations. Controlling for diet, smoking, exercise and blood pressure they found that these factors could explain only one-third of the variation in disease between the different grades. Marmot and colleagues argue that the psychosocial processes around the experience of inequality have an important impact on our sense of control, social affiliations and support, self-esteem, life events and job security and expose us to chronic psychosocial stress (**alienation**). It is these rather than lifestyle factors which account for the social gradient of disease (Marmot, M., Smith, G., Stanesfield, S., et al. 'Health inequalities among British civil servants: the Whitehall Study', *The Lancet*, 337: 1387–93) (**Black Report**; **occupation and health**; **risk factor epidemiology**; **social inequality**).

WOLLSTONECRAFT, MARY (1759–97) English feminist and author of *A Vindication of the Rights of Women* (1792) in which she linked liberalism (**liberal feminism**) to the rights of women.

WOMEN'S HEALTH INITIATIVE (WHI) A large scale clinical trail in the US to examine the impact of menopause on women, and of the impact of hormonal interventions on their experience of menopause (**menstrual cycle**).

WOMEN'S NARRATIVES (memory work).

WORKING CLASS That sector of society – largely unskilled, uneducated and with low social status – whose work is marked by physical exertion and repetition. While in significant decline in Western countries (from over 75 per cent of the workforce in the early 1900s to less than 50 per cent by the early 1980s) they die earlier and suffer from more preventable diseases than those above them. Members of the working class are regularly blamed for their situation (**blame the victim**) and for choosing health damaging **lifestyles** (**alienation**; **Black Report**; **class**; **class analysis**; **diseases of poverty**; **ideology**; **social inequalities**; **social gradient of disease**; **socio-economic status**; **Whitehall Studies**).

WORLD FEDERATION OF PSYCHIATRIC USERS Established in 1991 to provide support and act as a lobby group for psychiatric patients. The federation sought to secure the human rights of those labelled mentally ill and to lobby for consumer input into mental health policies, arguing that neither the provision of treatment nor the management of symptoms, was in itself sufficient to address the problems individuals faced when diagnosed as mentally ill. Individuals had to have choice about their life conditions, independence, involvement in decisions about their living conditions and employment, if they were to lead a meaningful existence (**antipsychiatry**; **consumerism**; **mental illness**).

WORLD HEALTH ORGANIZATION (WHO)
Founded in 1948 as part of the United
Nations and with triumphs to its credit
such as the worldwide eradication of smallpox in 1979. While it has singled out
poverty as the largest single cause of disease
and early death, its policies tend to be
idealist – strong on intent, but not backed
up with resources – and therefore almost
impossible to translate into actions which
relieve the burden of **disease**. With the rise
of **neoliberalism** its role has been overshad-
owed by the International Monetary Fund
and the World Bank, institutions whose
policies of **privatization** lead to greater
inequality, disease and preventable early
death (**Alma Ata Declaration**; **Chile**; **health
determinants**; **market**; **Ottawa Charter**).

X

XENOTRANSPLANTATION The transplanting of organs from animals to humans. The development of the ability to cross human and animal bodies raises complex cultural questions about what is human, as well as more practically, the problem of transferring diseases from animals to humans (Brown, N. and Webster, A. (2004) *New Medical Technologies and Society: Reordering Life*. Cambridge: Polity Press) (**cyborgs; organ transplantation**).

Z

ZINSSER, HANS (1878–1940) Hans Zinnser was a bacteriologist and is famous in medicine for developing a vaccine for rickettsias. However, like other early medical researchers such as **Virchow** and **Fleck**, he rejected any simple monocausal explanations of disease. In his study of typhoid, *Rats, Lice and History* (1935, Boston, MA: Little Brown) he showed how cultural, political, religious and economic variables shaped the spread of an infectious epidemic, thus making a contribution to the early development of a sociology of health and to public health.

ZOLA, IRVING (1935–94) American sociologist of health, disabilities rights activist, and founder of the Society for Disability Studies (he survived both childhood polio and a serious car accident at the age of nineteen). Zola wrote some of the landmark papers in the sociology of health. In 'Medicine as an institution of social control' (1972, *Sociological Review*, 20: 487–504) he made the argument that while medicine's scientificity and apparent basis lay in a value free natural science epistemology, the profession actually functioned to police deviancy. In 'Pathways to the doctor: from person to patient' (1973, *Social Science and Medicine*, 7: 677–89) he showed how the decision to go to the doctor was the outcome of social processes and not biological or physiological experience of disease (**lay culture; social control**).

Index